First-Person Anonymous

For Brett Fried, Alice Easley

and all those 'who were once at an early stage of their rise in the world, and were cherishing very large hopes in very small lodgings'

– George Eliot, Mill on the Floss

First-Person Anonymous

Women Writers and Victorian Print Media, 1830–70

ALEXIS EASLEY

LONDON AND NEW YORK

First published 2004 by Ashgate Publishing

2 Park Square, Milton Park, Abingdon, Oxfordshire OX14 4RN
52 Vanderbilt Avenue, New York, NY 10017

Routledge is an imprint of the Taylor & Francis Group, an informa business

First issued in paperback 2019

Copyright © 2004 Alexis Easley

The author has asserted her moral right under the Copyright, Designs and Patents Act, 1988, to be identified as the author of this work.

All rights reserved. No part of this book may be reprinted or reproduced or utilised in any form or by any electronic, mechanical, or other means, now known or hereafter invented, including photocopying and recording, or in any information storage or retrieval system, without permission in writing from the publishers.

Notice:
Product or corporate names may be trademarks or registered trademarks, and are used only for identification and explanation without intent to infringe.

British Library Cataloguing in Publication Data

Easley, Alexis
    First-person anonymous : women writers and Victorian print
    Media, 1830-70. - (The nineteenth century series)
    1.English literature - 19th century - History and criticism
    2.English literature - Women authors - History and
    criticism 3.English periodicals - History - 19th century
    4.Periodicals - Publishing - England - History - 19th
    century
    I.Title
    820.9'352042'09034

Library of Congress Cataloging-in-Publication Data

Easley, Alexis, 1963-
    First person anonymous : women writers and Victorian print media, 1830-1870 / Alexis
Easley.
        p. cm.
    Includes bibliographical references (p.) and index.
    ISBN 0-7546-3056-0 (alk. paper)
       1.English literature--Women authors--history and criticism. 2. Women and
literature--Great Britain--History--19th century. 3. English literature--19th
century--History and criticism. 4. Printing--Great Britain--History--19th century. 5.
Anonymous writings, English--History and criticism. 6. Anonyms and pseudonyms,
English--History. I. Title.

PR115.E25 2004
820.9'9287'09034--dc21

2003045334

ISBN 13: 978-0-7546-3056-2 (hbk)
ISBN 13: 978-0-367-88776-6 (pbk)

Contents

The Nineteenth Century Series General Editors' Preface	vii
List of Figures	ix
Acknowledgements	xi
Introduction	1
1 Beginnings: The 1830s	15
2 Defining Women's Authorship: Harriet Martineau and the Women Question	35
3 Periodical Journalism and the Gender of Reform: Christian Isobel Johnstone	61
4 Elizabeth Gaskell, Urban Investigation, and the 'Abused' Woman Writer	81
5 Gender and Representation: George Eliot in the 1850s and 60s	117
6 Christina Rossetti and the Problem of Literary Fame	153
Afterword	177
Works Cited	187
Index	201

The Nineteenth Century Series
General Editors' Preface

The aim of the series is to reflect, develop and extend the great burgeoning of interest in the nineteenth century that has been an inevitable feature of recent years, as that former epoch has come more sharply into focus as a locus for our understanding not only of the past but of the contours of our modernity. It centres primarily upon major authors and subjects within Romantic and Victorian literature. It also includes studies of other British writers and issues, where these are matters of current debate: for example, biography and autobiography, journalism, periodical literature, travel writing, book production, gender and non-canonical writing. We are dedicated principally to publishing original monographs and symposia; our policy is to embrace a broad scope in chronology, approach and range of concern, and both to recognize and cut innovatively across such parameters as those suggested by the designations "Romantic" and "Victorian." We welcome new ideas and theories, while valuing traditional scholarship. It is hoped that the world which predates yet so forcibly predicts and engages our own will emerge in parts, in the wider sweep, and in the lively streams of disputation and change that are so manifest an aspect of its intellectual, artistic and social landscape.

Vincent Newey
Joanne Shattock

University of Leicester

List of Figures

1.1	'The Fraserians' by Daniel Maclise	28
1.2	'*Regina's* Maids of Honour' by Daniel Maclise	29
2.1	'Miss Harriet Martineau' by Daniel Maclise	42
3.1	Title page, *Tait's Edinburgh Magazine*	64
3.2	Advertisement for *Edinburgh Tales*	74
4.1	Title page, *Howitt's Journal*	85
6.1	Frontispiece to *The Germ* by William Holman Hunt	159

Acknowledgements

Throughout the writing and revision process, I was blessed with a fine network of family, friends, mentors, and colleagues who were willing to devote their time, talent, encouragement, and good humor to this project. I am deeply grateful to my husband, Brett Fried, for his advice and patience throughout the writing process. I am also indebted to Professor Richard Stein, my doctoral advisor, for his insightful commentary on multiple drafts of this book when it was still a dissertation. Professors Richard Stevenson, Marilyn Farwell, Ian Duncan, and Randall McGowen provided valuable feedback during the revision process, as did Suzanne Bordelon, Pamela Parker, and Roxanne Kent-Drury. Members of the Research Society for Victorian Periodicals were generous with their feedback and encouragement when I presented various drafts of my research at their annual conference. I also want to thank my mother, Alice Easley, my sister, Roxanne Easley, and my parents-in-law, Maurice and Enid Fried, for their inspiration, encouragement, and guidance.

The revision of this manuscript would not have been possible without the support of my colleagues at the University of Alaska Southeast, especially Don Cecil and Mary Lou Madden, who allowed me time away from teaching responsibilities to devote to this project. I am also indebted to the University of Alaska Southeast for providing support for my frequent research trips abroad. The following organizations also provided valuable financial assistance as I developed this manuscript: the University of Oregon Center for the Study of Women in Society, the Eugene Chapter of the American Association of University Women, the University of Oregon English Department, and the University of Oregon Graduate School. Finally, I would like to acknowledge Beatrice Franklin and the staff of the Egan Library, University of Alaska Southeast, for their invaluable assistance in accessing materials for this project.

Portions of this manuscript were published in different form in academic journals and anthologies. Earlier versions of chapter two were published in *Nineteenth-Century Prose* (24.1), *Victorian Women Writers and the Woman Question* (Cambridge, 1999), and *Defining Centres: Nineteenth-Century Media and the Construction of Identities* (Macmillan, 2000). Earlier versions of chapters five and six were published in *Women's Writing* (3.2) and *Critical Survey* (13.2), respectively.

Introduction

Who was the Victorian woman author? We feel more confident answering this question today than we did twenty-five years ago. Efforts toward expanding the canon have led us to include the work of Elizabeth Gaskell, Christina Rossetti, and Charlotte Brontë on course syllabi and to rediscover authors such as Harriet Martineau and Margaret Oliphant. As successful as these efforts have been, it must be admitted that we are still very far from understanding the full scope of Victorian women's literary careers. Women's novels and poems, after all, were only a small part of their total contribution to literary discourse during the nineteenth century. Just as important to the development of women's careers as professional writers were their contributions to Victorian journalism. Most major nineteenth-century women authors—including the writers featured in this study, Harriet Martineau (1802-76), Christian Johnstone (1781-1857), Elizabeth Gaskell (1810-65), George Eliot (1819-80), and Christina Rossetti (1830-94)—made significant contributions to the periodical press. Their involvement in periodical journalism had important implications for the development of their book-length works of poetry, fiction, and non-fiction. Moving between journalistic and literary media, they were able to develop wide-ranging intellectual interests as critics, poets, novelists, and social theorists. They were also able to capitalize on the narrative conventions of diverse media as a way of constructing and complicating their authorial identities.

In the broadest sense, this book is intended as a contribution to the history of gender and authorship during the Victorian period. It draws attention to the ways women were able to capitalize upon the conventions of journalistic and literary print media as a way of making their way in a male-dominated profession. On one hand, women were drawn to high-profile careers as authors and cultural sages. By publishing books under their own signatures and participating in the construction of their public identities, women were able to achieve fame, influence literary culture, and attain economic self-sufficiency. However, literary celebrity was not without its perils. Famous women authors were often held accountable to confining definitions of 'female authorship', which constrained their choice of subject matter and exposed their personal lives to public scrutiny. For this reason, many women writers were attracted to careers in periodical journalism. One factor that made periodical journalism attractive to women authors was the policy of anonymous publication associated with most journals, magazines, and reviews until the 1860s. Anonymous publication provided women with effective cover for exploring a variety of conventionally 'masculine' social issues. It also allowed them to evade essentialized notions of 'feminine' voice and identity. Even after women established themselves as famous authors, they often returned to the periodical press as a medium for expressing their most controversial viewpoints, for retaliating against their critics, and for playfully spoofing the gendering of the author position in their society.

To be a woman author in Victorian society was to be 'first-person anonymous', that is, to both construct and subvert notions of individual authorial identity, manipulating the publishing conventions associated with various print media for personal and professional advantage. By investigating ways that women negotiated and capitalized upon these publishing conventions, we can begin to complicate our understanding of the construction and gendering of the authorial role during the Victorian period. Likewise, we can begin to deepen our understanding of the literary texts that women produced. Women often employed some of the same narrative techniques in their fiction as in their periodical journalism. There was consequently a great deal of cross-pollination between women's contributions to signed and unsigned print media—both in terms of narrative form and subject matter.

An investigation of women's authorship necessarily begins with an exploration of the periodical medium itself, which enabled women's literary careers in a number of significant ways. Though the focus of this study is the *intersection* of women's careers as celebrity authors and anonymous journalists, it is built upon the assumption that periodical journalism was instrumental in the rise of the woman author during the nineteenth century. Over 1,500 women are known to have contributed to the periodical press during the Victorian era.[1] In 1865 Bessie Rayner Parkes remarked that 'if editors were ever known to disclose the dread secrets of their dens, they would only give the public an idea of the authoresses whose unsigned names are Legion; of their rolls of manuscripts, which are as the sands of the sea' (*Essays* 121). Today this 'legion' of Victorian women journalists remains relatively unknown to us: we still know very little about their working lives—why they entered the field of journalistic publishing and what working conditions they encountered there. The work of Barbara Onslow, E. M. Palmegiano, Margaret Beetham, and the Research Society for Victorian Periodicals has begun to provide insight into this history,[2] but there is still much work to be done before we can claim to have gained an adequate understanding of the role of periodical journalism in women's literary careers. This study attempts to address this gap in scholarship by focusing specifically on the role of journalistic anonymity in the work and careers of five prominent women of letters, demonstrating the tension and productive interplay between their anonymous texts and their more well known works of fiction, poetry, and non-fiction.

The anonymity of periodical journalism enabled women to address broad audiences and subject matter, writing on subjects as diverse as slavery, women's emancipation, parliamentary reform, and industrialism. As Valerie Sanders has pointed out, the periodical press provided some conservative women with the means for developing an anti-feminist politics,[3] but as I will demonstrate, it provided other women writers with the means for developing a proto-feminist political consciousness. This proto-feminism first found expression in the radical periodicals and popular literature movements of the 1830s and '40s and later

INTRODUCTION

developed in women's journalism and public protests of the 1850s and '60s.[4] As a medium closely associated with these interdependent movements, the Victorian periodical played a key role in formulating new cultural stereotypes of the politically active woman writer. During the 1830s and '40s, the economic hardships faced by the poor prompted some middle-class women—especially those from radical, liberal, and dissenting backgrounds—to engage in forms of philanthropic writing intended to ameliorate class-based social inequities. Some edited reformist periodicals while others wrote political essays and social problem novels. By mid-century, however, as living conditions for the poor improved, class issues no longer seemed to provide sufficient justification for women's participation in public discourse. With the growing debate over the Woman Question, gender soon replaced class as a motivating cause for women's social radicalism. As an anonymous forum for political debate, the periodical press provided women with opportunities for self-advocacy that would lead to the development of an organized women's movement in the late 1850s.

Ironically, it was the suppression of individual identity through anonymous publication that enabled the development of new definitions of women's political subjectivity and liberal individuality. In anonymous contributions to the discourse on the Woman Question in the periodical press, women debated what role their sex should have in the political realm.[5] Many women who contributed anonymously to the discourse on the Woman Question—including Martineau, Johnstone, Gaskell, Eliot, and Rossetti—were reluctant to associate themselves with the high-profile public activities that characterized the women's movement during the 1850s and '60s. As Denise Riley has pointed out, the term 'woman' had developed many positive and negative associations within Victorian culture; consequently, women could not offer their 'own uncontaminated, self-generated understandings' of the term (68). Anonymous publication provided women with an opportunity to address the Woman Question from a position less 'contaminated' by gender definitions.

Although the periodical press provided expanded opportunities for women to enter debates on the Woman Question and other public issues, it was also the primary medium concerned with constructing negative stereotypes of the female author. As Gaye Tuchman and Nina Fortin have demonstrated, *ad feminam* attacks in periodical reviews resulted in the creation of a critical double standard that defined women's writing as a lesser genre of literary accomplishment (175-202).[6] These reviewing practices, they argue, had the effect of limiting the range of narrative forms and subject matter available to women. While it is undoubtedly true that the Victorian critical establishment was male-dominated and discriminatory, the periodical press was more contradictory in its attitude toward women's writing than has hitherto been allowed. As Ellen Casey has pointed out, Victorian reviewers sometimes expressed a 'grudging acceptance of women novelists as the equal of men' (152).

The contradictory attitudes of reviewers towards women's writing reflect women's changing roles within the critical establishment. By mid-century a significant number of women, including Jane Sinnett, Catherine Gore, and Margaret Oliphant, were employed as anonymous contributors to major periodicals. And a surprising number of women, including Eliza Cook and Bessie Rayner Parkes, were editors of their own journals. Consequently, Victorian women were not merely the objects of critical attacks; they also meted out their own criticism as editors and reviewers. Women retaliated against fellow critics who maligned their books and published their own theories and evaluations of women's literature. Thus, at the same time that the periodical press restricted women's literary practice by imposing gender stereotypes on their signed publications, it also provided them with the tools to participate in the debate over how those stereotypes were constituted.

The degree of women's involvement in journalistic reviewing and editing varied from periodical to periodical. Some periodicals, such as the Tory *Quarterly Review,* employed few women reviewers and were especially harsh critics of political texts written by women. Others, such as the liberal *Westminster Review,* employed more women and tended to respond more positively to their texts. In general, radical and liberal periodicals were more accepting of women writers since these journals were connected to social and ideological movements that sometimes sponsored women's educational and political advancement: utilitarianism, religious dissent, and the popular literature campaigns. In addition to having different political affiliations, periodicals had wide ranging audiences, formats, and subject matter. Many magazines, for instance, were especially accessible to women writers because their miscellaneous format implied a mixed-gender audience. Conversely, high-brow literary periodicals, such as the *Edinburgh Review,* were slow to include women on their lists of contributors. These sorts of differences make it difficult to generalize about the narrative conventions of the periodical press and women's relationship to these institutional arrangements. However, it is still safe to say that the narrative conventions associated with the periodical press as a whole were instrumental in facilitating the development of Victorian women's literary careers.

When selecting journalistic sources for this project, I focused on middle-class periodicals read by Victorian literati between 1830 and 1870. This included *Fraser's Magazine, Blackwood's Magazine,* the *Westminster Review,* the *Edinburgh Review,* the *Quarterly Review,* and the *British Quarterly Review.* These periodicals reveal the extent to which women were represented (both as contributors and the objects of criticism) in mainstream literary journalism. To a lesser extent, I surveyed radical and religious periodicals of the 1830s and '40s, such as the *People's Journal,* the *Monthly Repository,* and *Howitt's Journal,* because of their important role in establishing women's literary careers. I did include some references to women's periodicals in this study, especially the *English Woman's Journal*; however, I did not include extensive analysis of these periodicals because I wanted to examine how women participated in mainstream literary and political discourse aimed at a mixed-gender audience.

My investigation of middle-class literary periodicals revealed many patterns of growth and change in women's patterns of authorship. During this period, there was a steady increase in the number of women contributors to most mainstream literary periodicals. While during the 1830s women only rarely contributed to these journals, by the 1850s their numbers had increased dramatically. The increasing participation of women contributors resulted in a golden age of women's journalism, roughly spanning the years 1850 to 1870. This period saw the rise of some of the most prolific and influential women journalists of the day, including Margaret Oliphant and Anne Mozley. During the 1860s, the practice of anonymous publication came under attack, and by the end of the century, many literary periodicals, including the *Fortnightly Review* and *Macmillan's Magazine,* began publishing the names of their contributors. By requiring signature, editors made it increasingly difficult for women to engage in low-profile literary careers. While the celebrity associated with signed publication was attractive to many women who wanted to make names for themselves, it was a barrier to those who relied upon anonymity as a means of separating their private and public identities. The personal exposure associated with signed publication also made it more difficult for women to exert political influence since as female writers they might have a more difficult time treating conventionally masculine subject matter in their work. Likewise, women found it more difficult to gain access to the broad audiences and subject matter they had addressed as anonymous writers. As forms of signed publication took on high-culture literary status, anonymity came to be seen as a low-brow form of literary production. This had important implications for women writers, who had relied on anonymous journalism as a back-door entry into the literary establishment.

The rise of the woman of letters at mid-century had a destabilizing effect on cultural definitions of literary authority. At the same time women were contributing anonymously to periodicals in unprecedented numbers, they were publishing a diverse array of book-length texts under their own names. Increasingly, the political and social subject matter women addressed in their periodical essays spilled over into their signed texts—social problem novels, didactic stories, and sociological studies. The appearance these texts created a crisis of representation as critics struggled to come to terms with the social, economic, and cultural role of the author in their society. Since cultural authority had been historically associated with male authorship, the participation of women in debates over public issues disrupted the expected gendering of the authorial role and called into question the ideology of separate spheres. At stake was the notion of cultural authority itself: Who had the right to participate in public debates and under what circumstances? How was the right to participate in these debates determined by issues of gender? Was it possible for writers to speak outside their identities, roles, and life experiences? These questions, which today inform the most lively academic discussions, have their root in critical debates over cultural authority and identity politics within early and mid-nineteenth-century popular print culture.

6 FIRST-PERSON ANONYMOUS

Over the past twenty years, scholars have become increasingly interested in examining the ideological role of the author within Western cultural history. Beginning with Michel Foucault's 'What Is an Author?' scholars have explored how the author was constructed in legal and literary discourse of the nineteenth century.[7] While these studies have increased our understanding of the material and cultural history of the nineteenth-century author, they often rely on the mistaken assumption that the construction of an individualized authorial subject was uncontested within nineteenth-century print culture. Such studies fail to take into account the ways in which the anonymity of periodical journalism challenged the notion of an individually authored literary text and singularized authorial voice. Recent work by Laurel Brake and David Latané has provided a more in-depth picture of how notions of the popular author were challenged, subverted, and reinscribed in the anonymous periodical press. What remains to be investigated is how the conflict between literary anonymity and celebrity informed debates over the gendering of the authorial role within early and mid-nineteenth-century print culture.

Of course the issue of gender and authorship has been a critical concern among Victorian scholars for decades. Elaine Showalter's *A Literature of Their Own* (1977) and Gilbert and Gubar's *Madwoman in the Attic* (1979), for example, examine the ways in which women's voices and gender were suppressed by a patriarchal literary establishment during the nineteenth century. Anonymity, in these critical accounts, is a form of self-repression that women imposed upon themselves in order to participate in an overwhelmingly masculine literary culture. Such an interpretation is complicated by theoretical reconceptions of authorial identity, which interpret narrative obscurity as a means of resisting notions of essential gender. Viewed from this perspective, anonymity is not just a form of self-repression but also a response to the identity politics associated with popular authorship.

Increased understanding of the role of anonymity in Victorian print culture has caused us to question the assumption that nineteenth-century gender stereotypes were stable—that the Victorian sage was always a high-profile man of letters who cultivated literary fame as a way of influencing public opinion and promulgating middle-class values.[8] While it is true that the Victorian publishing industry was discriminatory and that the Victorian author was often characterized as a man in critical writing of the period, the masculinity of the popular author was far from stable.[9] Indeed, the existence of an anonymous press during most of the century demonstrates that the development of the author as an individualized male identity was countered by a tendency toward anonymous forms of authorship, wherein specificities of sex and gender were complicated and obscured. Likewise, the rapid increase in the number of reviews theorizing the gender, sex, and class status of the author testifies to the instability of the authorial role in Victorian culture. An understanding of the complexity of Victorian authorship may cause us to re-think our assumptions of literary authority and power that would cast women writers as the victims of an all-encompassing masculine literary tradition. Rather than simply tracing the ideological function of the female author in Victorian society, we can begin to examine the ways that women constructed and resisted these gender stereotypes in their own literary practice.

Of course, to discuss resistance to gender is to rely on a concept of the woman author as an individualized, gendered agent within literary history—a notion that has come under fire within the critical establishment in recent years. The death of the author theorized by Barthes has made some feminists uncomfortable with the project of recovering the woman author in literary history.[10] Many believe that to claim the woman writer as an agent in this history is to use biography as a means of imposing false unity, order, and essentialized definitions of women's writing on a series of texts. According to these critics, this kind of feminist biographical criticism often imposes the same kinds of constraining gender definitions meted out by Victorian critics in their critiques of women's writing. In response to this argument, other feminist critics have claimed that to question the viability of the 'woman author' and 'women's writing' as critical concepts is to assume that sex and gender played no historical role in the production, distribution, and reception of literary texts.[11] They also claim that the death of the author relegates women writers to the all-too-familiar role of passive invisibility within literary history. One of the only ways to contend with this theoretical impasse within feminist scholarship is to develop what Cheryl Walker has called a 'new concept of authorship that does not naively assert that the writer is an originating genius, creating aesthetic objects outside of history, but does not diminish the importance of difference and agency in the responses of women writers to historical formations' (560).

By examining discontinuities in women's authorial identities and texts, rather than assuming individualized, consistent authorial personae, we can explore the ways that anonymity allowed women to appear and disappear in their work—to be at once creators and constructions, cultural agents and culturally produced texts. Likewise, it enables us to view pseudonymous publication as a strategy designed to complicate the authorial position, rather than a defensive means of obscuring an essential 'self' or 'voice'. Such an approach operates under the contradictory assumption that women were active yet indeterminate agents within literary history. As Catherine Gallagher has pointed out, 'to concentrate on the elusiveness of these authors, instead of bemoaning it and searching for their positive identities, is to practice a different sort of literary history' (*Nobody* xviii). We can begin by investigating how women constructed complex literary identities—simultaneously representing and calling into question the existence of a sexed body behind their literary texts. In such an analysis, women's use of anonymity and pseudonymity is just as interesting as their desire to be named or to name themselves within popular print culture.

It is within this theoretical context that we can begin to deepen our understanding of the careers of Harriet Martineau, Christian Johnstone, Elizabeth Gaskell, George Eliot, and Christina Rossetti. I chose these writers for this study in order to highlight key moments in their careers that roughly correspond to and illuminate three broad movements in the history of women and authorship: 1830-40 (Johnstone and Martineau), 1840-60 (Gaskell), and 1850-70 (Eliot and Rossetti). That is, rather than providing a full overview of each writer's career, I focus on key events in their professional lives that help to illuminate the kinds of social, political, narrative, and institutional arrangements that shaped women's literary practice during successive decades of the Victorian period. I interpret these writers' experiences as typical in the sense that they illustrate the kinds of barriers and opportunities faced by women writers under changing historical circumstances. Of all the writers in the study, Christian Johnstone's career can be seen as most typical since she, like most other writers of the Victorian era, remained relatively obscure and unknown throughout her professional life. I chose the other writers in this study not only for their typicality but also for their atypicality: Martineau, Gaskell, Eliot, and Rossetti not only wrote anonymously for the periodical press but also became known as the famous authors of book-length works of fiction, poetry, and non-fiction. The confluence of their careers as anonymous authors and literary celebrities prompted me to investigate the extent to which the gender issues changed as they moved between and across media.

Through an examination of these writers' multi-faceted careers, this study highlights the intertextuality between literary and journalistic genres. Victorian books and periodicals shared audiences, authors, themes, subject matter, and narrative conventions. This was especially true of the social problem novel and the reformist periodical, which often integrated the same political and domestic subject matter.[12] There were of course conflicts inherent in women's participation in these intersecting media. The anonymity associated with the periodical press and the publicity associated with signed publication constituted a major difference between journalistic and literary genres. As women writers moved between media, they encountered various personal and professional dilemmas. Their literary texts attempt to mitigate these conflicts by employing some of the narrative devices and subject matter of their periodical journalism. By blurring the distinction between fiction and non-fiction, as well as between masculine and feminine writing, they extended the range of subject matter and audiences for their work.

While there have been many full-length studies of Martineau, Gaskell, and Eliot that include discussions of their overlapping careers as journalists and the high-profile authors of book-length texts, none of these studies has fully analyzed the role journalism played in the construction of their complex literary identities. Likewise, while most biographers of Rossetti note her periodical publications, they do not explore the role of journalism in shaping her career. What little critical attention Christian Johnstone has received in recent years has highlighted only a fraction of her substantial periodical contributions.

In most of accounts of the history of women's authorship, journalism is treated as a stepping stone to more prestigious careers in book publication. In the typical biographical narrative, journalism is treated as an obligatory apprenticeship, a day job undertaken to pay the bills until the writer's break into literary stardom. Often the journalistic texts of these writers are mined as a source of information about their philosophical, social, and moral beliefs. Even more frequently, the periodical essays of these writers are completely overlooked in critical studies of their work. Most of the periodical essays by Martineau, Gaskell, and Johnstone have not been anthologized let alone studied by Victorian scholars, and the minor essays of Eliot have been all but ignored in recent criticism.[13] Likewise, the periodical context for the publication of many of Rossetti's poems has been overlooked. This study aims to bring some of this journalistic 'background' into the foreground of Victorian studies. Rather than privileging literary over journalistic media, as in a conventional critical analysis of Victorian women writers, this study acknowledges the multiplicity of women's writing careers, drawing attention to the ways they crossed boundaries of gender, identity, and media in their development as writers.

The first chapter of this study focuses on the debate in the 1830s over the role of the author in post-Romantic literary culture. This investigation begins by exploring the work of Carlyle, Thackeray, and a variety of lesser known journalists, who theorized new forms of 'useful' authorship to counter what they saw as the decadence of the Romantic sensibility and the volatility of radical journalism. These debates over literary authority were closely connected to controversies over the popular literature movement, the freedom of the press, working-class rights, and most importantly, the Woman Question. As women became increasingly involved in periodical reviewing and began addressing political subject matter in their book-length works, debates over social and literary authority became explicitly gendered. Cultural stereotypes of the eighteenth-century female author were thus redefined in terms of class and gender, leading to a new definition of the politically engaged middle-class woman author.

One of the most important of these writers during the 1830s and '40s was Harriet Martineau. Chapter two examines Martineau's early career, especially focusing on the development of her proto-feminist activism. After publishing *Illustrations of Political Economy* (1832-34), Martineau became the focal point for debates over the proper role of the female author. By daring to publish a political work of fiction under her own name, Martineau came to be defined as a feminine transgressor and accordingly was subjected to a number of attacks in the press. In addition to analyzing the ways that Martineau's public image was constructed in the popular media, this chapter investigates how she was able to resist these definitions through anonymous publication in periodicals. Anonymity enabled Martineau to express what she saw as a de-personalized and disinterested perspective on the Woman Question. In her early sociological works, *Society in America* (1837) and *How to Observe Morals and Manners* (1838), she defines how this objective journalistic perspective could be adapted to the goals of social progress, particularly the emancipation of women. She further examines this theme in *Deerbrook* (1839), a novel that dramatizes the role of middle-class women as politicized observers of domestic sociology.

The participation of women in the discourse on social investigation was facilitated by the development of the reformist periodical press in the 1830s and '40s. Instrumental in shaping this new medium of discourse was Christian

10   FIRST-PERSON ANONYMOUS

Johnstone. Johnstone was the co-editor of the *Inverness Courier, Edinburgh Weekly Chronicle, Schoolmaster and Edinburgh Weekly Magazine,* and *Johnstone's Edinburgh Magazine.* When Johnstone assumed the editorship of *Tait's Edinburgh Magazine* in 1834, she became the first woman to serve as paid editor of a major Victorian periodical. Chapter two investigates Johnstone's career as a journalist, demonstrating ways that she used the anonymity of periodical journalism to build a career as an influential editor and reviewer. As editor of *Tait's Edinburgh Magazine* (1834-46) Johnstone developed a new kind of mixed-gender reformist journalism that brought women's issues to the attention of middle-class readers and provided a forum for emerging women writers. During the 1840s, Johnstone made a rare break with her usual anonymity by publishing fiction under her own name in *Tait's Edinburgh Magazine* and in *Edinburgh Tales* (1845-6). In this way, Johnstone attempted to capitalize upon her name and the notoriety of her female contributors as a marketing device. Her editorial innovations did not establish her as a literary icon, partly due to her own efforts at self-effacement; however, they did pave the way for later experiments in reformist journalism that would be influential in debates over the Woman Question.

The social upheavals of the 1840s demanded a more politically active role for the middle-class woman writer. The first part of chapter three examines the development of the middle-class radical press and its connection to women's increasing involvement in philanthropic forms of literary activism. In particular, it explores the early career of Elizabeth Gaskell, who wrote anonymously for *Howitt's Journal* while composing her first novel, *Mary Barton* (1848). Gaskell's first novel is best understood as an extension of her work in the reformist periodical press, especially in terms of its ideological stance on working-class issues. While reformist periodicals claimed to sympathize with working-class interests, their effect was to dramatize how the lower-class home could be de-politicized through the philanthropic efforts of the middle classes. Similarly, the social problem novel dramatized the politicization of middle-class domestic space and emphasized the importance of women's writing as a form of philanthropic interventionism. The radicalization of middle-class domesticity corresponds with women's increasing involvement in philanthropic projects and changes in domestic reading practices.

The second part of chapter three examines a general shift in Gaskell's career during the 1850s, from an engagement with the discourse on the Condition-of-England Question to an emphasis on the Woman Question. This shift corresponded to a broader change in the motivation and goals of women's writing during this period. While during the 1830s and '40s women's participation in political debates was justified by their usefulness in stabilizing class relations, by the 1850s social conditions no longer seemed to warrant such philanthropic activism. The increased participation of women in periodical journalism and in high-profile book publishing ignited debates in the periodical press over the social value of women's writing and the proper role for the woman writer in the public sphere. By this time there were many prominent women journalists who rose to the defense of the 'abused woman author'. The discourse on the female author carried over into biography, most significantly Elizabeth Gaskell's *The Life of Charlotte Brontë* (1857), which reemployed the language and imagery of philanthropy for the purpose of defending the female author from the critical establishment. The publication of Gaskell's biography was a watershed event in the redirection of women's activism because it reinvigorated critical debates over gender and literary authority, debates that spilled over into gender-based criticism in the years that followed.

The arrival of George Eliot on the literary scene during the 1850s transformed definitions of women's authorship during the Victorian era. The first part of chapter five examines Eliot's 'Silly Novels by Lady Novelists' (1856) and 'Amos Barton' (1857), highlighting the connection between the fashioning of her complex literary persona and periodical discourses on authorial gender and identity. In these texts, Eliot replaced the image of the philanthropic or radical woman writer with an image of the cultured and ambiguously gendered author. After 'Amos Barton' appeared anonymously in *Blackwood's Magazine*, critics undertook an extensive search for the author's identity. When Eliot's identity was discovered, she reestablished gender complexity in her novels by maintaining her pseudonym. This enabled her to distance her work from the feminine and proto-feminist journalism and fiction being produced in the 1850s.

During the 1860s, Eliot's literary practice was informed by two major controversies within popular print culture: the debate over signature in the periodicals and the discourse on women's enfranchisement. The second part of chapter five analyzes Eliot's contributions and responses to these controversies, especially her social problem novel, *Felix Holt* (1866), and its companion essay 'Felix Holt's Address to Working Men' (1868). In these texts, Eliot employs narrative genres conventionally associated with the rise of the middle-class woman writer—social fiction and anonymous journalism—only to point to the ineffectuality of these genres in the modern age. Instead of intervening in debates over class relationships and women's enfranchisement, Eliot identified a subtly political role for the woman author: through cultured forms of literary representation and self-representation she could elevate the status of her work within the masculine literary canon.

Another writer whose work intersected with the periodical discourse on signature and women's authorship during the 1850s and '60s was Christina Rossetti. Chapter four investigates Rossetti's contributions to the short-lived Pre-Raphaelite journal, *The Germ*. This discussion focuses on how Rossetti's authorial image was constructed through her poetry and mediated through her brothers' editorial activities. Though *The Germ* was an important early venue for Rossetti, it did not provide her with the artistic control necessary to develop an authorial identity separate from the Pre-Raphaelite Brotherhood. Conflicts between her desire for authorial notoriety and her fear of self-display inform her contributions to *The Germ* and her contemporaneously written novella, *Maude*. An exploration of these intersecting texts reveals the opportunities and barriers Rossetti faced as a beginning writer and as a participant in a masculine literary community. These experiences led Rossetti to publish in a women's periodical, *The Bouquet from Marylebone Gardens*, and ultimately to pursue publication in *Macmillan's Magazine*, one of the first periodicals to promote a policy of signed publication. The emergence of Rossetti as a literary icon in the 1860s was thus inseparable from the development of new journalistic media that relied on authorial signature as a marker of literary value. As Rossetti's work increasingly fell subject to biographical criticism in the latter part of her career, she employed strategies designed to problematize direct correlation between her authorial name and private identity.

The careers of Martineau, Johnstone, Gaskell, Eliot, and Rossetti tell us a great deal about the relationship between women writers and gendered definitions of Victorian authorship. The conclusion to this study explores how the conditions of authorship changed in the final decades of the century. In addition, it provides some commentary on the future of research on gender issues in Victorian print media. My hope is that this study will provide critical tools that will enable scholars to read and appreciate periodical texts by women and consequently to become more informed readers of their book-length works of poetry, fiction, and non-fiction. With a deeper understanding of women's relationship to the complex narrative practices of Victorian print media, we can begin to comprehend the multiplicity of their texts, identities, and careers.

Notes

1   See Christ, whose estimate is based on a survey of entries in the *Wellesley Index to Victorian Periodicals* (21). Since this index contains references to only a fraction of the total number of periodicals published, Christ's estimate must be viewed as conservative.

2   Barbara Onslow's recently published study, *Women of the Press in Nineteenth-Century Britain*, is an especially good source for understanding women's overall contribution to the periodical press. Also important are the combined efforts of the scholars associated with the Research Society for Victorian Periodicals (RSVP). Founded in 1969, the RSVP has played an important role in broadening scholarly understanding of women's contributions to nineteenth-century periodical journalism. Most recently, RSVP devoted two special issues of *Victorian Periodicals Review* (1996, 1998) to women journalists and editors.

3   See Sanders' *Eve's Renegades* for a discussion of the role of the periodical press in facilitating the development of anti-feminist discourse.

4   Barbara Caine's recently published article, 'Feminism, Journalism, and Public Debate', provides further information about the role of journalism in the Victorian women's movement.

5   I have been careful not to label these texts as 'feminist' since the term was not used by Victorians to describe women's political activism (Caine, *Victorian* 4).

6   See also Showalter (73-99) and Thompson (*Reviewing Sex* 8-24).

INTRODUCTION 13

7 Two recently published collections of essays, for example, address this history: Burke's *Authorship from Plato to the Postmodern* and Jaszi and Woodmansee's *The Construction of Authorship*. See also studies by Cross, Sutherland, and Erickson on the history of authorship during the Victorian period.

8 Christ, Swindells (24-5), and Corbett (59-64), for example, tend to define the Victorian man of letters as a stable, monolithic category.

9 Many critical reviews during the Victorian period attempted to theorize a new kind of masculinity at the same time that they were redefining authorship as a profession. See Poovey (*Uneven Developments* 89-125) for a discussion of masculinity and authorship during the Victorian period.

10 See, for example, Toril Moi (62-3).

11 See Cheryl Walker and Nancy Miller.

12 Many recent scholars, including Lennard Davis and Frank Donoghue, have noted that the novel as a narrative form is closely connected to journalistic media, especially the periodical press. Recent studies of the social problem novel, such as Joseph Kestner's *Protest and Reform,* Catherine Gallagher's *Industrial Reformation of English Fiction,* and Rosemarie Bodenheimer's *The Politics of Story in Victorian Social Fiction,* have provided scholars with increased insight into the ideology of gender and class in social fiction by women. What remains to be investigated is how the emergence of periodical journalism and social fiction as complementary narrative forms enabled women to participate in public discourse over the state of the poor. Of course, to discuss the social problem novel is to rely on a generic term that is rather slippery, especially considering the diversity of political fiction published in the nineteenth century. For the purposes of this study, I define it as a form of fiction focused on depicting the effect of industrialist practices on the working classes and the role of the middle classes in facilitating mutual understanding between class interests.

13 I am referring to Martineau's articles in the *Monthly Repository* (1822-31) and the *Daily News* (1852-69); Johnstone's contributions to *The Schoolmaster and Edinburgh Weekly Magazine* (1832-33), *Johnstone's Edinburgh Magazine* (1833-34), and *Tait's Edinburgh Magazine* (1834-46); Gaskell's contributions to *Howitt's Journal* (1847-48) and *Fraser's Magazine* (1851-65); and Eliot's early essays in the *Coventry Herald and Observer* (1846-49) and *The Leader* (1851-56).

CHAPTER ONE

Beginnings: The 1830s

Victorian women's authorial careers during the 1830s took shape against a backdrop of shifting definitions of popular authorship. It was during this decade that literary critics attempted to theorize a new role for the post-Romantic author and to reconfigure class and gender stereotypes associated with popular authorship. With the deaths of Keats, Shelley, and Byron in the 1820s and the deaths of Goethe, Coleridge, and Scott in the following decade, the age of great writers seemed to end prematurely. As Carlyle writes in 1831,

> The old ideal of Manhood has grown obsolete, and the new is still invisible to us, and we grope after it in darkness, one clutching this phantom, another that; Werterism, Byronism, even Brummelism, each has its day ... . The Thinker must, in all senses, wander homeless, too often aimless, looking up to a Heaven which is dead for him, round to an Earth which is deaf ('Characteristics' 26).

Carlyle's central metaphor in this passage—the 'homelessness' of the author—reflects an overall sense of cultural dislocation in critical discourse of the 1830s.[1] Located outside the boundaries of domestic space and outside conventional definitions of masculinity, the author lacks a moral center that would direct his aimless wandering. This sense of dislocation and ambiguity led critics to redefine the identity of the popular author in terms of both gender and class, a process of redefinition that had important implications for the direction and aims of women's literary careers in the 1830s.

Carlyle, like many critics of his day, felt that the homelessness of the contemporary author was caused in part by the mechanization of literary production.[2] The invention of steam presses and machine-made paper had led to an increase in reading materials of all kinds: pamphlets, novels, newspapers, magazines, journals, and self-help books.[3] Likewise, the reduction of the advertisement tax in 1833, the stamp duty in 1836, and the paper tax in 1837 expanded the availability of cheap periodicals.[4] The expansion of the periodical press created a demand for a new kind of middle-class author who made an independent living writing miscellaneous reviews and essays (Heyck 24-46). Though most critics acknowledged that the expansion of the periodical press had provided new opportunities for middle-class writers, they also felt that it had resulted in an overall decline in the quality of literature. As William Maginn put it in 1831, 'quantity, and not quality, is the thing nearest to the author's heart' ('Novels' 9). Suddenly literature had become an industry, and the author, by extension, had become a producer of commodities.

16   FIRST-PERSON ANONYMOUS

Carlyle's project—along with many other critics of the 1830s—was to reestablish a sense of ethical responsibility in the literary marketplace, thereby reinstilling moral values in the process of literary production. This project seemed especially urgent for middle-class critics of the 1830s because of the increasing radicalism of popular print culture. The expansion of the radical press, led by William Cobbett in the first decades of the century,[5] was seen by many as an example of the kind of journalism that, left unchecked, could undermine class hierarchies. Thackeray's 1838 review of several working-class publications confirmed the worst fears of many:

> Suffice it to say, that ribaldry so infamous, obscenity so impudently blackguard and brazen, can hardly be conceived, and certainly never was printed until our day ... . Thanks to the enlightened spirit of the age, no man scarcely is so ill-educated as not to be able to read them; and blessings on cheap literature! no man is too poor to buy them ('Half-a-Crown' 290).

Thackeray argues that the radical promoters and publishers of this cheap literature are to blame for its pernicious effects. In his estimation, the notion of the author as a popular educator was ridiculous because most working-class people desired ribald entertainment, not moral improvement, in their reading materials.

Despite Thackeray's objections, the image of the author as a popular educator was gaining increasing currency among those in the print trade. As Richard Altick points out, the call for a more improving literature emerged in the early decades of the century in response to utilitarian and evangelical critiques of imaginative literature (*English* 132).[6] These groups attempted to expand the availability of cheap reading material, though for different purposes: 'the religious parties to point the way to the kingdom of God, the utilitarians to insure the greater glory of the workshop of the world' (132). In other words, rather than serving as an end in itself, literature would have a clear moral or economic purpose that would lead to social improvement. Organizations such as the Society for the Diffusion of Useful Knowledge published scores of cheap magazines and books claiming to improve the morals and practical knowledge of working-class readers.[7] In reviews of these publications, critics attempted to formulate their own definitions of morally beneficial literature, often emphasizing its role in promoting social stability. As one critic for the *Penny Magazine* put it, an education founded in improving reading materials would allow workers 'to understand that a good and just government cannot consult the interests of one particular class or calling, in preference to another ... and that if each were to insist upon having everything its own way, there would be nothing by the wildest confusion, or the merest tyranny' ('What Is Education?' 110).

The discourse over the role of the post-Romantic author corresponds with an overall cultural preoccupation with defining the authorial subject during the 1830s. Biographies, obituaries, portraits, and encyclopedias of famous authors emerged as major literary forms during this period. The discourse on the author encompasses a large number of cultural texts. Examples include Thomas Moore's *Life of Byron* (1830), John Croker's *Life of Samuel Johnson* (1831), James Boaden's *Memoirs of Mrs. Inchbald* (1833), William Roberts' *Memoirs of the Life and Correspondence of Mrs. Hannah More* (1834), Henry Chorley's *Memorials of Mrs. Hemans* (1836), and John Gibson Lockhart's *Memoirs of the Life of Sir Walter Scott* (1837-38). The most significant literary medium concerned with constructing the author in the 1830s was the periodical press. Periodicals such as *Blackwood's Magazine* and *Fraser's Magazine* published literary portraits and biographical criticism.[8] This cultural fascination with the author was also represented in legal discourse, which further defined copyright protections and other rights associated with professional authorship.[9]

These critical and legal speculations often concentrated on the gender and class identity of the popular author. In these accounts, the upper-class male writer is often presented as the antithesis of the ideal public educator:

> These *littérateurs*, amateur authors; *dilettanti virtuosi*, writing gentlemen, men of nice taste and fastidious criticism, carpers at syllables, affected connoisseurs of style, hunters after polished phrases and elegant periods; these are not the class to educate the million (Roebuck, 'Useful Knowledge' 379).

Here the upper-class dilettante is depicted as one who pays more attention to style than social good. The popular author, in contrast, must have

> Bold and masculine understandings—men possessed of a thorough knowledge of the mental and physical wants of the people—men imbued with a high spirit, of undaunted courage, seeking not reputation by their productions, but wishing to instruct ... promoting virtue and happiness among the people—these are the men alone fit to be popular instructors, alone capable of diffusing useful knowledge (379).

What is remarkable about this definition of authorship is the way that it configures the authorial role according to both class and gender. The modern author is able to communicate across class boundaries by virtue of his masculinity—defined as his breadth of knowledge, courage, and disinterestedness. Presumably it is the effeminacy of the aristocratic author, defined as limited personal experience and vain self-interest, that makes him incapable of communicating effectively with the lower classes.

Though women writers are not directly mentioned in this passage, they are by implication excluded from the category of those capable of 'diffusing useful knowledge' by virtue of their gender since 'masculine understanding' of class relations would be considered outside their realm of experience. Indeed, the tendency to masculinize definitions of authorship was a dominant feature of critical discourse during the 1830s. As Mary Jean Corbett and Mary Poovey have demonstrated, the project of defining the male author was premised on separate spheres ideology and the construction of idealized definitions of middle-class femininity.[10] The creation of the Victorian professional man of letters, they argue, was dependent upon the construction of a domestic woman who would preside over the private sphere, exerting moral influence that would serve as a corrective to the degraded values of the literary marketplace. Conversely, the female author became a social anomaly whose work lowered the overall moral and aesthetic quality of contemporary literature. By distinguishing between what they considered to be serious masculine literary production and more ephemeral feminine texts, critics attempted to define a new canon of English letters.

Though by most accounts women novelists were in the majority during the late eighteenth century,[11] they were represented as a minority in the canon of literary authors as constructed by critics of the 1830s. The periodical press of this period was notable for its attacks on women authors as well as for its canonization of male authors, especially Walter Scott. This emphasis on constructing a masculine canon of literature carried over into English authors and great Englishmen anthologies and portrait collections published during this period. For example, in Arthur Malkin's *Gallery of Portraits* (1833-37), William Jerdan's *National Portrait Gallery* (1830-34), and Henry Chorley's *The Authors of England* (1838), portraits of men outnumber those of women.[12]

While it is undoubtedly true that women were often excluded in the process of canon formation in the 1830s, it is important to realize that the critical project of masculinizing literary authority by no means went uncontested. The discussions surrounding the passage of the Reform Bill (1832) brought the issue of women's enfranchisement to the attention of parliament and the general public (Fulford 32-40). Likewise, the participation of women in anti-Catholic, abolitionist, and Chartist movements suggested ways that women might assume an expanded public role.[13] Women's involvement in social movements corresponded with an increase in the number of political, scientific, and philosophical texts written by women during the first decades of the nineteenth century. The works of Mary Somerville, Harriet Martineau, and Jane Marcet, though very different in their audiences and aims, together had the effect of calling into question the notion of separate realms of literary authority for male and female writers.[14]

The most influential critic to participate in debates over the gender and identity of the author during the 1830s was Thomas Carlyle. Most scholars credit Carlyle with formulating distinctly masculine stereotypes of authorship in his early essays. Carol Christ, for example, claims that Carlyle constructs the profession of letters as a 'world of heroic masculinity' and defines the Victorian sage as 'exclusively male' (20). Indeed, in his biographical criticism of Goethe and others, Carlyle often seems to exclude women from his definition of heroic authorship.[15] However, in his early essays Carlyle's constructions of authorial gender are far from stable. At the same time he was constructing the male author-hero in his biographical criticism, he was making the contradictory claim that the most productive forms of authorship were dissociated from egotism and individualized identity.[16] That is, he advocated low-profile forms of public activism that would enable writers to transcend the limits of individual identity and thereby express truth. This diffusion of authorial identity also had a way of destabilizing—at least partly—critical constructions of authorial sex and gender.

In his essay, 'Characteristics' (1831), Carlyle defines the ideal author as one who operates outside social constructions of identity and marketplace definitions of value. For Carlyle, the artist does not desire public display like a 'Demonstrator' (4) or 'hawker' (15). Rather, true genius arises from 'that domain of the Unconscious, by nature infinite and inexhaustible; and creatively work[s] there. From that mystic region, and from that alone, all wonders, all Poesies, and Religions, and Social Systems have proceeded' (35). In this way, Carlyle defines artistic creation and social activism as private, unconscious activities that transcend the market for literary commodities. It is through self-cultivation, rather than through public adulation and remuneration, that authors can develop a wide-ranging perspective on social issues that will enable them to have a positive impact on society.[17]

In his review of Lockhart's *Life of Sir Walter Scott* (1838), Carlyle expands upon this definition of literary production by analyzing the damaging effects of fame and wealth on the career of one of the most renowned writers of his age:

> It is one of the comfortablest truths that great men abound, though in the unknown state. Nay, as above hinted, our greatest, being also by nature our *quietest*, are perhaps those that remain unknown! ... [If] Walter Scott, as a latent Walter, had never amused all men ... or gained and lost several hundred thousand pounds sterling by Literature ... he might have been a happy and by no means useless,—nay, who knows at bottom whether not a still usefuler Walter! However, that was not his fortune (77-78).

According to Carlyle, Scott's desire for name and fame kept him from achieving moral usefulness in the final years of his career. Likewise, Scott's desire for commercial success turned his work into a commodity. Rather than attempting to uncover universal truths, Scott was 'writing daily with the ardour of a steam-engine, that he might make | 15,000 a-year, and buy upholstery with it' (98). Carlyle felt that by writing for the marketplace and consciously constructing his own literary celebrity, Scott served the interests of self rather than the interests of society as a whole.[18] His novels offered 'no divine awakening voice' that would provide moral guidance and inspiration to readers (101).

Though Carlyle's essay is focused on a male writer, its message was applicable to women, who were often accused of writing for money and fame rather than for social good. His definition of authorship fit well within socially constructed definitions of femininity and domesticity. Like the ideal woman, Carlyle's ideal author was concerned with values and morality rather than with egotism, self-consciousness, and public display. Further, the work of the Carlylean hero, like that of the domestic woman, was separated from the marketplace economy and the laws of supply and demand. Defined in opposition to both upper-class superficiality and lower-class vulgarity, the middle-class author, like the middle-class woman, must constantly cultivate a sense of depth, moral value, and quiet political activism. The compatibility of Carlyle's notions of the ideal author with socially constructed notions of the domestic woman suggests ways that middle-class women might enter political discourse without sacrificing domestic privacy. Indeed, many Victorian women writers, including Martineau, Gaskell, and Eliot, expressed their indebtedness to Carlyle.[19]

Of course this is not to say that Carlyle consciously was feminist in any sense of the word. However, Carlyle's essays reveal an indeterminacy in gender categories that was becoming prevalent during the 1830s. In 'Biography' (1832), Carlyle's gendering of authorship is especially slippery. He begins his essay by singling out effeminate/feminine genres of writing, especially the fashionable novel, as examples of the 'lowest of froth Prose' (54).[20] But he includes both men and women in his definition of popular authorship:

> These Three Thousand men, women and children, that make up the army of British Authors, do not, if we will well consider it, *see* anything whatever; consequently *have* nothing they can record and utter, only more or fewer things that they can plausibly pretend to record (63).

For Carlyle, it is this mixed-gender, often naively child-like 'army' that needs to be reformed. This reformation comes from developing a more universal sense of self that is premised on understanding of 'the Universe, of Man and Nature' (63). Instead of ascribing to limiting definitions of self, perhaps including those based on sex and gender, Carlyle asks writers to look beyond the 'pitiful Image of their own pitiful Self, with its vanities, and grudgings, and ravenous hunger of all kinds' (64). Through close observation of transcendental reality writers could contribute to social improvement, functioning as so many 'watch-towers, to instruct us by indubitable documents' (64). Located above society, the author gains an expanded vision of the world and can thereby communicate a more truthful message.

Carlyle's watchtower metaphor suggests that good writing is the product of social observation, which in turn produces social discipline. But how was a woman writer to gain the broad perspective on contemporary literature, politics, and society necessary to perform this disciplinary function when her culturally defined place was in the domestic sphere? This was a question Carlyle was unwilling or unable to answer directly. But for women authors during the 1830s this was a question that could not be avoided because it exposed a basic contradiction in their professional lives: they must be separated from the commercial marketplace in order to maintain a sense of middle-class propriety and to preserve their claim to producing works of culture rather than of profit; at the same time, they must claim to have broad knowledge of issues outside the domestic sphere—to demonstrate understanding of the social and political issues associated with all classes of society.[21] Put another way, they must claim to be amateur writers lest they be considered lower-class hacks who write for money, yet they must establish their authority as professionals lest they be considered upper-class dilettantes who write for vanity. How were they to overcome these contradictions?

Domesticity, Class, and the Woman Author

The contradictions associated with definitions of women's authorship in the 1830s have their root in popular print culture of the 1790s when enlightenment ideology altered the terms of debate over the position of women in society. For many enlightenment thinkers, the march of the intellect promised to promote educational advancement and political equality among of all classes of society.[22] As a product of this ideology, late eighteenth-century republican writers such as Mary Wollstonecraft and Germaine de Staël as well as bluestocking writers such as Elizabeth Montague, Elizabeth Carter, and Hannah More attempted to construct a more rational femininity that would enable women to assume more responsible social roles.

In *Vindication of the Rights of Woman* (1792), Wollstonecraft argues that educational institutions train middle-class women to adopt the idleness of the upper classes, 'to fly from themselves to noisy pleasures, and artificial passions, till vanity takes place of every social affection' (51). The cultivation of female vanity, rather than 'well regulated affections', prevents them from acting out the 'indispensable duty of a mother' and from exerting a moral influence on society as a whole (142). 'I cannot help lamenting', she writes, 'that women of a superior cast have not a road open by which they can pursue more extensive plans of usefulness and independence' (147). If women received a practical education, she argues, they would be capable of pursuing careers in politics, business, and medicine (148). Both political and domestic, the useful middle-class woman embodied the contradiction between the ideology of separate spheres, which defined an exclusively domestic role for women, and new definitions of liberal individuality, which promised equal citizenship for all members of society (Eisenstein 102-8).

The tension between these contradictory ideological positions continued to inform the development of women's writing careers during the early decades of the nineteenth century. The resurgence of religious conservatism in the years following the French Revolution made many wary of the rhetoric on women's rights and the participation of women in public life (B. Taylor 9-15). 'Bluestockingism' was increasingly used as a pejorative term in critical discourse, and Mary Wollstonecraft's ideas were obscured by controversies over her personal life.[23] Suddenly the discourse on women's rights had become as controversial as radicalism, and the political woman was defined as a contaminating social influence.

For many early nineteenth-century critics, Hannah More seemed to embody the ideal of the socially concerned woman writer. Though More expressed ideas similar to those put forth in Wollstonecraft's *Vindication,* she couched these viewpoints in terms that were more compatible with conservative views of domestic womanhood in a post-revolutionary age. In *Strictures on Female Education* (1799), for example, More promotes educational programs that 'enable [a woman] to regulate her own mind, and to be instrumental to the good of others', but only in a way that is 'fitted for home consumption' (2: 2, 3). Through her efforts as a popular educator, prolific author, and cultural icon, More's career came to epitomize this sense of feminine usefulness. As many recent critics have pointed out, though More's brand of activism undoubtedly served the interests of middle-class patriarchy, it also provided a model for how women writers could participate in the public sphere while still maintaining a sense of domestic propriety.[24] As Lucinda Cole demonstrates, More's conservative activism allowed 'her to claim a separate realm of action for women, to argue that, as natural sources of compassion, they have both the right and the duty to institute the kind of social reform that begins with Christian virtues—public charity, social work, ministering to the poor' (118). More's *Cheap Repository Tracts* (1795-97) and her work in the Sunday School Movement (1789-1800) demonstrated how women could use their domestic morality and connections to religious and philanthropic organizations as springboards for careers in mass market publishing.[25] By transforming popular culture to suit her own personal and political agenda, More exerted influence on a large scale while still claiming a higher moral purpose as schoolmistress to the lower orders. From this base, More soon expanded her audience to include middle- and upper-class readers by publishing moral treatises, conduct books, and a best-selling novel, *Coelebs in Search of a Wife* (1809). These publishing projects made More one of the most influential—and wealthy—writers of her age.

When More died in 1833, she was one of the first English women writers whose *oeuvre* had been published in a multi-volume set.[26] Likewise, the posthumously published *Memoirs of the Life and Correspondence of Mrs. Hannah More* (1834) established her as one of the most exemplary lives of the post-revolutionary era. Though More's high-profile literary career had been controversial during her own time, by the 1830s, her image was reconstituted as one of conservative, pious activism. Likewise, the transgressiveness of More's forays into the masculine world of public education and administration were reinterpreted as extensions of her middle-class domesticity.[27] The frontispiece of More's *Works* (1838), for example, displays a picture of her home at Barley Wood along with the usual portrait of the author.[28] In the accompanying description, More is depicted as the creator of a home rather than as the creator of texts. The improvements made by the More sisters and their picturesque garden are described in great detail. Most significantly, it is the exemplary home, not More herself, that is depicted as the agent of social change:

> But Barley Wood is not merely an object of grateful attachment to the inhabitants of a particular district or county; its fame is spread to the eastern and western world. In 1823 there was published in America a view of this interesting spot, for the purpose of contributing to the support of a female missionary school, to be called Barley Wood, in the island of Ceylon (2: 3).

Instead of More's books being spread across the world, it is her home that is endlessly replicated in exotic locations, exerting its moral influence in the service of colonialism. Such a displacement conflates homemaking with writing and colonization with domestic economics.[29] Though on one hand the personification of Barley Wood seems to downplay More's agency as the writer of influential texts, it also suggests ways that an idealized domesticity could be adapted for political purposes. The conflation of domestic and political spaces, activities, and agendas provided a useful model for later women writers whose literary activity also complicated notions of public and private spheres.

For periodical critics of the 1830s, More epitomized the ideal middle-class woman writer and activist.[30] In the *National Portrait Gallery of Illustrious and Eminent Personages* (1830), William Jerdan praises More's 'Tales for the Common People' as 'plain, simple, adapted to the comprehension of those to whom they were addressed; encouraging by good example, and imbued with a strong spirit of religion' (3: 3). Jerdan suggests that More took 'religion as the only guiding principle of action', rather than pursuing a radical agenda (3: 1).[31] In critical appraisals of her *oeuvre,* More's character was also defined against the image of the lower class hack writer who wrote novels for financial gain. As the *Quarterly Review* points out, 'none of Hannah's books were written under pressure of poverty' but for the 'best and noblest of purposes' (Lockhart 417, 435). In this way, More's model of authorship came to be defined as a contradictory form of middle-class moral activism that exerted influence in public debates without subverting class and gender hierarchies.

The terms by which More was constructed as a model of the new socially concerned woman writer were also employed in periodical criticism of women's literature in general during the 1830s. Though many critics defined literary discourse as a realm of masculine privilege, they still devoted a great deal of energy to defining the roles and responsibilities of the woman writer. Anthologies, memoirs, and portraits of renowned women, including many women of letters, emerged at the same time that volumes focused on male authors were published.[32] In addition, portraits of women writers and reviews of their texts increasingly appeared in periodicals.[33] Far from being exclusionary, most periodicals of the 1830s demonstrate a fascination with women's writing. Though these reviews were sometimes derogatory, their sheer number testifies to the vitality of authorial sex and gender as a critical concern.

In these critical reviews, the new woman writer, like her male counterpart, was constructed in opposition to stereotypes of lower- and upper-class authorship. In assessing the progress of women in contemporary society, many critics focused on the inadequacy of educational institutions for promoting the right kind of middle-class female subjectivity:

> An accomplished woman of the present day is, therefore, peculiarly unfitted for any useful pursuit, since usefulness in any capacity of life is not the specific object of the instruction given ... The model upon which the education of every class of women is formed is an aristocratic model; and one of the attributes of an aristocracy is, and always has been, to have the women of their order totally unfitted for every purpose, but that of being mere ministers to their own idle vanity (Roebuck, 'Madame Roland' 83).

Women's frivolousness is thus attributed to aristocratic models of femininity promoted by educational practices and institutions. The 'useful' middle-class woman is defined in opposition to notions of upper-class (ef)feminacy that promoted vanity and self-indulgence rather than the production of socially beneficial works or texts. She would create a demand for more improving reading materials among disenfranchised groups rather than providing escapist entertainment.

While most critics agreed that the new woman writer needed to express a distinctly middle-class sensibility, they disagreed on whether women should be equal participants in public debates on social, economic, and political issues. According to many reviewers, the most socially useful women's writing depicted the morals and manners of middle-class domesticity.[34] The appearance of books by women on conventionally masculine subjects such as politics, economics, and social policy problematized this definition of feminine writing. Works such as Harriet Martineau's *Illustrations of Political Economy* (1832-34), Frances Trollope's *Domestic Manners of the Americans* (1832), and Caroline Norton's *A Voice from the Factories* (1836) challenged stereotypes of proper feminine subject matter. The political subject matter of women's fiction was often ascribed to their close association with male writers and influences.[35] For many critics, this was the only way to explain political subject matter for women since respectable middle-class women by definition had no contact with the world of politics.

The growing critical concern over the politicization of women's writing is expressed in William Maginn and Daniel Maclise's 'Portrait Gallery of Illustrious Literary Characters', published serially in *Fraser's Magazine* from 1830 to 1838. This series satirizes some of the most eminent personages of the day, including Harriet Martineau, Letitia Landon, John Gibson Lockhart, John Wilson Croker, and Mary Russell Mitford. In the text accompanying a portrait of Landon, contributing writer Francis Mahoney makes it clear that he will praise the achievements of the female author as long as she is a 'very nice, unbluestockingish, well-dressed, and trim-looking young lady, fond of sitting pretty' (433). If she ventures to write on political topics, she is fair game for the harshest criticism:

> Is she to write of politics, or political economy, or pugilism, or punch? Certainly not. We feel a determined dislike of women who wander into these unfeminine paths; they should immediately hoist a mustache—and, to do them justice, they in general do exhibit no inconsiderable specimen of the hair-lip (433).

Mahoney interprets the tendency of women to write on 'masculine' subjects as a violation of both gender and sex. In another portrait included in the series, William Maginn suggests that such violations justify exceptions to the rules of social decorum that prohibit the ill treatment of a respectable woman. He writes of Caroline Norton, 'We think that a lady ought to be treated, even by Reviewers, with the utmost deference—except she writes politics, which is an enormity equal to wearing breeches' (222). The woman author's disregard for the categories of gendered writing is figured as a disruption in conventional sexual codes.[36] This attempt to connect critical analysis to illustrations of the authorial body and costume is a dominant feature of biographical criticism of both men's and women's writing during this period. However, for women writers the public display of these images was more socially damaging. Although, as Patricia Marks points out, the publication of portraits of women authors undoubtedly 'ceded them some measure of literary influence', it also gave the impression that women authors sought such attention due to an 'unfeminine' love of public adulation (33).

Even though many critics imposed gender-based stereotypes on women's writing, it was not without a certain amount of self-consciousness. A number of articles appear in the 1830s that express anxiety about the role of the critic in constructing the gender of popular authors. For example, 'The Cant of Criticism', published in *Fraser's Magazine* in 1839, satirizes excessive criticism of women's writing by describing a conversation between a male poet and a critic over the meaning of Felicia Hemans' poem, 'The Burial in the Desert'. The critic insists on demonstrating 'that it is all inconsistent, not merely with fact or truth or common sense, but also with religion, morality, and good taste' (96). He then takes the poem apart line by line, ridiculing 'the bad taste displayed in the choice of words and images' (103). At various points, the critic employs explicitly gendered terms. For example, in response to a positive characterization of the 'Norman race' in Hemans' poem, he states, 'the page of history has not space to record their reckless, brutal acts of outrage ... [Yet] here we have a most *high* and ladylike compliment paid them by the highly professing poetess!' (100). Following the critical conventions of the period, he attacks the poem based on the presumed inexperience of its female author: ''Tis easy to be seen that this is a lady's composition', he writes. 'Had she ever been in camp, under a fire, or on burial duty, her experience would have led her to have used another epithet [than "soldier love"]' (100). Such remarks finally cause the poet to run out of the room, 'forswearing poetry and its parasitic plague for ever' (103).

The *Fraser's* essay aims to illustrate the folly of criticism run amok but even more specifically addresses the problem of gender-based criticism of literary works. It is not coincidental that a woman's poem is the designated victim of the worst kind of critical attention or that its defender is a male poet. As the passive author behind the text, Hemans does not speak in her own defense. This is not the case in a similarly self-reflexive article published in *Fraser's Magazine* in 1835 titled 'Miss Fanny Kemble and Her Critics'. The article recounts that in the early years of Kemble's career, critics praised her talent as an actress and writer, each 'surpassing his brother scribes in the extravagance of the eulogies which he heaped upon her' (327). After publication of her *Journal,* the critics turned against her, opening 'heavy fire upon the authoress, who was pronounced vulgar, coarse-minded, [and] destitute of all right feeling' (327). The reason for this change, the essay points out, was Kemble's harsh criticism of the press in her *Journal.*

While the essay condemns the 'bad taste' of Kemble's remarks, it is even more critical of those journalists who would 'run open-mouthed at one whom a few short months previously they had lauded' (327, 328). Such poor journalistic practice is 'exercised not in obedience to the laws of truth and fairness, but in subserviency to personal predilections or personal hostility' (328). By exposing the hypocrisy of the press and defending the female author from her attackers, this essay follows in the same vein as 'The Cant of Criticism' discussed above. However, in this review, Kemble's condemnation of journalists is presented alongside critiques of her work. In the excerpts included in the *Fraser's* essay, Kemble declares her 'aversion' to newspaper writers. She also writes, 'except where they have been made political tools, newspaper-writers and editors have never, I believe, been admitted into good society in England' (327). Thus, rather than being depicted simply as a victim of male critical attacks, she is represented as a critic in her own right. This representation reverses the usual order of critical reviewing where the journalist constructs the public image of the woman writer. At least in this review, the act of turning the tables on journalistic critics is depicted as a brave if somewhat tasteless literary maneuver on Kemble's part.

Women as Periodical Journalists in the 1830s

The self-consciousness of periodical reviews during the 1830s demonstrates the instability of the female author as a critical construct and expresses anxieties about the role of journalism in formulating gender categories. As we will see, women writers actively sought media that would enable them to resist restrictive definitions of gendered writing and to participate in the construction of their public identities. The most important of these media was the anonymous periodical, which provided women with the tools to expand their knowledge of popular thought and to write on issues of political and social concern with less fear of damaging publicity. With the expansion of the popular press in the 1830s, middle-class women gained greater access to reading materials on political, economic, and social issues. Prior to the reduction in stamp duties, women most often obtained these materials from neighbors, reading groups, and circulating libraries.[37] Consequently, women who could afford the subscription fee could gain access to the latest in popular thought. The reduction in the price of periodicals, books, and newspapers brought on by the partial remission of the stamp duties enabled middle-class women to purchase their own copies of reading materials, which could then be read privately.[38] As one critic remarked, journalism had become so ubiquitous in the middle-class home that 'the public goes to bed with a periodical in her hand, and falls asleep with it beneath her pillow ('Periodicals' 182). Consumed primarily within private spaces, the periodical came to be associated with a feminized domestic sphere. The serial and miscellaneous nature of the periodical made it particularly adaptable to the life of the middle-class woman, whose private time was often interrupted by social and domestic responsibilities. By reading periodicals and other popular literature, the intellectually inclined woman was thus able to broaden her education and to form opinions on public issues without having to leave the domestic environment.[39] As Margaret Beetham points out, even women's magazines of the period, such as the *Christian Lady's Magazine,* encouraged their readers to educate themselves on political issues and to 'use their influence for the common good' (52).

In addition to having greater access to periodicals during the 1830s, women had increasing opportunities to pursue careers as literary critics. Prominent authors of book-length critical studies such as Germaine de Staël and Anna Jameson pointed the way to a more politicized and gendered critical practice for women writers.[40] However, as many women realized, it was difficult to engage in such high-profile forms of politicized literary criticism in a society that still accepted the idea of women's natural domesticity. For this reason, the anonymity of journalistic publishing was especially attractive to women because it enabled them to engage in public careers while still maintaining the privacy and customs of domestic life. Because periodical editors sometimes attempted to essentialize authorial gender in graphic and prose sketches, women often sought to dissociate their private identities from their written work.[41] During the 1820s and '30s, writers such as Priscilla Buxton, Sarah Austin, and Lucy Aiken first began publishing anonymous reviews in prestigious periodicals such as the *Dublin Review, Edinburgh Review,* and *Westminster Review.* Though women contributors were usually in the minority, there were some exceptions. Mary Margaret Busk, for example, was a major contributor to the *Foreign Quarterly Review* during the 1830s, publishing over 50 critical reviews on European literature and culture.

The most accessible journalistic media for women during the 1830s were the magazines and miscellanies, especially the *Monthly Repository, Blackwood's Magazine,* and *Fraser's Magazine.* The *Monthly Repository* employed eight women writers during the 1830s, including Harriet Martineau, Mary Leman Grimstone, and Letitia Kinder.[42] The *Wellesley Index to Victorian Periodicals* lists six women contributors to *Blackwood's Magazine* and seven contributors to *Fraser's Magazine* during the 1830s. Though these periodicals often included women among their contributors, they were still careful to create the illusion of a male editorial board. *Fraser's Magazine,* for example, represented its contributors as a strictly male group of 'Fraserians' in one of its most famous 'Gallery Portraits' (Figure 1.1). This is also reflected in the masculine gender markers associated with its 'editorial we', which is most often personified as a male character, Oliver Yorke.[43] As Patrick Leary has pointed out, these narrative devices mask the contributions of several women to the magazine, including Agnes Hall and Anne Matthews.

Interestingly enough, when the editors of *Fraser's* did publish a group portrait of women writers in 1836, titled *'Regina's* Maids of Honour', they included only one of their women contributors, Letitia Landon, in the illustration (Leary 118).

1.1 The 'Fraserians' by Daniel Maclise. Reproduced courtesy of the British Library

1.2 '*Regina*'s Maids of Honor' by Daniel Maclise. Reproduced courtesy of Memorial Library, University of Wisconsin, Madison

Instead, they featured women writers who had been the objects of satire in their 'Gallery Portraits' series, including Harriet Martineau and Sydney Morgan (Figure 1.2). Whereas in the 'Fraserians' illustration the male writers sit around a table with most of their faces turned toward the viewer, in the 'Maids of Honor' illustration the group of women writers face each other and are engaged in private conversation over tea. In this way, the editors of *Fraser's* construct the reader as a male voyeur of a female domestic circle. Paradoxically, the woman writer is represented as both a commodified public image and an emblem of domestic privacy.

At the same time that *Fraser's* constructed non-Fraserian women writers as the public-private objects of the critical gaze, it included anonymous articles by women writers that created a disruption in the implied masculinity of the periodical as a whole. For example, Harriet Downing's 'Remembrances of a Monthly Nurse' (1836)—a series of stories about the adventures of a middle-class midwife—brings a sense of femininity into an otherwise masculine periodical. As in the 'Maids of Honor' illustration, this series turns a journalistic gaze on a feminized domestic space, thus complicating notions of domestic privacy and public discourse. The contradictory relationship between publicity and privacy, masculinity and femininity in *Fraser's* reflects the indeterminacy of gender in the periodical as a literary medium. Because of their anonymity, periodicals functioned so as to confuse the very gender definitions they attempted to construct in critical reviews. Disguised behind the collective 'editorial we', women to some extent lost the privileges of fame: copyright protection and artistic control. However, as they shed their identities, they gained freedom, at least partly, from the gender stereotypes attached to the feminine authorial name. The 'editorial we' sometimes proved to be a thin disguise for women since readers could usually find out the names of contributors through informal channels (Shattock 15-18). But not all readers would have had access to this informal network, and a great many others were not likely to trouble themselves. Consequently, it is probably safe to assume that anonymity provided relatively effective cover for women who wanted to write on political and social issues.

The expansion of the periodical press, especially the practice of literary reviewing, was part of an ongoing cultural project of retheorizing, reimaging, and regendering the popular author. By imposing notions of masculinity and femininity on literary works, many mainstream periodicals attempted to formulate a distinctly middle-class cultural identity. At the same time, the anonymity of the periodical press also enabled many writers—especially women—to subvert gender hierarchies in their literary practice. The next chapter explores the role of anonymous publication in the career of one of the most important women writers of the early Victorian period: Harriet Martineau. As we will see, Martineau's contributions to the Woman Question emerged from within the context of her career as a periodical journalist and led her to redefine women's authorial roles and responsibilities.

Notes

1   R. H. Horne also uses the 'homeless' metaphor in his discussion of the status of authors in the new literary marketplace (1). See Stein (63-71) and Brantlinger (11-14) for discussion of the sense of cultural dislocation and historical self-consciousness during the 1830s.

2   See, for example, Carlyle's commentary on mechanistic literary production in *Sartor Resartus* (35-6) and 'Sir Walter Scott' (104-6). Lee Erickson provides further examples (104-23).

3   Steam printing was introduced into England by publishers of *The Times* in 1806 and was first applied to periodical and book publishing during the 1830s. Machine-made paper came into use after 1812. See Altick, *English Common Reader* (277-80), Olivia Smith (159-61), and Williams, *Long Revolution* (156-72).

4   According to Thomas Heyck, 'between 1830 and 1880, more than 100 [periodicals] were founded each decade' (33). Popular print culture expanded rapidly during the 1830s even though the 'taxes on knowledge' were not eliminated until 1861. As Altick points out, the 1830s saw the publication of the first mass-market periodicals, including the *Penny Magazine* and *Chambers' Edinburgh Journal*, both of which achieved circulations of over 50,000 (*English* 393).

5   The stamp duties on newspapers were expanded in 1819 to include publications that printed commentary on the news. This change was intended to suppress the radical print trade, specifically Cobbett-style newspapers and periodicals. Instead, it led to a black market industry of unstamped papers. See Altick *(English* 318-332), Collet (1: 17-40), and Croker ('Conduct' 296-303).

6   See Nesbitt (96-129) and Brantlinger (19-28) for further background on utilitarian and evangelical critiques of imaginative literature.

7   The Society for the Diffusion of Useful Knowledge was a charitable organization that subsidized publication of the *Penny Magazine* and a series of inexpensive books and pamphlets. Its goal was to provide 'useful information to all classes of the community, particularly to such as are unable to avail themselves of experienced teachers or may prefer learning by themselves' (qtd. in Roebuck, 'Useful Knowledge' 365).

8   Of course the discourse on the author begins much earlier in periodicals such as the *Monthly Review* and the *Critical Review* (Donaghue). Significant early book-length texts focused on defining the author include Johnson's *Lives of the Poets* (1779-81), Disraeli's *An Essay on the Manners and Genius of the Literary Character* (1795), Barbauld's *The British Novelists* (1810), Scott's *Lives of the Novelists* (1821-24), and Hazlitt's *The Spirit of the Age* (1825). See Duncan (4), Altick (*Lives and Letters* 112-45), and H. Brown (179-85) for additional examples.

9   In 1837, Thomas Talford introduced a bill into parliament that would extend authorial copyright from 28 to 60 years. This led to a lively debate that involved many prominent writers, including Wordsworth, though significant changes in copyright law were not enacted into law until the 1840s. See Jaszi and Woodmansee (4-5) and Erickson (60-69). During this decade there was also a great deal of discussion of the rights of authors to pensions, annuities, and other professional benefits. See R. H. Horne's *Exposition of the*

False Medium (1833) and the *Fraser's Magazine*'s review of Horne's book ('Genius and the Public'). Cross also provides a useful overview (38-89).

10 Corbett (56-82), Poovey (*Uneven* 89-125).

11 See Watt (298), Tuchman and Fortin (45-50), and Lovell (42-3).

12 In the *Gallery of Portraits,* four women are depicted in a series of 168 portraits; in the *National Portrait Gallery,* nine women are represented in a collection of 184 portraits; and in *Authors of England,* four women are represented in a series of 14 medallion portraits.

13 Linda Colley provides a useful overview of the role of women in anti-Catholic, abolitionist, and other movements during the early decades of the nineteenth century (278, 333). See also Barbara Taylor for an analysis of the connections between Chartism and the development of socialist feminism (265-75).

14 See Somerville's *Connection of the Physical Science* (1834), Martineau's *Illustrations of Political Economy* (1832-4), and Marcet's *Conversations on Political Economy* (1816).

15 A good example is Carlyle's little-known essay, 'Schiller, Goethe, and Madame de Staël', published in *Fraser's Magazine* in 1832. His essay aims to show that the 'spiritual Amazon' Madame de Staël was a 'mortal woman' (171). He quotes several passages from the letters and journals of Schiller and Goethe written during Staël's visit to Weimar in 1803-4. These excerpts depict Staël as an ill-mannered and egotistical intruder who disrupts the peace of Weimar's masculine intellectual community.

16 See Vanden Bossche (28-62) and Rosenberg (1-44) for a discussion of Carlyle's formulation of his authorial role (28-62).

17 As Carlyle writes in his 1829 essay, 'Signs of the Times', 'To reform a world, to reform a nation, no wise man will undertake; and all but foolish men know, that the only solid, though a far slower reformation, is what each begins and perfects on *himself*' (245). See DeLaura, Riede, and Williams (*Culture and Society* 71-86), for further discussion of Carlyle's definitions of 'culture' and social activism.

18 For further elucidation of Carlyle's concept of 'silent' authorship, see 'Characteristics' (1831) and 'On Hero Worship: The Hero as Poet' (1840).

19 See Tillotson (150-56) and George Eliot's 'Thomas Carlyle'.

20 The (ef)feminization of 'trash' literature is a device Carlyle often uses in his essays. For example, in his second essay on Richter, he writes, 'But the new Literary man, on the other hand, cannot stand at all, save in stays; he must first gird up his weak sides with the whalebone of a certain fashionable, knowing, half-squirarchal air . . '. (208). This is also reflected in *Sartor Resartus* where he satirizes the 'Highpriests and Highpriestesses' of 'dandiacal' fiction (210).

21 To some extent, male writers also faced this dilemma. As Corbett points out, both Wordsworth and Carlyle negotiated the demands of the literary marketplace and their own desire for high-culture literary status. However, women writers faced 'very different imperatives' based on their class and gender status as they negotiated their place in a male-dominated literary marketplace (55).

22 See further discussion of these trends in Barbara Taylor (1-18) and Rogers (181-203).

23 For discussion of some of the negative connotations attached to the term 'bluestocking' in the early nineteenth century, see S. Myers (290-303). See Barbara Taylor for a discussion of the conservative backlash against Wollstonecraft's feminism (11-15).

24 More is a controversial figure in feminist criticism. Some critics (e.g., Grogan and Kirkpatrick) view her work as representing a patriarchal middle-class perspective. Others (e.g., Krueger, *Reader's Repentance,* and M. Myers, 'Hannah More') see her as a contradictory figure, whose work served the interests of patriarchy but also provided a new model for women's writing and social activism.

25 More was the author of over 50 *Cheap Repository Tracts* on political and moral issues, which were distributed widely among the poor in 1790s. Her efforts toward reforming the morals of the aristocratic classes were also legendary, especially her essay, *An Estimate of the Religion of the Fashionable World* (1790). See Olivia Smith's discussion of More's constructions of class relationships (91-6).

26 More's *Works* were first published in 1778 and were published in expanded form in 1801. Very few women writers had been honored with the publication of their complete works, let alone during their own lifetimes.

27 More's career was especially controversial after the so-called Blagdon controversy, yet she maintained her reputation by 'strategically adapting feminine prescription while decorously observing all rules' (M. Myers, 'Peculiar Protection' 244).

28 Ford Brown notes that after the publication of More's *Cheap Repository Tracts,* her home became 'a shrine where earnest people came from near and far to meet the celebrated Christian woman' (151). Visits to literary shrines became popular in the early years of the nineteenth century, especially tours of the Lake District and visits to Scott's home at Abbotsford. Thus, domestic space and authorial identity became inextricably linked in the minds of many readers of the period.

29 The appropriation of More's image in colonialist discourse can be seen as a precursor to the kinds of social constructions that represented Florence Nightingale as an instrument of colonialism at mid-century. See Poovey *(Uneven* 164-98).

30 Other critical appraisals of More's work published in the 1830s include 'The Life and Correspondence of Mrs. Hannah More' (1834) and 'Biographic Sketches: Hannah More' (1834).

31 More played an important role the construction of this public image by distancing herself from Wollstonecraft's radicalism. She claimed never to have read *Vindication* and often expressed conservative views on the role of women in society. However, at the same time, through her own example, she was expanding the boundaries for women's participation in political discourse. See Rogers (209-13) and M. Myers, 'Peculiar Protection' (244).

32 For example, see Mary Elliott's *Female Biography; or, Virtue and Talent Exemplified in the Characters of Eminent British Females* (1822), Mary Hays' *Female Biography, or Memoirs of Illustrious and Celebrated Women* (1803), Samuel Burder's *Memoirs of Eminently Pious Women of the British Empire* (1815), and Mary Roberts' *Select Female Biography, Compromising Memoirs of Eminent British Ladies* (1829).

33 This was especially true for women's poetry in the 1830s. As Courtney points out, 'the astonishing thing is not the neglect of the women poets, but the adulation that was paid to them' (6). This is not to say that all women writers received positive attention from critics; rather, it is to suggest that women's texts received a great deal of attention in literary discourse of the period.

34 See, for example, Lister's review of Catherine Gore's *Women as They Are* (1830).

35 For example, a review entitled 'Miss Edgeworth's Tales and Novels' (1832) ascribes the '*manly* character' of her unembellished, clear writing style to her collaboration with her father (550).

36 As Sidonie Smith observes, 'nineteenth-century representations of the intellectual woman oftentimes turn on the disalignment of her bodily parts, as if to suggest that the very exercise of the intellect pulls natural phenomena into grotesque postures' (15).

37 See Altick (*English* 322-32) and Moers (82-4).

38 See Beetham (46) and Moers (82-4) for further discussion of this issue. Moers points out that women often had to wait for the male members of their households to finish reading newspapers and periodicals before they could gain access to them.

39 Charlotte Brontë, Elizabeth Gaskell, Harriet Martineau, and many other women writers refer to their reading of periodicals (see Moers 82-4).

40 Key texts are Staël's *De la Littérature* (1800) and Anna Jameson's *Characteristics of Women* (1833), both of which discuss literature in the context of the Woman Question. See Peterson's 'No Finger Posts' for more discussion of the difficulties women faced in pursuing careers as professional writers in the early Victorian period.

41 Of course, as Peterson points out, women often included images of themselves in the frontispieces of their books ('No Finger Posts' 42-3). Harriet Martineau, for example, selected images of herself to be included in her *Autobiography* ('Notes Toward' 3). Martineau, like other famous women, tried to control what texts were associated with these images, but sometimes this was impossible. Once portraits of Martineau were published, they became commodities over which she had little control. Mary Gillies sold etchings based on her 1833 portrait of Martineau for profit ('Notes Toward' 3). In addition, several *carte de visite* photographs of Martineau were apparently sold without her permission (5).

42 The other writers were Sarah Flower Adams, Catherine Hering, Caroline Southwood Smith, Emily Taylor, and Harriet Taylor (see Mineka 401-28).

43 Interestingly enough, though the fictionalized editor was male, the periodical as a whole was often referred to as the feminized 'Regina'. Most often this personification was used for satirical purposes. For example, in a scathing review of Catherine Gore's novels, Maginn writes, 'The truth must be spoken by REGINA, one of Mrs. Gore's "own sex", and that in uncompromising and fearless language' ('Novels' 12).

CHAPTER TWO

Defining Women's Authorship: Harriet Martineau and the Women Question

During the 1830s, many women became involved in the debate over women's rights, what came to be known as the Woman Question.[1] This involvement was prompted by Chartist and Owenite movements as well as debates over women's enfranchisement and the Infant Custody Act (1839). The expansion of the print trade provided middle-class women with increasing opportunities to bring their views on women's rights to the attention of the general public. The 1830s saw the publication of several book-length studies of women's roles in Victorian society, including Sarah Lewis' *Woman's Mission* (1839), Sarah Strickney Ellis' *The Women of England* (1839), and the anonymously published *Woman as She Is and Should Be* (1835). One of the dilemmas faced by women writers of the 1830s was how to participate in debates over the Woman Question without losing a sense of middle-class respectability. As Caroline Norton and other high-profile women activists of the period discovered, to be known as an advocate for women's rights was to risk having one's personal relationships brought under public scrutiny.[2] The rapid expansion of an anonymous periodical press provided women writers with an effective medium for speaking out on the Woman Question with less fear of public exposure.[3]

Perhaps no writer was more aware of the opportunities and dilemmas faced by women activists during the 1830s than Harriet Martineau (1802-76). During this period, Martineau published articles on women's issues in *Tait's Edinburgh Magazine* and the *London and Westminster Review*.[4] She also published several works that addressed the Woman Question, including a book-length sociological study, *Society in America* (1837); a guidebook to sociological method, *How to Observe Morals and Manners* (1838); and a domestic novel, *Deerbrook* (1839). Through these early publishing efforts, Martineau helped to crystallize a new definition of women's authorship: as a private yet politicized activity that would enable women to exert influence on key social issues while still avoiding the public gaze. Central to Martineau's definition of authorship was the notion that women would be successful in entering the debate over the Woman Question only if they argued their points from a de-personalized point of view. Though Martineau was a life-long advocate of women's rights,[5] she disapproved of women who drew attention to their personal lives when debating the Woman Question. In her *Autobiography,* Martineau criticizes the activist who '[violates] all good taste by her obtrusiveness in society ... oppressing every body about her by her epicurean selfishness every day, while raising in print an eloquent cry on behalf of the oppressed' (1: 400-401). Such selfish activism, Martineau claimed, had the effect of drawing attention to the identity of the writer instead of furthering ideas and actions that would enable women to overcome confining social roles.

Martineau believed that the woman writer must cultivate a sense of personal distance from her subject matter lest she be accused of writing for reasons of egotism or vanity. Yet she did not propose a strictly objective or scientific approach to writing on issues of concern to women. She also demonstrated ways that women could develop sympathetic understanding of the barriers faced by women in British society. By utilizing the conventions of anonymous journalism and formulating her own system of sociological observation in book-length works of fiction and non-fiction, Martineau attempted to define strategies for women to develop a sympathetic understanding of gender-based social inequities and to communicate their insights from a position less contaminated by personal self-interest. Martineau redefined and complicated conventionally feminine genres of writing, such as the domestic novel and the travel narrative, to include discussion of women's social, political, and economic roles. Likewise, she incorporated the self-effacement, reticence, and sympathy conventionally associated with the middle-class woman into a redefinition of the woman activist as a sociological observer. This redefinition of women's authorship had important implications for Martineau's later career and for the development of feminist thought in general.

Martineau's Early Years

In 1829, Martineau marked the beginning of her literary career by recording a series of private resolutions in her journal.[6] She writes, 'After long and mature deliberation, I have determined that my chief subordinate object in life shall henceforth be the cultivation of my intellectual powers, with a view to the instruction of others by my writings' (*On Women* 33). Inspired by the radicalism of Lant Carpenter, Joseph Priestley, and other Unitarian activists, Martineau readily committed herself to the cause of social reform (*Selected* 15). In order to construct herself according to a socially beneficial model of female authorship, Martineau realized she needed to develop a broader educational background, so she outlined a program of self-instruction and vowed 'to consider [her] own interests as little as possible, and to write with a view to the good to others; therefore to entertain no distaste to the humblest literary task which affords a prospect of usefulness' (*On Women* 35). These 'humble' literary tasks included periodical essays, religious tracts, and devotional texts, works inspired by the interests and concerns of her Unitarian mentors. In this way, Martineau defined herself as a national instructor who would transmit 'useful' knowledge to society at large. That is, rather than viewing authorship as an egotistical process of asserting her own individuality, she saw herself an instrument of social progress.

When defining herself as an author and social reformer, Martineau identified few women who served as positive role models. In her *Autobiography*, Martineau claimed that Mitford and Austen were important early influences (1: 418-19). However, she apparently did not feel that they provided a model of women's writing that would enable her to promote social reform. In an early letter to William J. Fox, she refers to herself as a 'solitary authoress, who has had no pioneer in her literary path but steadfastness of purpose' (*Selected Letters* 32). The work of Mary Wollstonecraft would seem to have provided Martineau with a more applicable model of female activism; however, though Martineau agreed with many of Wollstonecraft's views on the Woman Question, she, like many of her contemporaries, was repelled by Wollstonecraft's scandalous public persona. Martineau would later claim that in her youth she found Wollstonecraft to be one of those women writers whose

> advocacy of Woman's cause becomes mere detriment, precisely in proportion to their personal reasons for unhappiness, unless they have fortitude enough (which loud complainants usually have not) to get their own troubles under their feet, and leave them wholly out of the account in stating the state of their sex (*Autobiography* 1: 400).

For Martineau, the controversy over Wollstonecraft's personal life detracted from her reformatory project. Martineau suggests that Wollstonecraft devalued her personal image and political message by bringing them simultaneously to the attention of the reading public. What was needed was a depersonalized voice that could speak more objectively about social inequities faced by women.

In addition to distancing herself from Wollstonecraft, Martineau was also wary of being identified as a literary bluestocking. As Sylvia Myers points out, while in the eighteenth century the term 'bluestocking' was used to refer to a specific circle of writers, by the early nineteenth century it was used more broadly—and often pejoratively—to refer to any woman with literary ambitions (290-303). In the popular press of the early nineteenth century, bluestocking writers were often viewed as intellectual exhibitionists who publicly displayed their knowledge and achievements in upper-class salons and *conversazioni.* Though during various periods of her career Martineau was cast into the bluestocking mold by critics,[7] she always attempted to distance herself from what she saw as a negative stereotype. In her *Autobiography,* for example, she tells how at age eighteen she made a practice of conducting her studies surreptitiously, lest she be accused of 'bluestockingism which could be reported abroad' (1: 100).

Martineau was especially interested in distancing herself from what she saw as a tendency toward self-display among bluestocking writers. After her literary success in London, she was often invited to intellectual dinner parties where she met a variety of prominent women authors. At one such gathering, Martineau reports that she was 'boarded by Lady Stepney, who was then, as she boasted, receiving seven hundred pounds apiece for her novels. She paraded a pair of diamond earrings, costing that sum, which she had so earned' (1: 371). Here and elsewhere in the *Autobiography,* material display is closely associated with the exhibition of a false intellectualism premised on literary publication. Martineau defines Lady Stepney's novel as a commodity that is exchanged for a pair of diamond earrings—signifiers of upper-class vanity and decadence. As a form of self-aggrandizing literary production, Lady Stepney's novel serves as personal decoration rather than as an instrument of social good. In this way, Martineau defines her own brand of intellectualism and activism against the materialism and display of upper-class salons, where sex and identity were used as a means of self-promotion.

This is not to say that Martineau did not feel an affinity for some bluestocking writers, especially Anna Letitia Barbauld and Hannah More. In one of her earliest essays for the *Monthly Repository,* 'Female Writers on Practical Divinity' (1822), Martineau expresses her admiration for these writers, applauding their creation of 'some of the finest and most useful works' of devotional literature (593). She analyzes their texts as a means of 'doing justice' to their achievement but also for the purpose of 'exciting the emulation of those of their sex who are capable of imitating such bright examples' (593). Martineau's glowing response to More's work is interesting considering that privately she rebelled against More's evangelicalism and conservatism on women's issues (Peterson, 'Household Education' 184-6). Though during the 1820s Martineau wrote popular education tales modeled after More's *Cheap Repository Tracts,* she looked on these productions with a certain amount of self-disgust. She writes to her sister Helen Tagart in 1824, 'I don't know how I shall manage, but I generally make my stories so *vulgar,* worse than Mrs. H. More's' (Letter). More's career and writing style thus became a kind of obligatory mold for Martineau that simultaneously facilitated and constrained her literary practice.

However much Martineau was repelled by More's 'vulgar' evangelicalism, her career resembled More's in one important aspect: both writers capitalized on popular print culture in order to establish themselves as professional writers and moralists. One of the most important factors that facilitated Martineau's entry into the field of letters was the convention of anonymity in early and mid-Victorian periodicals. When writing for the *Monthly Repository,* the *London and Westminster Review,* and *Tait's Edinburgh Magazine* in the 1830s, Martineau used anonymity to avoid the publicity associated with authorship, writing on subjects as diverse as abolition, theology, and political economy.[8]

To distance her work from what she saw as self-indulgent forms of feminine writing, Martineau modeled her rhetorical style after the works of masculine sages such as Thomas Carlyle and William Cobbett.[9] As Linda Peterson has pointed out, Martineau appropriated the sage discourse of the masculine sphere as a way of 'dispensing truth, wisdom, and sometimes judgment' on the state of contemporary society ('Masculine Discourse' 172). Since the narrative voice of many reform-minded periodicals was assumed to be masculine, Martineau often adopted a male persona in her essays. This enabled her to speak out on the Woman Question with the appearance of objectivity since as a 'man' she could not be accused of writing on behalf of her own sex or in reference to her own personal difficulties.

In her essay, 'On Female Education' (1822), for example, Martineau placates conservative readers by claiming that a woman's primary role is to serve as 'domestic companion' to her husband (*On Women* 91). But interspersed with this essentializing discourse on women's nature is a persuasive defense of women's right to equal education:

> In our own country, we find that as long as the studies of children of both sexes continue the same, the progress they make is equal. After the rudiments of knowledge have been obtained, in the cultivated ranks of society ... the boy goes on continually increasing his stock of information, it being his only employment to store and exercise his mind for future years; while the girl is probably confined to low pursuits, her aspirings after knowledge are subdued, she is taught to believe that solid information is unbecoming her sex, almost her whole time is expended on light accomplishments, and thus before she is sensible of her powers, they are checked in their growth (*On Women* 89).

In this way, Martineau expresses progressive views on women's education without seeming to commit herself—and readers—to an extremist stance. This was especially important considering that the readers and editors of the *Monthly Repository* were more likely to support women's right to educational opportunity than their right to equal treatment under the law (Mineka 284-85).

Later in the same article Martineau presents her argument from the perspective of a bourgeois male journalist in order to obscure any traces of femininity in her journalistic voice. She writes, 'I do not desire that many females should seek for fame as authors' and goes on to outline a course of reading that includes study of 'living languages' (92). Such statements are of course ironic—and perhaps hypocritical—considering that Martineau was herself an author who signed her article with a Latin pseudonym, Discipulus. But such a stance was unavoidable for women who participated in public discourse during the 1820s, a time when there were few positive cultural stereotypes of professional women writers. Of course, as Linda Peterson, Deirdre David, and Mary Jean Corbett have suggested, Martineau's appropriation of masculine discourse also to some extent reflects her internalization of patriarchal ideology.[10] By adopting a male persona, she reinforced the very system that necessitated a masculine disguise. However, by insisting that women be 'heard but not seen' in political debates, Martineau also intended to secure the right of women to participate in public discourse by constructing a contradictory role for the woman activist that was neither strictly public nor private. Writing in the privacy of her own home, a woman writer could make a living for herself and participate in public debates while still avoiding accusations of egotism and personal bias. Likewise, while she might employ masculine rhetoric in her reviews and essays, she might also broaden the audience for discussion of women's issues.

40 FIRST-PERSON ANONYMOUS

Once Martineau began publishing books under her own name in 1832, she had more difficulty maintaining the sense of personal distance she desired for expressing her viewpoints on the Woman Question. After the publication of *Illustrations of Political Economy* (1832-34), a serialized collection of didactic stories based on the principles of political economy, Martineau was catapulted into literary stardom. Suddenly she was no longer just an obscure journalist; she was a newly crowned female genius, whose growing literary reputation was called upon to be of service to a variety of radical causes. She writes to William Tait in 1832,

> You make me wish to send you papers on all of the subjects you mention: but what can I do? I am all but overwhelmed with the materials of useful labour [which] are heaped upon me, & perplexed with the choice of channels thro' [which] to issue my writings.— You know that my Series is no small task; & I have now direct access to the Cabinet, & feel that nothing is so important as to preach my sermons there. The radicalism of a woman does not alarm them, & I learn not a little from them as to how much the aristocracy does actually know of the people (*Selected Letters* 37-38).

The publicity of Martineau's first high-profile publishing venture thus enabled her to exert influence on the most sensitive political subjects. Ironically, her status as a woman radical provided her with greater access to the reins of power since she was viewed as the popularizer of masculine theories rather than as the creator of her own radical viewpoints. Martineau was thus able to turn a negative gender stereotype to her own advantage, advancing her viewpoints under the guise of popularization.

The success of *Illustrations* not only provided Martineau with increased authority to write on political questions but also enabled her—at least privately—to renew her commitment to the advancement of women. Even though *Illustrations* did not directly address the Woman Question, Martineau felt that the story behind its creation and publication had direct relevance to debates over the status of women in Victorian society. Martineau interpreted her own narrative of literary struggle and success as a new social script that other ambitious literary women might follow. She writes to one woman admirer in 1833,

> None of the many rewards of my humble exertions gratify me more than the appreciation by my own sex of my endeavors to prepare a way for them to more elevating objects & more extensive usefulness than at present, except in a few cases, desired by them, or willingly yielded to them. I wish the timid & doubting of my own sex would take the assurance of my experience in this matter, as well as read what I write about it (*Selected* 40).

In this way, Martineau uses her fame as a means of promoting women's overall usefulness as authors and activists. She becomes the 'exemplary life' that will guide fellow women from a life of 'apathy & frivolity' and encourage them to exert the 'true humanizing influence of woman' in the public sphere (40-41).

At the same time that Martineau's celebrity provided her with greater access to the kinds of audiences and subject matter she most desired to address, it also imposed limitations on her career. After the publication of *Illustrations,* Martineau became not only the most famous woman writer in England but also the most infamous.[11] By daring to publish serious literature under her own name, Martineau came to be defined as a female transgressor, a public identity that subjected her to a number of personal attacks in the press. Though almost all reviewers praised Martineau's genius, they also tended to focus on her emotionality and inexperience. As one critic for the *Edinburgh Review* suggested, 'A young lady can scarcely possess the experimental knowledge of mankind, without which a confident imagination must occasionally run wild in the paradise of its own conceptions' (Empson 10).[12] The political implications of Martineau's *Illustrations of Political Economy* were seen as being beyond the scope of a woman, whose proper purview was the domestic sphere. As *Fraser's Magazine* put it, 'it was indeed a wonder that such themes should occupy the pen of any lady, old or young, without exciting a disgust nearly approaching to horror' (Maginn, 'Miss Harriet' 576). In the accompanying illustration, she is shown in an unfeminine posture, with her feet on the grate. Witch-like, she stirs her brew and enjoys the caresses of her feline companion (Figure 2.1).

The most damaging publicity, however, was instigated by a review article published in the *Quarterly Review* in 1833. Focusing on Martineau's treatment of Malthusian theories of population growth in *Illustrations of Political Economy,* this article questioned the propriety of a woman—let alone an unmarried woman—who dared to discuss the sexual themes implied in Malthus' theories:

> But no;—such a character is nothing to a *female Malthusian. A woman* who thinks child-bearing a *crime against society!* An *unmarried woman* who declaims against *marriage!!* A *young woman* who deprecates charity and a provision for the *poor!!!* (Croker et al. 151).

By focusing on Martineau's character—highlighting her social status as an unmarried female—this review attempted to criticize not only the Malthusian principles behind Martineau's work but also her right to address issues outside of her proper sphere of influence. Though Martineau claimed to have learned a great deal about the importance of courage in authorship from reading this review, she also acknowledged that it had damaging effects on her career. 'For ten years', she writes, 'there was seldom a number which had not some indecent jest about me,—some insulting introduction of my name' (*Autobiography* 1: 208). During this time, Martineau's books were subjected to various forms of social censorship. She heard stories of parents who out of fear of impropriety kept her books out of the reach of their children (1: 209). Likewise, she heard tales of unnamed 'literary ladies' who claimed that in her place, they 'would have gone into the mountains or to the antipodes, and never have shown their faces again' (1: 206).

Martineau was not one to take such attacks without thought of retribution. Martineau often used the anonymity of the periodical press to turn the tables on her detractors. In her article 'Criticism on Women' (1839), for instance, Martineau discusses the unwarranted abuse suffered by women writers in periodical reviews. Though she claims she will not lower herself to 'name either the men or the journals' who deal out this abuse, she coins the term 'Crokerites', after her nemesis John Wilson Croker, in order to skewer the worst 'reptiles' of the reviewing profession (460, 458). Martineau points out that it is not so much the subject matter of

2.1 'Miss Harriet Martineau' by Daniel Maclise. Courtesy British Library

women's writing that Crokerites object to as it is that women '[dare] to differ from them in politics' (459). With neither legal recourse nor the 'miserable protection of the duel', women authors become the 'most piquant and the safest objects of abuse a reviewer can select' (460). Thus, the name of the woman author becomes associated with 'ideas of disparagement and contempt' in the public imagination (466). In place of this gender-based criticism, Martineau proposes a more 'scientific' critical practice that promotes aesthetic appreciation rather than 'abuse and slander' (474-75).

Though Martineau suggests that femininity be excluded from scientific literary analysis, she does not reject masculinity as a term in her own critical practice. She criticizes the unmanliness of the abusive male journalist who 'skillfully avoids duellable matter when attacking men' and is even unable to 'give an utterance in shouts from the great heart of manhood' in honor of the Queen's accession to the throne (458-9). Martineau finds it especially unmanly that these writers publish their attacks anonymously in the periodicals: 'The women who are slandered are known: they stand clearly and distinctly in the public gaze—the men who slander them are hidden: their names are denied; their deeds are repudiated even by themselves' (470). Thus, Martineau attempts to reinscribe gender on the anonymous male author as a way of disciplining his literary practice.

Martineau's attack on the anonymous male author was ironic considering that she published most of her own articles anonymously in the periodical press. Indeed, in 'Criticism on Women', Martineau uses her anonymity to lash out at those who have done the same to her in past reviews. She discusses herself in the third person, pointing out the many injustices she has been dealt in the popular media. She writes, 'we have found it to be impossible to give any examples from ... the worst and coarsest attacks which they have made on this lady' (469). She then goes on to point out that even though she has been criticized for her deafness, there are 'very few persons indeed [who] surpass her in the ability with which she collects information, whether from seeing or listening' (469-70). The anonymity of the periodical press thus enables Martineau to participate in the construction of her own public image.

The anonymity of periodical publishing also helped Martineau to evade what she considered to be excessive forms of positive attention. The high-profile status she achieved after the success of *Illustrations* made her uneasy about the potential negative effects of public adulation. Her discomfort is recounted in 'Literary Lionism', an essay published in the *London and Westminster Review* in 1839. In this essay Martineau expresses concern about the tendency of society to 'lionize' its writers: to admire their public personalities more than their work. Such lionism, she claimed, would have a damaging effect on intellectual production because it encouraged egotism and mediocrity rather than moral sympathy and literary excellence. Literary lionism was especially hazardous for the female writer, who might arrive at a private dinner party only to be

> seized upon at the door by the hostess, and carried about to lord, lady, philosopher, gossip, and dandy, each being assured that she cannot be spared to each for more than ten seconds. She sees a 'lion' placed in the centre of each of the first two rooms she passes through ... and it flashes upon her that she is to be the centre of attraction in a third apartment (267).

Such attention not only placed women writers in the uncomfortable position of being public performers but also exposed their work and lives to the scrutiny of the general public, which reserved its 'hardest treatment' for female authors (268).

As an example of the ideal conditions of authorship, Martineau turned to the Middle Ages where 'literature was cultivated only in the seclusion of monasteries' and where the 'prospect of influence and applause was too remote to actuate a life of literary toil' (262-63). In order to recreate these ideal conditions of authorship,

> The author has to do with those two things precisely which are common to the whole race—with living and thinking .... The very first necessity of his vocation is to live as others live, in order to see and feel as others see and feel, and to sympathize in human thought. In proportion as this sympathy is impaired, will his views be partial, his understanding, both of men and books, be imperfect, and his power be weakened accordingly (272).

In this way, Martineau defines authorship as a sympathetic rather than an egotistical process. She then quotes liberally from Ralph Waldo Emerson's 'Literary Ethics' (1838), emphasizing the importance of intellectual independence and modesty in the composing process. Building on Emerson, she argues that authors can express universal truth only by avoiding public display and by sympathetically observing daily human life. For Martineau, the message was more important than its messenger, whose egotism and vanity could interfere in the process of communicating vital moral and political lessons. She thus characterizes the ideal author in universal terms: as a 'godlike human mind' that transcends individual identity (281).

Though in 'Literary Lionism' Martineau seems to propose a genderless model of authorship, she does not completely discount gender as an important consideration in addressing the role of the author in contemporary society. After all, she is very careful to point out the special struggles faced by famous women writers. In addition, Martineau hints at her own identity as a woman author in the article. Though she does not sign the essay, she does include her initials after the final paragraph. Given Martineau's fame during the 1830s, many readers would have been able to guess the identity of 'H. M'. Thus, in a sense, Martineau undermines her own argument about sexless authorship by fastening a marker of her individual identity to her work. Though the struggles of women authors are discussed in generalized terms in the article, astute readers might interpret them as anecdotes from Martineau's personal experience.

'Literary Lionism' illustrates Martineau's struggle with the problem of how to speak out from a position of authority—as a famous author and as a woman— while still giving the impression of personal distance from her subject matter. Writing for the periodicals, Martineau had discovered a medium that would enable her to construct the voice she felt she needed in order to participate in debates over the Woman Question. Throughout her career she would continually return to the periodical press as a way of expressing her viewpoints on women's issues. Yet the periodical press did impose limitations on her writing. Writing for the periodicals, Martineau could not undertake a broad study of the state of women in society nor could she effectively capitalize on her own notoriety as a way of influencing public opinion. What Martineau needed was a medium and method that would enable her to present an individualized, yet de-personalized, perspective on the Woman Question. This search led her to the travel writing genre. From 1834 to 1836 Martineau toured America, recording her thoughts and observations in preparation for writing her major sociological works, *Society in America* (1837) and *How to Observe Morals and Manners* (1838). In these texts, Martineau described and illustrated techniques of sociological inquiry that women could use to uncover sources of social inequity in foreign cultures and within their own domestic circles.

Domestic Observations: *How to Observe Morals and Manners*

In writing *Society in America*, Martineau claimed that her goal was to 'compare the existing state of society in America with the principles on which it is professedly founded; thus testing Institutions, Morals, and Manners by an indisputable, instead of an arbitrary standard' (48). With this goal in mind, Martineau conducted a minute examination of American society from a variety of domestic, social, and political standpoints, including a sharp critical analysis of the disenfranchisement of women and slaves.[13] By claiming to address women's issues in the context of another country's political and domestic culture, Martineau was able to give the impression that she was speaking on behalf of the citizens of another country rather than in her own personal or national interest. Of course in reality Martineau intended her cultural critique to extend far beyond America's national borders.[14] In a letter to William J. Fox, she writes that the purpose of *Society in America* was in part to promote the 'revision in [parliament] of all laws regarding Woman; to set watch on all legal proceedings [which] relate to women; & to expose her whole state' *(Selected* 45).

Martineau provides readers with the tools to understand and question conventional gender roles by encouraging them to observe other cultures from a detached yet gender-sensitive point of view. She suggests that women are especially qualified for such a task by virtue of their access to and understanding of domestic and moral institutions. As Maria Frawley points out, even though Martineau never explicitly genders the role of the 'traveler' in *Society in America,* she does suggest that her gender is an asset rather than a detriment in her investigatory enterprise (16). In the introduction to *Society in America,* Martineau writes,

> I am sure, I have seen much more of domestic life than could possibly have been exhibited to any gentleman travelling through the country. The nursery, the boudoir, the kitchen, are all excellent schools in which to learn the morals and manners of a people:

46   FIRST-PERSON ANONYMOUS

and, as for public and professional affairs,—those may always gain full information
upon such matters, who really feel an interest in them,—be they men or women (53).

Martineau evokes feminine gender not to emphasize her subjective response or the
limitations of her knowledge but rather to establish the superior breadth of her
understanding and vision. Likewise, domestic institutions become schools for
learning about culture and society rather than circumscribed retreats from the world
of politics.[15]

In order to examine the specific forms of gender-based social criticism
Martineau was promoting in *Society in America*, it is useful to examine its
companion text, *How to Observe Morals and Manners* (1838), which spells out her
techniques of cultural criticism. In her *Autobiography,* Martineau claims that this
how-to book was originally 'written at sea' during her Atlantic crossing (2: 117).
Its purpose was to train tourists to develop their 'powers of observation', which
would enable them to come to a broader, more scientific, understanding of the
morals and manners of other cultures *(How to Observe* 13). Instead of travelers
drawing inferences from limited interactions with individuals, she suggests that
they analyze 'Institutions and Records, in which the action of the nation is
embodied and perpetuated' (73). Under these headings are instructions for
investigating the rituals, organizations, values, and manners of foreign societies,
including their marriage practices, literary achievements, cultural heroes, civil
liberties, religious beliefs, and class relationships. In addition to training observers
to be more objective in their analysis of these institutions, Martineau urged her
readers to adopt an explicitly politicized point of view. As Richard Stein points out,
Martineau was attempting to produce a kind of 'subjective objectivity' that
incorporated the individuality of the observer, producing 'not so much a neutral
record of impersonal facts as a passionate search for truths essential to individual
and social improvement' (181, 180). Martineau thus proposed that travelers
employ moral sympathy and systematic observation as a means of understanding
and judging the institutional practices of a given country according to her own
definition of social progress.

Martineau's proposals for analyzing social institutions from a gendered point of
view were especially innovative. 'The degree of the degradation of woman', she
writes, 'is as good a test as the moralist can adopt for ascertaining the state of
domestic morals in any country' (179). She then lists various benchmarks against
which societies must be measured in order to determine their level of social
'progress':

> Where he [the observer] finds that girls are committed to convents for education, and
> have no alternative in life but marriage, in which their will has no share ... [he may
> presume that] domestic employments of the highest kind are undesired and unknown. He
> may conclude that ... for one more generation at least, there will be little or no [social]
> improvement. But where he finds a variety of occupations open to women; where he
> perceives them not only pursuing the lighter mechanic arts, dispensing charity and

organizing schools for the poor, but occupied in education, and in the study of science and the practice of the fine arts, he may conclude that here resides the highest domestic enjoyment which has yet been attained, and the strongest hope of a further advance (184-85).

Here Martineau associates the development of society with the occupational and vocational status of women. Of course by suggesting that British Protestantism and progressivism are the 'strongest hope' for overall human advancement, this passage also presents a colonialist perspective. Indeed, in an earlier passage, Martineau compares the 'slavery' of the 'Indian squaw' to that of the women of 'France, England, and the United States ... [who are] less than half-educated, precluded from earning a subsistence ... and prohibited from giving or withholding their assent to laws which they are yet bound by penalties to obey' (179). In this way, Martineau privileges Western society while at the same time suggesting that it bears the vestiges of 'savage' cultures.[16]

In addition to analyzing the overall social status of women, Martineau encourages travelers to focus their analysis on the institution of marriage within foreign cultures. She argues that 'by no arrangements yet attempted have purity of morals, constancy of affection, and domestic peace been secured' (172). Problems with marriage as an institution are attributable to the social construction of gender roles. On one hand, males are brought up to prize a 'shallow' sense of honor and a sense of 'feudal ambition' in their relationships with women (173-74). Women, for their part, are 'educated to consider marriage the one object in life, and therefore to be extremely impatient to secure it' (180). In discussing problems associated with marriage as an institution from a transnational perspective, Martineau goes beyond the boundaries of her original project of giving travelers the tools to observe and understand foreign cultures; here, and elsewhere, the observant gaze is turned on British culture as a means of judging its collective health against a series of benchmarks. Only by undermining the 'feudal' relationships that characterize the institution of marriage will British culture be worthy of its privileged status.

By providing readers with the tools to analyze other cultures—and their own—from a gender-sensitive perspective, Martineau provided a new form of gender-based social criticism that could be employed on an international journey or a walk down the streets of London. Martineau encouraged travelers to convert these gendered observations into writing. In a chapter titled 'Mechanical Methods' she suggests that readers keep a journal in which to record 'facts and impressions' gathered during their journey (235). She recommends that travelers not clutter their journals with 'personal feelings' or 'changes of mood ... sufferings from heat or cold, from hunger or weariness' (235). Instead, they should 'record as little as possible about [themselves]', leaving room for 'things much better worth recording'—thoughts on the social, political, and domestic state of the country they are analyzing (235). Though Martineau does not go so far as to suggest that these impressions be published or shared with others, her proposals are still intended to produce moral activism. She suggests that through close observation and note

48 FIRST-PERSON ANONYMOUS

taking, readers will develop a politicized point of view that will alter their understanding of institutional practices.

Thus, *Society in America* and *How to Observe Morals and Manners* propose gender-sensitive observation and sociological analysis as tools readers can use to gain a distanced viewpoint on institutional practices, thereby establishing universal benchmarks for social progress among diverse cultures. Of course, by suggesting that readers measure other cultures according to the standards of British progressivism, Martineau was participating in a larger colonialist enterprise. At the same time, by providing readers with the tools to analyze other cultures—and their own—from a depersonalized yet gender-sensitive point of view, she was fostering a proto-feminist consciousness, which interpreted gender roles as categories generated by a given set of institutional arrangements, rather than as natural, God-given identities. When viewed as dynamic and socially constructed, gender roles become a temporary problem that must be overcome in order to facilitate overall social progress.

By focusing her critique on other cultures, specifically on America, Martineau attempted to create a distanced perspective on women's issues by employing a scientific approach to writing that examined facts and institutions instead of individual cases. In this way, she built upon her earlier anonymous contributions to the periodical press, which aimed to present a disinterested perspective on the Woman Question. Martineau's claim to 'objectivity' shielded her from the accusations of bias, self-interestedness, and vanity that plagued many women activists. However, as Martineau turned her critical eye more directly on British culture, she found it increasingly difficult to gain a sense of personal distance from the women's issues she was committed to addressing. How was she to write directly about the institutional oppression of women in England without falling into the trap of 'epicurean selfishness' that she so disliked in public discourse on the Woman Question? Her answer—at least temporarily—was to turn to domestic fiction.

Fictionalized Observations: *Deerbrook*

Martineau claimed that her decision to write *Deerbrook* (1839), her first novel, was premised on her desire to escape the 'constraint of the effort to be always correct, and to bear without solicitude the questioning of my correctness' (*Autobiography* 2: 108). While in the past the claim to scientific observation had provided her with the authority to contribute to the Woman Question, it also had subjected her to criticism by those who questioned her ability to produce reliable data.[17] Martineau's discussion of women's issues in *Society in America* was interpreted as a form of self-advocacy rather than as a scientific analysis of gender relations in American culture. *Fraser's Magazine,* for example, claimed that the book was intended to 'press forward her [Martineau's] individual self as a crowning example of the equality of the sexes' ('Female Writers' 566). After reading many critical reviews of this sort, Martineau feared 'losing nerve' in her reformatory project (*Autobiography* 2: 108). This fear prompted her decision to turn to fiction as a means of more freely expressing her moral viewpoints:

> my heart and mind were deeply stirred on one or two moral subjects on which I wanted the relief of speech, or which could be as well expressed in fiction as in any other way,—and perhaps with more freedom and earnestness than under any other form (2: 108).

It is difficult to know what these 'moral subjects' might have been, but it is likely that women's issues—particularly problems associated with marriage as an institution and the lack of vocational opportunities for intellectual women—were still on her mind as she began her first novel.[18] Martineau no doubt felt that such issues could be addressed with more freedom in a domestic novel, since as a socially acceptable form of women's writing, it was held to a lower critical standard than most forms of non-fiction, such as political tracts and sociological studies.[19] For this reason, it provided her with more license to analyze the social roles of women in contemporary British culture.[20] After all, her earlier contributions to the debate over the Woman Question had been either in the form of anonymously published periodical essays or in the form of sociological analyses of distant societies; thus, in order to analyze gender issues in contemporary British culture without being branded as an exhibitionist bluestocking, she needed to address women's issues from behind the veil of fictionality.

Written contemporaneously with *How to Observe Morals and Manners*, *Deerbrook* demonstrates how gender-sensitive forms of observation can lead to a deeper understanding of the material and moral conditions that impede women's social progress. However, because the domestic novel by convention was focused on the fate of individuals rather than more broadly on the progress of social institutions, Martineau needed to employ narrative tools that would enable her to analyze the general social issues that the specific instances depicted in her novel were intended to illustrate. This was something she had already attempted in *Illustrations of Political Economy*, where she had used fiction to impart the principles of economic theory. In order to bring forth her didactic themes, she had concluded each story with a summary of the economic concepts it illustrated. Such an approach was not well-suited to the domestic novel since its narrative conventions were perceived as being less elastic than those of serially published short fiction. Martineau needed to find a way to work within the conventions of the marriage plot associated with domestic fiction[21] while at the same time criticizing marriage as a social institution in need of reform.

On the surface, *Deerbrook* seems to be a love story in the manner of Austen, where intricate and often humorous social relations are used to examine moral issues associated with domestic life. In the beginning of the novel we are introduced to two orphaned sisters of marriageable age: the beautiful and emotive Hester Ibbotson and her plain and well-tempered sister Margaret. The sisters arrive in the small town of Deerbrook to stay with their distant cousins, the Greys, until their inheritance is settled. Through the meddling of Aunt Grey, Hester is soon married to Edward Hope, a well-respected local doctor, who still harbors feelings of love for Margaret. Meanwhile, Margaret develops a close relationship with Maria Young, a disabled governess, and with Philip Enderby, brother to her Aunt's Grey's social nemesis, Mrs. Rowland. She soon falls in love with Philip, not realizing that he was once Maria's lover. Resenting both Hope's defection to the Grey camp and her brother's decision to make an undesirable match with Margaret, Mrs. Rowland sets out to destroy both alliances. First she turns the community against Hope, causing him to lose local patronage and fall into poverty. Then, through a number of ruses, she poisons the relationship between Philip and Margaret. However, in the end, the social evil represented by Mrs. Rowland is overcome when Philip and Margaret discover her treachery and the Hopes overcome social censure through hard work and devotion to duty. Both Maria Young and Edward Hope suppress their desire for true love, with Philip and Margaret respectively, settling instead for a life focused on service to others.

This seemingly conventional marriage plot has troubled feminist critics over the years because it seems to reinforce conventional gender relations and class hierarchies. As Valerie Sanders points out, *Deerbrook* is 'unsatisfying because of its refusal to follow through the implications of its many statements about love, self-repression, marriage, and women's career prospects: statements which are often made in impassioned, isolated speeches to other women' (*Reason* 70). Likewise, Deirdre David views the novel as evidence of Martineau's retreat into a more conservative political position that 'endorses many of the unpleasant "facts" of women's oppression which Martineau so bravely exposed and attacked in *Society in America*' (77). Indeed, it would be difficult to argue that *Deerbrook* is unconventional in its representations of gender relations. After all, Margaret's and Hester's highest aspiration is to find a husband and serve him faithfully. Maria Young works only because she cannot find fulfillment in love and entertains little hope of devoting her intellectual and sympathetic powers to any social or moral purpose beyond her limited domestic circle.

However, beyond the novel's marriage plot and the conventional gender relations it seems to endorse lies a deeper investigation of domestic issues of concern to women. By integrating the conventions of domestic fiction with those of sociological analysis, Martineau encourages readers to understand and to question the social conditions that narrowly define women's social and economic roles.[22] In *Deerbrook,* Maria Young's story continually interrupts the progress of the marriage plot, providing an outsider's perspective on issues of love and marriage. By asking readers to identify with the marginalized perspective of Maria Young, Martineau encourages them to develop an objective perspective on conventional domestic morality. As in *How to Observe Morals and Manners,* Martineau uses seeing as a metaphor for the kind of politicized cultural perspective she hopes readers will adopt. In this sense, Maria's perspective has much in common with Adam Smith's notion of the 'impartial spectator'. In the *Theory of Moral Sentiments* (1759),

Smith suggests that individual actions be viewed from the perspective of an objective yet sympathetic observer who judges their propriety. To the extent that the 'impartial spectator' would be able to sympathize with both the motives and the effects of a given action, it would be judged morally proper: 'If we place ourselves completely in his [the impartial spectator's] situation, if we really view ourselves with his eyes, and as he views us, and listen with diligent and reverential attention to what he suggests to us, his voice will never deceive us' (227).

Like Smith's 'impartial spectator', Maria represents a distanced yet sympathetic perspective on the novel's events by commenting on the motivations and actions of others. Of course, Maria's perspective represents a woman's *interpretation* of moral sympathy to the extent that she challenges the implied masculinity of Smith's 'impartial spectator'.[23] By expressing dissatisfaction with social institutions that oppress women, Maria embodies what Lucinda Cole, in her analysis of Wollstonecraft's fiction, calls the desire to transform the 'discourse of sympathy into the service of anti-hierarchical politics that transcend or resolve social and cultural differences' (130). That is, Martineau reformulates Smith's 'impartial spectator' as a philosophical, sympathetic woman whose access to domestic spaces and understanding of cultural politics provide her with broad moral vision of sexual politics in her society. Martineau suggests that just as Maria observes the marriage plot from a gendered critical perspective so should readers become more careful observers of conventional domestic institutions.

Unmarried, homely, and intellectual, Maria Young plays the role of the redundant woman, a literary trope that would later become a staple of domestic fiction.[24] Existing always at the margins of the novel's plot, Maria's point of view is at once objective and peripheral. Like an internal narrator, she seems to have a broad view of the moral and emotional issues that are being addressed in the novel but does not play an active, central role. She functions as a chorus or conscience that provides a distanced yet sympathetic perspective on the actions of others. Social activism for Maria, as for Martineau, is a kind of sympathetic interference in the lives of others that is carried out without thought of personal gain. By providing the perspective that others lack, she engages in public service without self-righteously displaying her own intellectual and moral superiority. Of course, unlike Martineau, Maria does not attempt to influence political and social affairs at a national and international level, nor does she attempt to enter into masculine discourse, but she does define social activism in similar terms—as a form of social intervention premised on politicized, gender-sensitive observation of others.

One of the reasons Maria's superfluity is so interesting is that at the beginning of the novel she seems almost to fulfill the role of protagonist. Though the Ibbotson sisters are introduced early in the novel, it is Maria who takes center stage. We learn that she is an educated, philosophical woman who would 'rather study than teach' and who reads the latest German philosophy (19-20). Though she is clearly exceptional, Maria seems to submit to a system of institutional relations that would require her to sublimate her intellectual talents as a provincial governess. 'There's no need to be sorry for me', she tells the Ibbotson sisters. 'Do you suppose that one's comfort lies in having a choice of employments?' (20). However, this sort of commentary is interspersed with criticism of social relations and institutions that oppress educated women:

> There is a great deal said about the evils of the position of a governess—between the family and the servants—a great deal said that is very true, and always will be true, while governesses have proud hearts, like other people: but these are slight evils in comparison with the grand one of the common failure of the relation (22).

In this way, Maria affirms and submits to her own marginal status while at the same time criticizing the system that assigns her to a subordinate social position. Throughout her discussion of the governess role, she is careful to point out that she speaks 'quite generally' about the issue, rather than seeming to complain about the difficulty of her own situation (21). In this way, she attempts to construct her views as objective and philosophical rather than as an expression of self-pity.

Early in the novel, Maria uses her marginality as the means of gaining a broad perspective on the events around her. In one of the only passages of extended monologue in the novel, Maria reflects on the kinds of vision provided by her marginal social position. Left alone for a few precious hours without the demands of her students, Maria analyzes the world outside her study:

> What is it to be alone, and to be let alone, as I am? It is to be put into a post of observation on others: but the knowledge so gained is anything but a good if it stops at mere knowledge—if it does not make me feel and act. Women who have what I am not to have, a home, an intimate, a perpetual call out of themselves, may go on more safely, perhaps, without any thought for themselves, than I with all my best consideration: but I, with the blessing of a peremptory vocation, which is to stand me instead of sympathy, ties and spontaneous action—I may find out that it is my proper business to keep an intent eye upon the possible events of other people's lives, that I may use slight occasions of action which might otherwise pass me by ... . Without daring to meddle, one may stand clear-sighted, ready to help (35).

In this way, Maria presents her marginality as the source of alienation but also as a source of power. By achieving a 'post of observation', a broad view of the social affairs of others, the single intellectual woman can 'feel and act' in a way that promotes overall social good. She sublimates her own desire for romantic fulfillment—her unrequited love for Philip Enderby—as a way of increasing her 'usefulness' to others. Like Martineau herself, Maria assumes a narrative position that allows her to rise above the personal, thereby exerting moral influence on issues of social and moral concern.

Maria's sympathetic observation is contrasted with forms of voyeurism in the novel, the meddling of Mrs. Grey and Mrs. Rowland, who peer at each other from behind the curtains as a means of gaining ammunition for their social rivalry. They are presented as examples of a general atmosphere of gossip and surveillance in the small town where there is little that escapes the eye and ear of public opinion. Hester and Margaret soon discover that one of the major sources of entertainment in Deerbrook is 'to witness all the village spectacles which present themselves before the windows of an acute observer' (25). Yet, even with their ability to observe the affairs of others, the gossips of Deerbrook never achieve the kind of vision that would enable them to transcend their limited points of view. Confined in the oppressive atmosphere of the Grey household, the Ibbotson sisters, like 'starlings in a cage', pine for outdoor activity, and thus a wider perspective on the world around them (27). Margaret, especially uncomfortable in Deerbrook society, continually chides Hester to rise above the 'opinions of the people' in the small community (102). But Hester is too self-involved to be able to achieve this emotional distance; only Maria Young seems to provide Margaret with the broader, more sympathetic, point of view she seeks.

One of the ways that Maria helps Margaret gain greater perspective is to prepare her for the torment of romantic love. Though she herself entertains passionate feelings for Philip Enderby, she is able to overcome these personal interests, presenting a more dispassionate view of love and marriage. In a remark which might have been quoted from *How to Observe Morals and Manners,* Maria says to Margaret,

> All girls are brought up to think of marriage as almost the only event in life. Their minds are stuffed with thoughts of it almost before they have had time to gain any other ideas. Merely as means to ends low enough for their comprehension. It is not marriage— wonderful, holy, mysterious marriage—that their minds are full of, but connection with somebody or something which will give them money, and ease, and station, and independence of their parents. This has nothing to do with love (159).

But even those women who find 'true love' still face the 'agony of a change of existence' that they must endure 'silently and alone' (159). Conditions are especially difficult for those women who must endure the 'abyss' of unrequited love, which drives some to 'a state of perpetual and incurable infancy' and leads others to 'sacrifice themselves, in marriage or otherwise, for low objects' (164). It is only by being 'philosophical', that is, by resigning themselves to the 'objects and conditions' of life, that they can transcend their individual circumstances and be of use to others (164). Thus, Maria defines the excessive feeling associated with romantic love as a problem that must be overcome in order for women to achieve self-fulfillment and moral usefulness.

The dangers associated with the self-indulgent expression of personal feeling take on larger social significance when an angry mob descends on Deerbrook, threatening to kill Hope, who is accused of stealing corpses from pauper graveyards for scientific experimentation. Spurred on by superstition and gossip, the lower classes have lost their ability to tell truth from hearsay. The arrival of the local nobility—Lord and Lady Hunter—promises to quell the passion of the rioters by providing rational leadership, but their own selfishness prevents them from

54 FIRST-PERSON ANONYMOUS

fulfilling this role. Lady Hunter's decision to go into town is premised on her desire to 'catch a glimpse of the ladies in their terrors' (311). She goes to Deerbrook not only out of prurient interest in the commotion caused by the mob but also as a means of self-display. Upon preparing for her journey home, she discovers that

> once in the carriage, in all the glory of being surrounded and watched by a number of gaping clowns and shouting boys, she could not resolve to bury herself in the seclusion of the Hall, without enjoying the bustle a little longer. She therefore suddenly discovered that she wanted to order a morning cap at Miss Nares' (316).

Thus, her seeming concern for the social well-being of her community is revealed to be her thinly disguised desire for public attention and adulation. As she departs Deerbrook with 'Miss Nares's newest cap and story', she has succeeded in fanning—rather than dousing—the flames of gossip and rumor, further exacerbating the social crisis centered upon the Hope household (317). As she drives by their 'dangerous abode', she stares in the window, shocked that they are calmly having dinner with all the ruckus outside (318). The inhabitants, for their part, do not return this invasive gaze, assuming that the Hunters are 'deriving all the excitement and amusement they could from an airing through the village', all the while unaware of the 'most atrocious stories about Hope that were now circulating from mouth to mouth, all round Deerbrook' (318).

Lady Hunter's voyeurism provides a contrast to Maria's sympathetic philosophical perspective. Though Maria is just as much of a voyeur as Lady Hunter, she uses her powers of observation to exert moral influence and to seek justice for those who are victimized by more unsympathetic forms of social interference. At the same time that Lady Hunter is retreating to her manor house, Maria breaks her leg as a result of being 'thrown down by the crowd' during the riot (324). When her injury is discovered, all present suddenly forget their troubles and remember the self-effacing Maria:

> How thankful were they all now, that some one had thought of Maria! She had been in extreme anxiety for them [Margaret and the Hopes]; and she would not certainly have sent for aid before the morning. It was indeed a blessing that some one had thought of Maria (324).

even though circumstances make Maria's presence in the plot redundant, she is never completely forgotten; like a conscience, she is 're-membered'—reconstructed and brought back into the central focus of the novel—just when she seems least important to its progress. A social anomaly in every way, her sympathetic, self-effacing presence is the only antidote to the vain emotionality and self-interested forms of social interference that absorb the common mind of Deerbrook.

As Margaret suffers the pain of rejection from Enderby and the hardship of her family's social ostracism, she, too, contains her self-interest in order to be of service to others. By transcending the personal and devoting herself to duty, Margaret is able to withstand the painful separation from her object of desire. During the most bitter stage of her romantic sorrow, she consults Maria about possible vocations that can provide her with emotional and material sustenance. She asks Maria, 'Cannot you tell me of some way in which a woman may earn money?' (448). Maria responds with a long speech about vocations for lower-class women, adding,

> But, for an educated woman, a woman with the powers which God gave her, religiously improved, with a reason which lays life open before her, an understanding which surveys science as its appropriate task, and a conscience which would make every species of responsibility safe,—for such a woman there is in all England no chance of subsistence but by teaching—that almost ineffectual teaching, which can never countervail the education of circumstances, and for which not one in a thousand is fit (448).

Here again, Maria becomes the mouthpiece for Martineau's viewpoints on the paucity of suitable vocations for intellectual women in her society. Maria points out that there are also literary professions available for women but that these should not be attempted merely to provide for 'lower wants' but rather to express 'some loftier meaning' (449). Since Margaret desires 'money' more than 'employment', she discounts the possibility of pursuing the 'higher departments of labour' (449). Thus, in order to be most useful to those around her, she is relegated to the role of housekeeper until the arrival of a plague that puts her into service as a nurse for the poor. Through her hard work and devotion to duty, she passes over the 'abyss of nothingness', finding a new outlet for her unfulfilled passion for Enderby (482).

After the plague runs its course, Philip and Margaret are reconciled, and Edward and Hester regain their social status along with their mutual regard, Maria once again re-enters the novel as a kind of loose end that cannot be incorporated into the conventions of the marriage plot. The last scene in the novel is devoted to a conversation between Maria and Margaret just before Margaret's marriage to Philip. Margaret worries about Maria's future, pointing out that she is 'infirm and suffering in body, poor, solitary, living by toil, without love, without prospect' (521). While Maria views her own situation with some pathos, she refuses to see it as hopeless. She says to Margaret, 'If I were without object, without hope, without experience, without the power of self-rule which such experience gives, you might well fear for me' (521). Though she laments that her solitude is 'very hard to bear', she admits that it also provides her with 'glimpses of heaven', which enable her to 'look forward without fear of chance or change' (521, 522). Maria thus submits to the will of providence, rising above her personal difficulties, social marginality, and romantic desire with her own sense of transcendent vision. While her future is unnarratable in terms of the conventional marriage plot, it is still a subject that the other characters cannot let go. Even in the last line of the novel, when Philip and Margaret walk in the twilight, they are 'talking of Maria' (523). Both admirable and pathetic, Maria is never fully incorporated into a domestic novel focused on love and marriage; she remains a redundant yet somehow vitally necessary observer and moral commentator who facilitates conventional domestic relations while at the same time interrupting and complicating the reader's understanding of them.

Through the characterization of Maria Young, Martineau attempted to create a distanced yet sympathetic perspective on the Woman Question. In this way, she was able to discuss the need for women's educational and vocational opportunity while at the same time working within the conventions of domestic fiction. Of course, by communicating her viewpoints through the voice of a marginalized character, Martineau in some sense downplayed her own commitment to the cause of women's emancipation. Likewise, by creating women characters who conform to conventionalized gender roles, she provided no clear models of the kind of intellectual activism she enacted in her own career. However, by having Maria enact the same kind of process skills she defined in *How to Observe Morals and Manners,* she demonstrated how the development of a radical consciousness would enable readers to understand and to question the morality of domestic relations within their own social spheres. The intellectual, solitary woman is defined as an individual with untapped social value who can provide clearer moral vision than those who are embroiled in everyday domestic and romantic entanglements. Marginality is thus defined not only as a source of exclusion but also as the source of socially useful knowledge.

Deerbrook, like Martineau's other contributions to the Woman Question in the 1830s, demonstrates how conventional domestic narratives and marginal social roles could be reconfigured to serve the cause of women's emancipation. Martineau's definition of the woman activist requires that she assume a contradictory role that spans both public and private spheres. She must be dispassionate yet sympathetic, objective yet moralistic, domestic yet political, reticent yet outspoken, visible yet invisible. In short, she must do the impossible: validate the patriarchal ideology of separate spheres, while at the same time challenging its underlying assumptions about women's natural roles and abilities.

This contradiction troubles many modern critics who object to her inconsistent feminist beliefs premised on a meliorist view of social change. Yet what many fail to realize is that Martineau's approach to gender politics is an important precursor to modern feminist thought. As Gayle Graham Yates points out in her introduction to *Harriet Martineau on Women*, Martineau's radicalism is a 'true progenitor of the intellectual mode that reigns in Anglo-American liberalism today and provides the dominant informing paradigm of mainstream Western feminism' (5). Just as modern feminists contend with the contradictions of their roles within patriarchal institutions, so did Martineau struggle with her own relationship to liberal ideology. On one hand she sought only to secure equal rights for women in a patriarchally controlled democratic society, that is, for women to be treated without regard to gender in educational, professional, and other social institutions. As she puts it in a letter to Henry Reeve, her ideal was not the promotion of 'abstract doctrines of rights' but rather that gender not inhibit individuals from 'giving their faculties fair play' (*Selected* 164). For a woman intellectual such as Martineau, this meant that her ideas rather than her sex ought to be the subject of public attention and criticism. To some extent, such an idealistic position exposes the limitations of liberal individualism in bringing about fundamental changes in women's social and economic roles. After all, as Ann Hobart points out, Martineau 'never directly confronts ... the sexual division of labor and property in the discourse of political economy and in the liberal theory of political representation' (227).[25]

However, though Martineau's liberalism in some ways constructed a limited role for the woman activist, it also laid the groundwork for a more militant feminism. As Zillah Eisenstein points out, 'liberal feminism, containing the seeds of its own transformation in the contradictory nature of it as a political theory and practice, sets into motion this heightened political understanding' (9). By encouraging women to engage in forms of gender-sensitive social observation and cultural criticism, Martineau helped to establish a proto-feminist consciousness among middle-class women that not only led them to demand equality within a patriarchally defined public sphere but also facilitated a questioning of patriarchy itself. Certainly Martineau's contributions to debate over the Woman Question in the 1850s and '60s demonstrate how her liberal individualism could be converted into more militant forms of social protest. The publication of Martineau's essay, 'Female Industry', in the *Edinburgh Review* in 1859 established 'female redundancy' as a key issue in the movement to expand professional opportunities for women (Sanders, *Reason* 179). Likewise, Martineau's anonymous leaders for the *Daily News* (1852-66) were influential in public debates on women's issues as diverse as divorce rights and rational dress. Perhaps the most important of these contributions was a series of letters on the Contagious Diseases Acts, which ignited public protests led by Josephine Butler in the 1870s.[26] As Judith Walkowitz has shown, these protests were part of a larger social movement that 'facilitated middle-class women's forceful entry into the world of publicity and politics, where they claimed themselves as part of a public that made sense of itself through public discourse' (7). However, while on one hand the women's movement was becoming increasingly 'visible', on the other hand it was becoming increasingly 'invisible' as women activists such as Martineau maneuvered behind the scenes.[27] Thus a proto-feminist consciousness developed not only in highly public cultural moments but also in innumerable private acts.

Essential to Martineau's campaign for women's rights was the anonymity of the periodical press, which enabled her to write from an depersonalized perspective. Many critics have viewed Martineau's use of this strategy as evidence of her unwillingness to take a firm stand on issues of concern to women.[28] However, Martineau's use of authorial obscurity can perhaps more profitably be viewed as a rhetorical technique that enabled her to expand the audience for the Woman Question and to strike a philosophical tone in public discussions of women's

58 FIRST-PERSON ANONYMOUS

issues. These techniques carried over into her book-length works of fiction and non-fiction, which employed devices intended to present a depersonalized yet sympathetic point of view on issues of concern to women. Throughout her long career, Martineau demonstrated how women could embrace the contradictions inherent in their positions as insiders and outsiders in debates over the Woman Question. Instead of imagining public activism as an either/or proposition—that a woman must choose between domesticity and public life—she demonstrated how women could achieve both simultaneously through politically engaged forms of writing and seeing. She showed how writers could speak out on issues of concern to women while still avoiding being labeled according to socially constructed stereotypes of literary bluestockingism. Though these activities were in some sense contained by patriarchally defined institutions and narrative media, they were also subtly transformative, gradually altering the terms by which women's issues would be presented and discussed.

Martineau's career demonstrates how she was able to manipulate the conventions of signed and unsigned print media in order to shape her own authorial image and radical agenda. However, in many ways Martineau's career was unusual for a woman of letters of her time. Most women who began their careers as journalists clung to authorial anonymity throughout their lives as a means of evading socially constructed definitions of the female author. This enabled them to harness the power associated with anonymity as a way of shaping Victorian public opinion from behind the 'editorial we'. One of the most remarkable and elusive of these women journalists of the 1830s and '40s was Christian Johnstone, whose career as an editor and critic would have important implications for the development of women's authorship in the Victorian period. The next chapter will explore Johnstone's career, examining ways that she contributed to the discourse on women's issues from within the context of periodical debates over the Condition-of-England Question.

Notes

1   See Thompson ('Responding') for an overview of women writers' contradictory responses to the Woman Question during the Victorian era.

2   Caroline Norton's high-profile participation in debates over women's rights had the effect of exposing her personal life. In 1836, Norton published a pamphlet describing her own struggles in attempting to gain custody of her children. As a consequence, Norton was attacked as an adulterous 'she-devil' in the *British and Foreign Quarterly Review* (Helsinger et al., 2: 8-13).

3   Many articles and reviews focused on women's issues appeared in literary periodicals during the 1830s. Palmegiano provides a comprehensive bibliography. See also two anonymous articles published in *Fraser's Magazine*: 'Female Education and Modern Matchmaking' (1836) and 'The Female Character' (1833).

HARRIET MARTINEAU   59

4   For example, in 'Literary Lionism', published in the *London and Westminster Review* in 1839, Martineau explores the challenges faced by literary women, and in 'The Achievements of the Genius of Scott', published in *Tait's Edinburgh Magazine* in 1833, Martineau critiques depictions of women in Walter Scott's fiction.

5   See Sanders and Pichanick (*Reason* 168-85) for a broad overview of Martineau's contributions to the Woman Question.

6   Though Martineau had been a published author since 1821, writing articles on various subjects for the *Monthly Repository,* it wasn't until the late '20s that she defined herself primarily as a professional writer.

7   For example, see Leigh Hunt's satirical poem 'Blue-Stocking Revels', which satirizes Martineau's Malthusianism: 'I own I can't see, any more than dame Nature, / Why love should await dear good Harriet's dictature!' (quoted in Mineka 389).

8   Mineka provides a complete listing of Martineau's essays published in the *Monthly Repository* (397, 414-17). A significant number of Martineau's contributions to other periodicals are indexed in the *Wellesley Index to Victorian Periodicals.*

9   Martineau's *Autobiography* includes a discussion of her literary influences (1: 120-23).

10   Peterson ('Masculine Discourse'), David (27-39), and Corbett (89-93).

11   See Hunter (38-54) for an in-depth discussion of the critical reception of *Illustrations.*

12   The tendency of these reviews to refer to Martineau as a 'young lady' are interesting considering that Martineau was 30 years old at the time *Illustrations* was published. Their emphasis on her supposed youthfulness was most likely intended to make her literary ambitions and choice of subject matter all the more shocking to Victorian readers.

13   In chapters on the position of 'people of color' and women, she asks why those who do not assent to the laws of their 'democratic' country should be held accountable to them. See Hoecker-Drysdale (62-69) and Frawley for an extended analysis of the feminist and abolitionist content of *Society in America.*

14   As R. K. Webb points out, in this regard Martineau was similar to other travel writers during this period whose 'intentions and conclusions were determined less by the country they visited than by their hopes and fears for society at home' (134).

15   Frawley provides an extended analysis of Martineau's complex treatment of gender and social observation in *Society in America.*

16   See Eva-Marie Kröller for a discussion of the 'author's multiple persona' in Victorian travel writing, 'which allows him or her to be both accomplice in, and critic of, the business of imperialism' (87).

17   For example, see John Croker's scathing response to *How to Observe Morals and Manners* in the *Quarterly Review,* which questions Martineau's ability to write about international travel, since she has not visited the 'continent of Europe, nor indeed in any country of which English is not the vernacular idiom' (62). See Webb for further background on the critical response to Martineau's work in the 1830s (157-161).

18   In her *Autobiography* and letters, Martineau gives many hints as to what these 'moral questions' might have been. However, she suggests that the major source for her novel

was the marriage woes of a childhood friend who was tricked into an unfavorable marriage by a 'match-making lady' (2: 113).

19 Elaine Showalter provides a useful overview the critical double standard applied to women's writing during this period (73-99).

20 See Valerie Sanders for a discussion of Martineau's theory of fiction, particularly her views on the social function of the novel (*Reason* 1-29).

21 Rachel Blau DuPlessis provides an analysis of the conventional marriage plot in nineteenth-century women's fiction. DuPlessis points out that these texts demonstrate a 'contradiction between love and quest in plots dealing with women as a narrated group' which is resolved with an 'ending in which one part of that contradiction, usually quest or *Bildung*, is set aside or repressed, whether by marriage or by death' (3-4). Of course, I am to some extent disagreeing with DuPlessis by pointing out the ways that Martineau worked both within and against the conventions the marriage plot associated with domestic fiction.

22   See Hobart for a discussion of Martineau's simultaneous reinforcement and problematization of women's social roles. Hobart argues that '*Deerbrook* is divided between representations of women who must be brought up to their crucial duties as wives and mothers and representations of a society insufficiently flexible to accommodate those whom exceptional circumstances have exempted from conventional womanly responsibilities' (242).

23 Cole provides an in-depth analysis of the 'anti-feminist sympathies' in Smith's *Theory of Moral Sentiments* and how the concept of sympathy was reconfigured in the work of Hannah More and Mary Wollstonecraft.

24 Sanders provides a useful discussion of this trope in Victorian fiction (*Reason* 59-60).

25 See Hobart for a discussion of the limitations of Martineau's liberal individualism. Though I agree with Hobart that there were contradictions within Martineau's program for women's emancipation, I do not agree that Martineau's work demonstrates the 'high cost of masculine identification' (228). I view Martineau as operating both within and against patriarchy during her career, constructing her radical viewpoints from multiple narrative and ideological positions.

26 The Contagious Diseases Acts (1864, 1868, 1869) proclaimed that women suspected of being prostitutes would be detained and inspected for venereal disease. Martineau criticized the sexual double standard inherent in this legislation by publishing several letters of protest in the *Daily News*. Inspired in part by Martineau's letters, Josephine Butler to found the social purity movement aimed at reforming male sexual morality. See Hoecker-Drysdale (143-47), Pichanick (24-26), and Yates (239-45).

27 Martineau's name did appear in a proclamation published in the *Daily News* by the Ladies' National Association for the Repeal of the Contagious Diseases Acts, but for the most part she participated in the campaign by writing letters to influential friends and members of parliament (see Hoecker-Drysdale 143-46). Partly due to Martineau's efforts, the Contagious Disease Acts were eventually repealed.

28 See, for example, Sanders (*Reason* 181-83) and Figes (114).

CHAPTER THREE

Periodical Journalism and the Gender of Reform: Christian Isobel Johnstone

The desire for social usefulness that motivated women's writing careers during the 1830s intensified with the emergence of a field of discourse focused on social reform: the Condition-of-England Question.[1] Debates over the Factory Acts (1833, 1842, 1847), the new Poor Law (1834), and the repeal of the Corn Laws (1846) emphasized the volatility of class relations and the necessity of public action on behalf of the poor. These debates spilled over into statistical and sociological studies, including James Kay-Shuttleworth's *Moral and Physical Condition of the Working Classes* (1832), Peter Gaskell's *Artisans and Machinery: The Moral and Physical Condition of the Manufacturing Population* (1836), Edwin Chadwick's *Report on the Sanitary Condition of the Labouring Population of Great Britain* (1842), and the *Report of the Children's Employment Commission* (1842, 1843).[2]

An equally important vehicle for the Condition-of-England debate was the periodical press, which during the 1830s and '40s became increasingly focused on social problems. Monthly periodicals such as *Fraser's Magazine* (1830-69), *Bentley's Miscellany* (1837-68), and *Blackwood's Magazine* (1817-1905) expressed concern over urban poverty and the threat of working-class violence. Many of the novels serially published in these periodicals—for example, *Oliver Twist* in *Bentley's Miscellany* (1837-39)—were often focused on investigating inner-city sociology and domestic spaces. Closely related to the serialized social problem novel was the urban sketch (e.g., *Sketches by Boz*), a short travelogue describing spaces unfamiliar to most middle-class readers: factories, gin shops, cellar apartments, and workhouses.

By reading and contributing to periodicals, women were able to participate both directly and vicariously in debates on the Condition-of-England Question. Periodicals such as the *Christian Lady's Magazine* (1834-49), the *British Mother's Magazine* (1845-55), and the *Mother's Friend* (1848-59) were important for encouraging women's social activism and intervention on behalf of the poor. However, these magazines also tended to reinforce women's conventional roles as keepers of the domestic hearth.[3] Even more important in facilitating women's participation in the discourse on poverty and industrialism were reformist periodicals such as *Eliza Cook's Journal* (1848-54), *Jerrold's Shilling Magazine* (1845-48), *Howitt's Journal* (1847-48), the *People's Journal* (1846-49). These periodicals claimed to provide middle-class readers with the information and tools needed to facilitate the process of social reform. As Brian Maidment has noted,

62   FIRST-PERSON ANONYMOUS

they were 'essentially literary magazines with interests in the intellectual and social progress of "the people", and in humanitarian and progressive causes' (83). In addition, they provided updates on philanthropic efforts and information about the domestic habits and morals of the poor—knowledge that was intended to provide a foundation for a more informed and enlightened social activism.

One of the most important of these reformist periodicals was *Tait's Edinburgh Magazine*, which from 1834 to 1846 was edited by a woman, Christian Isobel Johnstone (1781-1857). The career of Christian Johnstone today seems nothing short of miraculous. In addition to publishing two regional novels, *Clan-Albin* (1815) and *Elizabeth de Bruce* (1827),[4] Johnstone published a cookbook, the *Cook and Housewife's Manual* (1826), which went through several editions. Johnstone also co-edited the *Inverness Courier* (1817-24), *Edinburgh Weekly Chronicle* (1824-32), *Schoolmaster and Edinburgh Weekly Magazine* (1832-33), and *Johnstone's Edinburgh Magazine* (1833-34). When Johnstone assumed the editorship of *Tait's Edinburgh Magazine* in 1834, she became the first woman to serve as paid editor of a major Victorian periodical.[5]

Like Martineau, Johnstone shaped her career within the context of anonymous print media; however, while Martineau emerged into public visibility as the author of signed works of fiction and non-fiction, Johnstone was much more reticent about assuming a public identity.[6] This was partly due to the fact that Johnstone was a divorcée and consequently had good reason to avoid public attention.[7] However, Johnstone was no doubt also attracted to anonymity because it provided her with access to audiences that would have been inaccessible to a celebrity female author or editor. After all, during the 1830s, the role of the editor in mainstream magazines and quarterlies was gendered masculine by default.[8] By capitalizing on the convention of anonymity in the periodical press, Johnstone was able to enter the field of journalistic editing covertly without assuming an a feminine editorial identity. Though in some Edinburgh literary circles Johnstone's identity as the editor of *Tait's Edinburgh Magazine* was most likely an open secret, the anonymity of periodical editing still enabled her to address a broader audience without as much fear of personal exposure.

When Johnstone assumed the editorship of *Tait's*, she was entering a field of professional activity that was gaining increasing power and importance in Victorian culture. To be an editor was to assume the power of the fourth estate, to influence the direction of social policy by shaping public opinion.[9] As Carlyle points out in 'Signs of the Times', the Victorian editor functioned as a secular priest, 'admonishing kings themselves; advising peace or war[;] ... inflicting moral censure; imparting moral encouragement; consolation, edification' (241). Johnstone, more than any other woman journalist of her era, knew how to harness this power—to redefine the periodical medium in such a way as to facilitate social reform as well as to promote the careers of women writers. The first part of this chapter will focus on Johnstone's editorship of *Tait's Edinburgh Magazine* (1834-46), especially her techniques for selecting, arranging, and reviewing literary texts from a gender- and class-sensitive point of view. The second part of this chapter will focus on Johnstone's editorship of *Edinburgh Tales*, an anthology of short fiction published from 1845 to 1846. In this rare break with anonymity, Johnstone attempted, rather unsuccessfully, to establish herself as a celebrity fiction writer while at the same time continuing to function as the unknown but highly influential editor of *Tait's Edinburgh Magazine*. An exploration of Johnstone's editorial projects illuminates the complex relationship between class and gender in her work and within the reformist periodical press more generally during the 1830s and '40s.

Johnstone and *Tait's Edinburgh Magazine*

William Tait founded *Tait's Edinburgh Magazine* in 1832, just one month before the passage of the first Reform Bill (Figure 3.1). In his 1832 prospectus for the magazine, Tait writes, 'on the eve of great events, it has appeared to us not only desirable, but necessary, to provide an organ or vehicle through which the voice of a renovated people may be heard' (qtd. in Houghton 3: 476). Tait emphasized that his magazine represented 'no party but that of the country' and as such spoke for the 'good of THE PEOPLE' (476). By claiming to speak for 'the people', Tait was attempting to market his radicalism to a broad base of middle-class and artisan-class readers with diverse regional affiliations. With this marketing strategy, he hoped to promote a sense of national unity at a time when class interests were becoming increasingly divided. In addition, he hoped to provide a vehicle for his radical political viewpoints that would rival *Blackwood's Magazine* in popularity and sales. In order to pursue this goal, he solicited and published work by some of the most important thinkers of the day, including Leigh Hunt, Harriet Martineau, J. S. Mill, and John Roebuck. When establishing the magazine, Tait turned to Christian Johnstone as a major contributor and sub-editor. In the early years of the magazine, from 1833 to 1834, Johnstone also co-edited *Johnstone's Edinburgh Magazine*, a cheap monthly published by Tait.

When in 1834 *Johnstone's Edinburgh Magazine* was absorbed into *Tait's Edinburgh Magazine*, Tait and Johnstone became the magazine's co-proprietors. Johnstone was elected to serve as the primary editor, with William Tait as her sub-editor. Once Johnstone assumed the editorship of *Tait's*, it is difficult to determine the extent of her editorial responsibilities. According to one biographer, William Anderson, she was not 'strictly speaking' the magazine's editor, though she was a 'large and regular contributor' of literary articles (3: 713). However, most other accounts of Johnstone's editorship suggest that she had more wide ranging responsibilities. James Bertram, a clerk in the *Tait's* offices during Johnstone's tenure, notes that 'while Mr. Tait conducted the necessary correspondence with the actual and would-be contributors ... [Johnstone] generally passed judgment on the articles offered' (30). Apparently Johnstone performed most of these editorial duties from her home. Bertram would deliver the proofs of the magazine to Johnstone's house and take them back to the printing office when she had completed her work (5). The contents of the magazine, as cataloged by the editors of the *Wellesley Index to Victorian Periodicals*, suggest that Johnstone

TAIT'S

EDINBURGH MAGAZINE.

NUMBERS I.—VI.

FOR

APRIL, MAY, JUNE, JULY, AUGUST, AND
SEPTEMBER, 1832.

FIAT JUSTITIA.

VOLUME I.

EDINBURGH:
WILLIAM TAIT, 78, PRINCE'S STREET;
SIMPKIN & MARSHALL, LONDON; AND JOHN CUMMING, DUBLIN.

MDCCCXXXII.

3.1 Title page, *Tait's Edinburgh Magazine.* **Courtesy Memorial Library, University of Wisconsin, Madison**

often took responsibility for writing political editorials and notes to contributors. The editorship of *Tait's* was thus most likely a collaborative relationship between Tait and Johnstone, with Johnstone taking primary responsibility for selecting and arranging the contents of the magazine.

As editor, Johnstone instituted many changes to the magazine designed to make it more appealing to the working classes. She changed the format of the magazine to a larger, more popular size and reduced its price from half a crown to one shilling. In a note to subscribers, Johnstone and Tait write that the new price and format will allow the magazine to reach the 'most cultivated class of general readers; and from the unrivalled cheapness resulting from a large circulation, accessible to those of the most moderate pecuniary means' ('To Our Subscribers' 289). The reduction in price made *Tait's* for a time the best selling magazine in Scotland, surpassing even *Blackwood's Magazine* in its Scottish sales (289).[10] Another strategy Johnstone used to attract a popular readership was to increase the number of working-class contributors to the periodical, most notably Ebenezer Elliott and Robert Nicoll. In 1837 she also instituted an annual anthology of working-class poetry titled the 'Feast of the Poets'. In the introduction to the 1839 anthology, Johnstone remarks that it is the magazine's aim to publish poetry 'which reveals the expanding and brooding heart of the People, and which, wherever it may germinate, is sure first to break forth at the plough, the loom, the forge, in the village school, or in the workshop of the skilled artisan' ('A Chapter' 581). By providing a venue for working-class writing, Johnstone hoped to promote the careers of aspiring poets and to revitalize the rhetoric of reform.

Johnstone's definition of reformist journalism was premised on the idea that positive social change would result if the literary taste of the general public were improved. During her years at *Tait's,* Johnstone wrote a number of articles on periodical journalism as a trade, examining its social roles and responsibilities. These articles give us a sense of how Johnstone might have viewed her editorial mission. In an article entitled 'On Periodical Literature', for example, she defines the periodical as having a vital role to play in improving the self-culture and political consciousness of the British people. She argues that journalism has become 'trivial and fragmentary, deficient in dignified strength and high-raised endeavor' (494). As a result, she contends, the modern reader has become shallow and uninformed. The new periodical, she claims, must assume a central role in facilitating self-improvement. The role of the modern journalist is to give 'direction' to the 'onward current of mind' that will lead it to 'what is worthy, and pure, and faithful' (496). She writes, 'We consider its duties as no light or perfunctory undertaking; we insist upon the necessity of performing them in an earnest, nay, almost religious, spirit of truthfulness' (496).

Johnstone often uses feeding and hunger as metaphors for describing the supply and demand for better reading material.[11] In an article titled 'High Living and Mean Thinking', for example, she describes the mass of new readers that has arisen with the development of a democratic society. She is concerned not only for the poor, who survive on the 'potatoe diet of the press', but the rich, whose reading 'is generally lower than the reading in the servants' halls' (443, 444). She writes, 'The care of the mind has yet to have a commencement. Its servants and its food have hitherto been of the lowest sort; but on both the character of the ministration and the nutriment[,] the purity and soundness of the intellect must greatly depend' (444).

The periodical, by providing intellectual 'food', thus acts as a replacement for other forms of social action aimed at improving the material existence of the British people.[12] Interestingly, Johnstone's vision of the man of letters begins to sound more like a mother of letters—a maternal figure who nurtures and nourishes a growing population of readers. Such a view of the editorial role fits well within the middle-class discourse on reform during the 1830s and '40s, which sought non-violent, literary solutions to class-based social inequities and provided a utopian vision of communication across class boundaries. However, as Brian Maidment points out, magazines of popular progress such as *Tait's* were far from being the static organs of middle-class ideology. At the same time that they served as instruments of social control, they also made 'progressive attempts to replace cultural propaganda with a more open form of cultural dialogue' (87). Implicit in the overall project of reformist journalism was the notion that women had an important role to play as facilitators of this dialogue.

Johnstone and the Gendering of Reform

Johnstone's editorship of *Tait's*, though not widely publicized, can be seen as a marker of an important change in the Victorian publishing industry. While during the 1830s and '40s mainstream periodicals were assumed to have been edited, written, and read by men, this assumption of male control was challenged by the increasing participation of women in popular print culture. As Margaret Beetham has pointed out, during the early decades of the century women were often advertised as the celebrity editors and contributors to women's annuals and periodicals (42-4). Women were also closely associated with evangelical popular literature movements inspired by Hannah More and Sarah Trimmer (Beetham, 49-50). This included the publication of a variety of family periodicals directed to middle-class and working-class women that were designed to promote rational motherhood and Christian values.[13] The magazines Johnstone co-edited with her husband—*The Schoolmaster and Edinburgh Weekly Magazine* (1832-33) and *Johnstone's Edinburgh Magazine* (1833-34)—followed in the tradition of the popular literature movement, focusing on the dissemination of useful and entertaining knowledge to an audience of artisan and middle-class families. The *Schoolmaster*, priced at 3 ½ pence, included columns for children and ladies as well as a variety of short articles and stories, some of which were published with Johnstone's byline. *Johnstone's Magazine,* priced at 8 pence, also addressed artisans and middle-class readers, though it contained more well developed literary features such as serialized fiction and reviews of useful literature. The periodical's

CHRISTIAN JOHNSTONE 67

title page indicated that it was edited by John Johnstone and 'Mrs. Johnstone, authoress of "Clan-Albin", "Elizabeth de Bruce", "Nights of the Round Table", &c. &c.' As the named co-editor of the periodical, Johnstone assumed a role as schoolmistress to the lower orders, thereby giving the periodical a 'feminine' cast. Consequently, when *Johnstone's Magazine* merged with *Tait's Magazine*, the event was viewed as a symbolic union between masculine and feminine influences. Leigh Hunt, writing just before the merger of the two magazines, remarks,

> *Tait* has now exactly the size and look of *Johnstone*; and the two publications agreeably harmonize. They lie on the bookseller's counter like the two last peaches in a fruiterer's basket. It seems a pity, nay, impossible, to divide them ... Indeed the same writers appear to write in both; and as *Johnstone* has become more political, so *Tait* has become more storied, and domestic, like *Johnstone*, so that what with looking alike, and being printed by the same printer, and published by the same publisher, they seem like the man and wife of Magazines, each partaking the goods and graces of the other (qtd. in Johnstone, 'Union' 529).

Paradoxically, Hunt suggests that the subject matter and format of the magazines is so similar that it is difficult to distinguish them, yet, like man and wife, they retain essential, yet complementary, gender-based differences that make them suitable for 'marriage' in a single periodical.

Part of the reason that *Johnstone's Magazine* was considered the 'female' member of the union was that William Tait had advertised the fact that Christian Johnstone was the primary editor of *Johnstone's* in an 1833 article puffing the magazine. Tait writes of Johnstone, 'her mind is essentially versatile, and readily accommodates its energies to any task in which it may suit her convenience to engage; and hence, in the merest matter-of-fact pursuits, no less than in embodying, and, as it were, vivifying the creations of fancy, she has been pre-eminently successful' ('Johnstone's' 784). Johnstone was thus defined as a distinctly feminine, though clearly 'versatile' writer. Tait writes, 'In a word, if there be any author of the day, whether male or female, better qualified than another to conduct a periodical intended to combine instruction with amusement, and to render the latter the vehicle of the former, that author is Mrs. Johnstone' (784). Such a recommendation most likely still lingered in readers' minds when less than a year later the two magazines joined forces under a single title.

However, once Johnstone assumed the editorship of *Tait's*, the magazine did not actively publicize her name and credentials. William Tait's name, not Johnstone's, was advertised on the magazine's title page. Johnstone contributed to the creation of a masculine textual space by sometimes assuming a male identity in her articles and reviews. For example, in an article titled 'What Shall We Do With Our Young Fellows', Johnstone assumes the persona of a young man who laments the prohibition against genteel men entering careers in the trades. The narrator remarks, 'in fact, I am one of themselves and sympathize in all their real cares and difficulties' (528). In another article Johnstone assumes the identity (and Scottish

68   FIRST-PERSON ANONYMOUS

dialect) of a dealer in wool who writes a letter on current political issues directed to Sir John Campbell, MP for the city of Edinburgh ('Tam Glen'). Tam begins his letter, 'But it doesna suit the likes o' me to be holding correspondence with Sirs and other potentates of the land, though, for the matter of that, it hadna been for coporation reform—against which my wife, I thocht, wad ha'e gane clean wude—wha kens but I might ha'e been a barronight mysel'?' (539). Taken together, these and the many other masculine voices included in the periodical give the impression that the creators and readers of *Tait's Edinburgh Magazine* are part of a male community. Johnstone no doubt believed that this sense of homosociality would lend credibility to the magazine. After all, during the 1830s and '40s it was generally assumed that a mainstream literary periodical such as *Tait's* would have been written and read primarily by middle-class men. Consequently, Johnstone probably viewed the creation of a masculine voice as a prerequisite to a successful editorship.

Part of Johnstone's task in maintaining the implied masculinity of *Tait's Magazine* was to suggest to readers that William Tait was the magazine's real editor. Suppressing her own sex and identity meant creating a literary representation of William Tait that would serve as her stand-in. For example, in 'What Is Going On', a political article written in the form of a humorous dialogue, Johnstone assumes the character of a young man, Paul Pry, who has come to Edinburgh seeking work as a journalist. Walking into Tait's office, he sees the editor hard at work behind a large screen, surrounded by proofs, magazines, books, and other 'literary litter' (419). Through the eyes of Paul Pry, we are given the impression that Tait is the magazine's solitary editor. What makes this scene especially interesting, though, is how in the ensuing dialogue Johnstone subtly undermines the image of William Tait that she has created. Spotting William Tait behind the screen, Paul Pry says, 'O, Mr. Editor Tait, behind your screen all the while,—how droll! ... Told you are your own Editor;—circulate fifty thousand:—is that *correct*?' A bit perturbed, Tait responds, 'There's some slight mistake here, Mr. Paul' (419). It isn't clear if Paul Pry's 'mistake' is believing Tait to be the editor or believing that the circulation of *Tait's Magazine* is fifty thousand. Johnstone thus playfully leaves the question of Tait's sole editorship open ended.

Unfortunately, few readers would have understood Johnstone's inside joke since it was not widely known that she was the primary editor of *Tait's*. In fact, it was Johnstone's self-effacement, rather than her editorial playfulness, that struck most of her contemporaries and biographers as they reviewed her career at *Tait's*. They often emphasized her reticence as a writer and editor, pointing out that her self-effacement enabled her to pursue a literary career without compromising her feminine virtue. Thomas De Quincey, for example, remarks that she was one of the 'women of admirable genius' of her day who with 'absolutely no sacrifice or loss of feminine dignity' were able to work as professional authors (2: 209). Likewise, biographer William Anderson remarks that she was 'of unassuming disposition' and 'shrank from anything like publicity or conspicuousness' (3: 714). Within some Edinburgh circles, however, Johnstone was probably known as the editor of

CHRISTIAN JOHNSTONE

Tait's. James Bertram, for example mentions one Edinburgh subscriber 'who seemed never to tire of questioning me about Mrs. Johnstone' (16). News of Johnstone's editorship also seemed to reach London, where Carlyle remarked in an 1834 letter, 'Mrs. J., we often say here, would make half a dozen Cockney "famed women".' (*Collected Letters* 7: 311). In a later letter to William Tait, he praises Johnstone's radicalism and extends 'hearty remembrances, good-wishes and applause' to the 'good brave-hearted lady' (11: 234). Though clearly some readers were aware of Johnstone's role as the editor of *Tait's*, most readers probably would have assumed that Tait was in charge of the magazine. This was partly due to the convention of anonymous editing but was most likely also due to her own efforts at self-concealment.

Though as an editor Johnstone attempted to suppress her own identity and to construct *Tait's* as a male literary community, she also instituted editorial changes that seem intended to disrupt the implied masculinity of the periodical as a whole. Under her editorship, the number of female contributors increased from about 19% to 37%. While it is true that a large number of these contributions came from Johnstone's own pen, the magazine also employed a number of important women writers, including Catherine Gore, Eliza Meteyard, Amelia Opie, and Harriet Martineau. In addition to publishing her fellow women writers, Johnstone demonstrated a keen interest in women's issues and perspectives as a reviewer of contemporary literature.[14] In some reviews, she seems to assign a feminine gender to her 'editorial we'. For example in a review of a memoir written by a military officer, Johnstone writes, 'Taking it for granted that our readers, like ourselves, feel more interest in the Spanish ladies and Spanish interiors, than in the marchings and mishaps of the Legion, with whose operations we have all had abundant opportunities of making ourselves acquainted, we shall adhere to our favorite passages' ('Twelve Months' 694). This excerpt suggests that the readership of *Tait's* includes women, whose interest in the domestic realm provides a lens through which to critique literary texts.

In addition to modeling gender-sensitive reading practices, Johnstone played an important role in legitimizing women's authorial careers. She single-handedly reviewed most works published by women in the 1830s and '40s, including Mary Howitt's *Sketches of Natural History* (1834) and Catherine Gore's *The Banker's Wife* (1843).[15] Like Martineau, Johnstone often used her position as an anonymous reviewer to assert a proto-feminist critical sensibility. The most striking example of this proto-feminism is Johnstone's 1844 review of Marion Reid's *A Plea for Woman*. First published in 1843, Reid's *Plea* is today considered a foundational text in the British women's movement, serving as an important precursor to Harriet Taylor's 'The Enfranchisement of Women' (Burness 108-11). Though Reid's *Plea* was a controversial text during its own time, Johnstone still gave it a prominent notice in *Tait's*. This was partly due to the fact that it was published by William Tait; thus, Johnstone was probably drawing attention to the book as a way of increasing its sales. However, at the same time, the publication of the review seemed to reflect Johnstone's ongoing interest in the Woman Question. By 1844

70 FIRST-PERSON ANONYMOUS

Tait's had already become an important vehicle for proto-feminist discourse, most likely due to Johnstone's efforts as editor.[16]

Johnstone begins her review of Reid's *Plea* by briefly summarizing the contributions of Harriet Martineau and Mary Wollstonecraft to the Woman Question. She praises Martineau's critique of American gender inequities and defends Wollstonecraft against her detractors. She writes, 'modern female advocates for the rights of the sex, though contending for the principles of Mary Wolstonecraft [sic], are either ignorant that they are hers, or else are afraid to use a name which prejudice has covered with unmerited obloquy' (423). After this introduction, Johnstone assesses the progress of women's rights in Great Britain. Like Martineau, she views the status of women as an indicator of social progress:

> The last twenty years have been remarkable for the mental development, and social progress, of all the 'inferior orders of society:' that is, of the slaves of the British colonies, the working-classes of manufacturing England; and the women, at least those of the middle rank, in France, England, and America:—we may add, of the whole North of Europe. The great, if silent, change in the attainments and knowledge, and consequently in the social, if not civil, position of women which has already taken place, portends still greater changes; while it indicates the progress already made (423).

By grouping women with other 'inferior orders', Johnstone attempts to link their struggle for civil liberties with those who suffer oppression based on race and class. Yet in contrast to these other groups, women have advanced through 'silent' forms of self-advancement and improvement. Presumably, the anonymous periodical press is one possible vehicle for the type of 'great and increasing influence' women exert 'on public affairs', even without the vote (423). As she imagines what changes will need to be brought about before women will be allowed direct political representation, Johnstone argues for continued improvement of women's education but also an expansion in employment opportunities. Women, she argues, must 'be placed in circumstances where they may turn that education to account for their individual benefit,—like men' (424). In making an argument for equal employment opportunity, Johnstone casts aside sex difference as a valid justification for women's economic dependence. Likewise, she is skeptical of language that would essentialize socially constructed gender differences. She writes, 'The fallacies and injustice involved in the phrases "masculine", "women's sphere", and other favorable expressions, are, we fear, as strong as ever' (426).

Yet Johnstone is unwilling to join Reid in pleading for women's immediate access to equal rights under the law. She writes, 'We must confess, however, that we are not yet prepared either for mixed male and female juries, or deliberative or legislative assemblies' (427). Though as editor, Johnstone was eager to address the Woman Question, as a reviewer she was careful to assume a moderate, meliorist stance. This may have been due to her own lingering conservatism but perhaps also because of her fear of alienating readers with what would be considered an

CHRISTIAN JOHNSTONE 71

extremist point of view on the Woman Question. Nevertheless, by introducing Reid's work to a broad audience, Johnstone succeeded in putting the Woman Question at the forefront of the social agenda.

In her review of *A Plea for Woman*, Johnstone attempted to demonstrate how the plight of women was inseparable from the struggles of other oppressed groups. Indeed, for Johnstone the question of how to promote social justice for the working classes was inextricably linked to the problem of how to empower women within literary and political realms. The connection between Johnstone's explicit goal of promoting inter-class dialogue and her implicit goal of promoting women's participation in the discourse on reform is revealed in her 1832 review of Harriet Martineau's *Illustrations of Political Economy*. Throughout the article, Johnstone praises Martineau's fictional approach to illustrating the principles of political economy. She makes it clear that her intent is not only to praise Martineau's abilities as a national instructor but also to defend her right to participate in the dialogue on national and international economic policy. She writes,

After all, we believe that there is something in the female mind which particularly fits it for elucidating, in a familiar manner, the intricacies of political economy. The economy of empires is only the economy of families and neighborhoods on a larger scale. Now woman is eminently the best family manager. Let profane ones sneer if they please—we give it as our deliberate conviction that there never yet was a well regulated house in which the lady was not the master (613).

In this passage, Johnstone was responding to Martineau's critics, who considered *Illustrations of Political Economy* unfeminine due to its economic subject matter. On one hand, Johnstone's editorial persona seems to present a distanced, masculine perspective on Martineau's work; however, it also seems to provide an empathetic response to Martineau as a woman writer entering a male-dominated field. Johnstone envisions a political role for the woman writer in solving social problems, with the domestic sphere functioning as a microcosm of a broader political realm. In an expanded sphere of influence, the woman author has an important role to play in facilitating the improvement of the working classes. That is, she must '[free] men from the self-imposed fetters of ignorance and prejudice' through popular education (618). Johnstone remarks that as a new 'fellow-laborer' in this struggle, Martineau deserves a 'cordial' welcome (618). She thus welcomes Martineau into a cadre of 'gifted females whose writings have of late years so eminently benefited their country', women who view writing as a form of social activism on behalf of the poor (617). Writing anonymously, Johnstone doesn't necessarily include herself in the category of 'gifted females', but she still constructs a sense of community out of which women can participate in the process of solving social problems.

Key to the development of *Tait's* as a reformist periodical was the implicit knowledge that middle-class women had an important role to play as literary critics and national instructors. Though Christian Johnstone's name did not appear on the title page of *Tait's Edinburgh Magazine*, her influence is evident not only in periodical's list of contributors but also in its implicit dialogues over gender and literary authority. During the 1830s, *Tait's* became a multi-layered text, capable of being read by multiple audiences from diverse class- and gender-based perspectives, while at the same time maintaining its identity as a reformist periodical aimed primarily at middle-class men. Reading with and against the grain, readers could uncover explicit and implicit dialogues over class and gender that both confirmed and challenged the dominance of men as writers and editors in the discourse on social reform.

During the 1840s, the participation of women in *Tait's Edinburgh Magazine* became more 'visible' when Johnstone began publishing her own name and the names of female contributors along with selected works of serialized fiction. Johnstone's novella *Nighean Ceard*, Eliza Meteyard's *Scenes in the Life of an Authoress*, Elizabeth Thornton's *Truth and Falsehood*, and Catherine Gore's *Temptation and Atonement* appeared as signed serials in *Tait's* during the mid-1840s. It is difficult to know why Johnstone chose to include the names of women fiction writers in *Tait's*, but it is likely that she hoped to capitalize on the notoriety of her literary contributors in order to boost circulation of the magazine. In addition, she may have been attempting to capitalize on her own reputation in Edinburgh literary circles as a well regarded fiction writer and to create a name for herself as a literary contributor to *Tait's Magazine*. However, though 'Mrs. Johnstone' became known as a fiction writer for *Tait's*, her identity as the magazine's anonymous editor remained relatively unknown. Indeed, most readers probably would have viewed 'Mrs. Johnstone' as just another fiction writer employed by William Tait. It wasn't until the publication of *Edinburgh Tales* (1845-46) that Johnstone actively advertised her own role as a woman editor.

Johnstone's *Edinburgh Tales*

Perhaps building on the success of the publication of signed fiction in *Tait's Magazine*, Johnstone began work on *Edinburgh Tales*. This anthology, published by William Tait in weekly and monthly parts, then in bound volumes from 1845 to 1846, included selected stories and novellas reprinted from *Tait's* as well as a variety of new works commissioned specifically for the series. The two-column format of the *Tales* was identical to that of *Tait's Magazine*, thus providing a visual marker of the connection between the two publications. The cheaper price of the *Tales*, however, made it achieve a circulation far higher than its sister periodical. The weekly issues, priced at 3 ½ pence, achieved a circulation of 30,000 (Conolly 244). James Bertram, clerk for *Tait's Edinburgh Magazine*, noted that after the publication of the tales, the offices were 'inundated with offers of stories' from local writers (47). Part of the reason for the popularity of *Edinburgh Tales* was the list of celebrity contributors it employed. The table of contents included the names of Mary Russell Mitford, Thomas Carlyle, William Howitt, Mary Howitt,

Catherine Gore, and Robert Nicoll. In addition, Johnstone included a number of her own works, including two novellas originally published anonymously in *Tait's*: *Violet Hamilton* and *Blanche Delamere*. She also advertised her own name as editor of the series by printing 'Conducted by Mrs. Johnstone' on the serial's title page.

Advertisements for *Edinburgh Tales* published in *Tait's* in 1845 prominently display her name and emphasize her qualifications as the author of popular fiction (Figure 3.1). These ads include the names of her previous publications as well as excerpts from critical notices of her work. One excerpt reads, 'The writer unites the affection of a mother, the vigilance of an aunt, and the skill of a governess, with the grace and elegance of a well-bred lady' ('The Edinburgh Tales'). A later excerpt refers to her as the 'Edgeworth of Scotland', and another calls her 'one of the foremost female writers of the age' ('Opinions'). Taken together, these advertisements present Johnstone as an esteemed female author who is known for her work as a fiction writer. However, these excerpts do not mention Johnstone's role as editor of *Tait's Magazine*, instead referring to her as a 'pleasing contributor' ('Opinions'). Johnstone's identity as the author and anthologizer of serial fiction is further reinforced by the fact that her novel *Nighean Ceard* appeared under her signature in the same issues of *Tait's* as the advertisements for *Edinburgh Tales*.

After so many years of anonymous editing, it is difficult to understand why Johnstone chose to identify herself as the 'conductor' of *Edinburgh Tales*. On one hand, Johnstone, like many other Victorians, would have viewed the project of editing a collection of stories as a more appropriately 'feminine' activity than editing a radical magazine. In other words, Johnstone could claim the realm of 'light literature' since it was already a well established field for women writers. In this sense, *Edinburgh Tales* would seem to represent Johnstone's attempt to emerge from anonymity into the world of celebrity writing and editing. Indeed, by acting as 'conductor' to a cadre of esteemed writers, she in some sense claimed a visible role as a Scottish woman of letters with a prestigious literary past. The listing of her previous books and achievements in advertisements for *Edinburgh Tales* would seem to have been intended to create a sense of Johnstone's *oeuvre*.

However, since the serially published and bound versions of *Edinburgh Tales* did not include a preface, picture, or biographical sketch of 'Mrs. Johnstone' that would help to provide a context for her body of work, they did not successfully market her as a literary celebrity. Likewise, by editing *Edinburgh Tales*, Johnstone was not laying claim to her previous work as a reviewer, political thinker, or editor. The bulk of her anonymous *oeuvre* would remain unattributed until the late twentieth century.[17] Consequently, her work and her authorial identity were only half-revealed by the publication of *Edinburgh Tales*. Who is 'Mrs. Johnstone'? *Edinburgh Tales* raises this question but refuses to answer it fully, providing instead a variety of stories told by omniscient or first-person male narrators. Indeed, the stories in *Edinburgh Tales* represent a multiplication and diffusion of narrative identities, rather than a narrowing down of the authorial self. This follows

TAIT'S MONTHLY ADVERTISER,—JANUARY, 1845.

NEW WORK FOR THE PEOPLE.

Now Publishing, in Weekly Numbers, Price Three-halfpence,
And in Monthly Parts, Price Sevenpence, stitched in a Wrapper, handsomely printed in large 8vo,
with a clear type,

THE EDINBURGH TALES,

CONDUCTED BY MRS. JOHNSTONE,

Author of "Clan-Albyn," "Elizabeth de Bruce," "Nights of the Round Table," "Violet Hamilton," "Blanche Delamere," &c. &c.

Under this title will be published a Series of STORIES and NOVELETTES, illustrative of English, Irish, and Scottish Character, Domestic Manners, and Social Duties, by MRS. JOHNSTONE, and other well-known Writers of Fiction, whose Works have obtained a large share of public approbation. The Series will comprehend Historical, and also Biographical Tales, in the style of Mrs. Johnstone's stories of "The Three Westminster Boys," and "The Two Scotch Williams;" with selected specimens of such French, German, and other Continental Tales, as, possessing high literary merit, are also unexceptionable in point of taste and moral tendency.

Though the Tales in this Series will be all copyright, and part of them written expressly for the Work, it is the aim and hope of the Conductor to furnish literary amusement of a healthful and refined character, at the cheapest rate.

Opinions of the London Literary Journals of MRS. JOHNSTONE, *as a Writer of Tales.*

"The story [of 'Aunt Jane'] is told with a nature, and truth, and skill, which are found to be wanting in works of far higher pretension. The moral effect is all that might be wished. We cannot desire to infuse better notions into youth than such as are inspired, rather than inculcated, by the Authoress of 'Nights of the Round Table.'"—*Spectator.*

"Under a bad title ['Nights of the Round Table'] is here concealed one of the meritorious efforts of our fiction writers. The story of the 'Quaker Family,' which occupies the principal part of this volume, has more character, nature, and truth, than usually go to the composition of a whole shelf of the circulating library. . . . 'The Three Westminster Boys,' an exhibition in the magic-lantern style, following Thurlow, Hastings, and Cowper, (contemporaries,) through their several careers, and marking the striking stages, is a performance of excellent effect, and suggesting an admirable moral lesson."—*Examiner.*

"Mrs. Johnstone's Tales, or Domestic Pictures, at once pique the imagination and gratify the understanding, by a singular mixture of the genial and the prudential."—*Leigh Hunt.*

"We have seldom met with a work, aiming only at instruction, in which there are so many attractions. The writer unites the affection of a mother, the vigilance of an aunt, and the skill of a governess, with the grace and elegance of a well-bred lady."—*Athenæum.*

"The first Series of this publication, ['Nights of the Round Table,'] was received by us with more than a common warmth of approbation. Many parts of the work made a deep impression on our mind; and we are even yet accustomed to refer to the 'Widow of Spitalfields,' as a true picture of virtuous low life, and a most affecting example of patience and resignation under afflictions such as few know but the very poor. The praise we have to bestow on the 'Quaker Family,' a story which occupies nearly the whole of the present series, is not less than that deserved by the former one. It has convinced us that the authoress is a person of genius; and that her name ought immediately to be removed out of the list of bookmakers and other manufacturers of literature."—*The Spectator.*

W. TAIT, Edinburgh; CHAPMAN & HALL, London; J. CUMMING, Dublin.
M'LEOD, Glasgow; GALT, Manchester; PHILIP, Liverpool; WRIGHTSON & WEBB, Birmingham; BINGHAM, Bristol; FINLAY & CHARLTON, Newcastle.

In small 8vo, with a Frontispiece, price 5s.,

TALES OF GREAT AND GOOD KINGS.

BY M. FRASER TYTLER.

Author of "Tales of the Great and Brave," &c.

Contents:—James I. of Scotland.—Charles V. of Germany.—Gustavus Vasa, of Sweden.—Gustavus Adolphus of Sweden.—Henri Quatre, of France.—Henry V. of England.

WILLIAM TAIT, Edinburgh: SIMPKIN, MARSHALL, & Co. London.

3.2 Advertisement for *Edinburgh Tales*. Courtesy of Memorial Library, University of Wisconsin, Madison

CHRISTIAN JOHNSTONE 75

in the same vein as Johnstone's other book-length works of fiction and non-fiction, in which she assumes a variety of narrative personae, including 'Meg Dods' and 'Aunt Jane'.[18]

Edinburgh Tales begins not with an editorial foreword or list of acknowledgments but with a series of the editor's own stories, *The Experiences of Richard Taylor, Esq.* The *Richard Taylor* tales were first published anonymously in *Johnstone's Edinburgh Magazine* in 1833 and, after the merger of the two magazines, continued in *Tait's* until 1835. In her introduction to *Edinburgh Tales*, Johnstone assumes the voice of the 'editorial we' as she relates the story behind the genesis of the stories. She begins by introducing 'the Gentleman with the Umbrella', Richard Taylor, whose story she is about to communicate (2). We learn that Taylor suffered the loss of his father and his business early in life and subsequently turned to the study of domesticity and 'doing some little good to his fellow-creatures' as his sole occupation (2). As he says to his relatives, 'I am a domestic, an in-door reformer' (7). He then proceeds to visit the people in his neighborhood, especially young brides, dispensing advice along with a copy of his own self-published *Grammar of Good Housewifery*. At the end of this introduction, Johnstone breaks the flow of the narrative with the intrusion of her editorial persona: 'How it finally, along with his Diary, has come into our hands, must remain a secret. Its contents, which are all that is important about it, we mean, from time to time, to submit to the courteous readers of THE EDINBURGH TALES . . '. (11). After this introduction, Richard Taylor takes over as the first-person narrator of the tales. While the 'editorial we' and 'Richard Taylor' might have been perceived as being two separate authorial personae in the original context of anonymous publication, in *Edinburgh Tales* they are revealed to be the creations of 'Mrs. Johnstone'. She is both writer and editor, whose literary disguises are made transparent through authorial signature. Read with the knowledge of the author's sex in mind, Richard Taylor begins to resemble the reformist woman author and activist. He is a writer who is knowledgeable about charity work, cooking, child-rearing, and housekeeping. Likewise, he writes and publishes stories intended to illuminate the lives of working classes and to provide guidelines for domestic economy.

The first of his tales, 'Young Mrs. Roberts' Three Christmas Dinners', tells the story of Taylor's attempts to reform Maria Roberts skills as a housewife, training her to economize and avoid finery. Throughout his reformatory project, Taylor expostulates on women's morals and manners. For example, on observing Maria's penchant for fancy dress, Taylor remarks,

> How much of female time is consumed in this wretched way: time, valuable for health, for knowledge, for social enjoyment, for really productive labor, is thus wasted! Maria, when we obtain that nicely balanced constitution of King, *Ladies*, and Commons, of which we have so often talked, I hope Rachel Greene [Maria's thrifty neighbor], representative of the women of this district, will bring in a bill, decreeing that when a dress is once made in the proper form, there it shall remain till worn out, or, at least, till it require to be turned. I will have no remodelling, no adaptations to a new style (15).

Though Taylor claims to leave politics to others—in this case, to women of the future—he often emphasizes the political implications of domestic behavior. He bids Maria not to buy lace because it is made by fellow women who work in oppressive conditions. He asks, 'Do you know any thing of the state of the poor women engaged in that [lace] manufacture, or in what you term fancy articles,—married as well as single women?' (20). Later in the passage, he once again refers to a utopian future: 'In my Arcadia—my ideal republic—the beauty, health, and spirits of one order of the women shall never be sacrificed, that another may wear a thing about her face which Rachel Greene looks very pretty without, and Maria Roberts also' (21). In this way, Taylor reveals the ways that the personal is political, that is, how women can change society through their own private actions in the domestic sphere, always with the goal of achieving rationality as wives and mothers.

In this regard, Taylor seems to speak for Johnstone, whose cookery book and cheap periodicals demonstrated an equally strong commitment to facilitating rational motherhood and domestic economy. Yet in her original conception of *The Experiences of Richard Taylor, Esq.*, composed with the idea of anonymous publication in mind, Johnstone assumed a masculine persona to address these issues. Like Martineau, Johnstone no doubt believed that to address women's issues directly, as a woman, would be to lose the sense of objectivity she felt was necessary for speaking out on the Woman Question. When published under Johnstone's signature, the tales seem to draw attention of the masculine persona as a device employed by Johnstone in order to speak out on women's issues. That is, by assigning the name 'Mrs. Johnstone' to a text that had previously been anonymous, she was revealing the strategies she had formerly used to mask her gender and identity. The addition of the authorial name thus complicates the narrative structure and the subject matter of the story, drawing attention to multiple layers of women's concerns as authors, editors, and housekeepers.

Though the publication of Johnstone's signature along with her fiction revealed some of her concerns as a woman, a writer, and a social thinker, it did not otherwise expose the details of her personal or professional life in any significant way. While Johnstone's name was meant to lend credibility to the anthology, the contents did not establish her as a literary icon. Indeed, in reviews of *Edinburgh Tales*, Johnstone's contributions are often downplayed in favor of her celebrity contributors. The *Athenaeum* remarks, 'Mrs. Johnstone's own contributions [are] least likely to be popular, though we readily allow that they are not without merit of a certain kind' ('The Edinburgh Tales' 788). Johnstone thus came to be seen as the producer of ephemeral literary texts. She did not achieve the name recognition of Hannah More or Harriet Martineau, partly because of negative critical reactions to her work, however perhaps more importantly due to her own unwillingness to engage in self-promotion. Like so many other women journalists of the 1830s and '40s, Johnstone ascribed to a model of quiet social activism that was premised on anonymous publication and on the creation of literary personae. For Johnstone, these narrative techniques provided her with privacy that would have been denied to her as a celebrity writer. While *Edinburgh Tales* momentarily revealed Johnstone's concerns as a proto-feminist writer and exposed the devices she used to succeed in a male-dominated field, they did not otherwise provide a structuring narrative for her remarkable career as a fiction writer, journalist, and editor.

The fact that Johnstone's work has been lost to literary history would seem to suggest that her model of quiet, 'invisible' authorship was ineffective as means of securing a place in the canon of Victorian letters. Indeed, even today there are very few scholars who are familiar with Johnstone's work as a journalist and novelist. However, though Johnstone may have been lost to literary history, she nonetheless has had a lasting influence on the development of Victorian print culture. Johnstone was instrumental in the development of the reformist periodical press as a mixed-gender medium concerned with addressing the Woman Question and the Condition-of-England Question. By creating a mainstream periodical that incorporated the perspectives of women and working-class readers, Johnstone provided an important model for later reformist periodicals such as *Household Words, Eliza Cook's Journal, People's Journal,* and *Howitt's Journal.* Following Johnstone's model, these periodicals established a link between class and gender politics, a connection that would lead to the development of politicized reviewing practices, including a proto-feminist literary criticism. For Johnstone, as for many of the women editors who followed her, including Eliza Cook and Mary Howitt, the goal of facilitating cross-class communication was inextricably connected to the goal of promoting women writers as facilitators of this dialogue. For Johnstone, the question of what role women should have in the movement toward social reform was inseparable from the question of what role they should play in popular print culture. By capitalizing upon the convention of journalistic anonymity, Johnstone was able to mold the periodical medium to her own advantage, thereby setting the themes and narrative strategies that would shape the careers of women writers in the decades that followed.

The next chapter will demonstrate how the development of the reformist periodical press shaped the career of one of these writers: Elizabeth Gaskell. Gaskell's experiences as a journalist had important implications for the development of her social fiction. Unlike Martineau and Johnstone, Gaskell was not initially interested in exploring the Woman Question within the context of the periodical press. However, by employing the journalistic rhetoric of middle-class reform and the discourse on urban investigation in her social fiction, she constructed an expanded role for the middle-class woman author in defining and solving social problems. At the same time that the publicity and controversy surrounding Gaskell's social fiction seemed to define an expanded public role for the woman author, it also served to crystallize cultural anxieties about the role of women in the public sphere. Gaskell's contradictory public image served to create points of contact between the Woman Question and the Condition-of-England Question in the cultural project of redefining the role of the woman author during the 1840s and '50s.

Notes

1 For further elucidation of this term, see chapter one of Carlyle's *Chartism* (1840).

2 See Brantlinger (11-33) for an overview of the literature of reform during the 1830s.

3 Analysis of these periodicals is beyond the scope of this study. See Beetham for an in-depth discussion of the role of women's periodicals in simultaneously reinforcing and challenging conventional gender roles.

4 Johnstone's novels have received some recent critical attention. See Monnickendam ('The Good, Brave-Hearted Lady'), Anderson & Riddell (187-89), and Ferris.

5 According to James Bertram, a clerk in the Tait's offices, Johnstone received 20 pounds per month for her editorial services, in addition to her half-share in the magazine (36).

6 Very few of Johnstone's book publications were signed. For her *Cook and Housewife's Manual* (1826), she assumed the pseudonym 'Meg Dods', and published her novels *Clan-Albin* and *Elizabeth de Bruce* anonymously. Only *Edinburgh Tales* (1846) and *True Tales of the Irish Peasantry* (1836) seem to have included the name 'Mrs. Johnstone' on the title page. Though Johnstone co-edited *Johnstone's Magazine* with her husband, there is some indication that readers would have primarily associated the magazine with 'Mrs. Johnstone'. See discussion of this issue later in the chapter.

7 Johnstone, then Christian Todd, married a Mr. M'Leish and was divorced a short time later. She married John Johnstone, a Fife schoolmaster, in 1815. The two remained childless. Biographical information on Johnstone is scant, but see the *DNB* as well as the obituary published in *Tait's Edinburgh Magazine* ('Mrs. Johnstone').

8 Both *Blackwood's Magazine* and *Fraser's Magazine*, for example, created fictional male editors: Christopher North and Oliver Yorke, respectively.

9 See Weiner's Introduction to *Innovators and Preachers*.

10 For further discussion of the circulation of *Tait's Magazine*, see William Tait's 'Advertising in Scotland' and Hyde's 'The Role of "Our Scottish Readers".'

11 This is especially interesting considering that Johnstone was the author of the *Cook and Housewife's Manual*.

12 Eliza Cook, in many ways Johnstone's successor as a radical editor of *Eliza Cook's Journal* during the 1850s, also uses a culinary metaphor to describe her editorship. In her introduction to the first volume of the journal, Eliza Cook makes a pun on her own name in order to spell out her overall purpose as an editor. She writes, 'I simply prepare a plain feast, where the viands will be all of my own choosing, and some of my own dressing, hoping that if what I provide be wholesome and relishing, I shall have a host of friends at my board, whose kind words and cheerful encouragement will keep me in a proud and honourable position at the head of the table' (1).

13 A number of periodicals in the evangelical tradition were published during the 1830s, including The *Christian Lady's Magazine* 1834-49, which was edited under the signature of its founder, Charlotte Tonna (Beetham 51-4).

14 For additional examples, see Jessop (224-28).

15 Johnstone's reviews of her fellow women writers' texts were not always positive. See, for example, her negative review of Fanny Kemble's *Journal of a Residence in America*

CHRISTIAN JOHNSTONE 79

('Miss Fanny'). See Monnickendam ('The Odd Couple') and Jessop (224) for discussion of Johnstone's treatment of Maria Edgeworth.

16 The earliest example of this proto-feminist sensibility is Martineau's article, 'The Achievements of the Genius of Scott', published in 1833 when Johnstone was sub-editor of the magazine. The essay, second in a two-part series eulogizing Walter Scott, is less concerned with establishing Scott as a literary icon than it is concerned with establishing guidelines for a gender-sensitive literary criticism. Johnstone also explored gender issues in her reviews of Scott's fiction (Monnickendam, 'The Odd Couple'). There are of course examples of anti-feminist literary criticism in *Tait's,* but overall it provided an unusually open venue for proto-feminist criticism of literary texts.

17 Johnstone's contributions to *Tait's* are catalogued in the *Wellesley Index to Victorian Periodicals*. However, most of her other periodical writings (e.g., to the *Schoolmaster* or *Johnstone's Magazine*) have not been positively identified.

18 Johnstone used the pseudonym 'Meg Dods' as author of *the Cook and Housewife's Manual* and the persona 'Aunt Jane' in *Nights of the Round Table*.

CHAPTER FOUR

Elizabeth Gaskell, Urban Investigation and the 'Abused' Woman Writer

One of the most remarkable features of reformist periodicals during the 1840s was their gender inclusivity. While mainstream periodicals such as *Blackwood's Magazine* and *Fraser's Magazine* attempted to give the impression of a masculine literary community, reformist periodicals such as *Howitt's Journal* and the *People's Journal* were self-consciously gender balanced. Beginning in the late 1840s, reformist periodicals began publishing the names of male and female contributors. They also reinforced the inclusion of women in introductory prefaces and editorial remarks. Though there is some differentiation of conventionally masculine and feminine subject matter in these journals, women are listed as authors of articles on both social and domestic subjects. Often they are depicted as social investigators who wander through urban landscapes, documenting the harsh reality of working-class poverty. Reformist periodicals of the 1840s thus explicitly identified women writers as key players in the dissemination of diverse forms of knowledge that spanned both public and private spheres.

By including women as high-profile contributors to debates over the Condition-of-England Question, reformist periodicals created an accessible medium for women writers within the male-dominated discourse on urban investigation. By the 1840s, the discourse on urban poverty, employment, sanitation, and domestic life was a ubiquitous feature of British popular print culture. As Mary Poovey points out, the literature of urban investigation formed a 'dense network of interdependent theories, technologies, and political disputes about policy' (*Making* 116). Within this network, the urban investigator was often depicted as an objective recorder of the facts of poverty and as a sympathetic moral judge who intervened on behalf of the oppressed. At the center of this investigation was the degraded working-class home, which was seen as lacking the domestic comforts and moral influences necessary to promote social stability. For example, in *The Sanitary Condition of the Labouring Population of Great Britain* (1842), Edwin Chadwick states that it is the aim of his report to describe the effects of overcrowding, poor ventilation, and inadequate sanitation in 'places of work and dwellings' (79). In addition, he proposes to illustrate the 'good or evil moral habits promoted by the nature of the residence' (79).

In most sociological and statistical studies, the role of the urban investigator was gendered masculine by default.[1] To wander through lower-class neighborhoods was considered a compromising—and dangerous—activity for middle-class women. During the 1840s, Sunday schools and charitable organizations were defined as the primary venues for women's social activism. The expansion of manufacturing neighborhoods and the escalation of urban violence made any contact with the poor outside established religious and charitable institutions an increasingly dangerous prospect for middle-class women. As Deborah Epstein Nord points out, middle-class women who walked the streets in industrial neighborhoods ran the risk of being mistaken for prostitutes and other morally suspect urban wanderers (3). At the same time, the reformation of working-class domestic space was represented as an activity middle-class women were uniquely qualified to fulfill: with their superior morality and knowledge of domestic economy, philanthropic women were seen as having the skills necessary for reforming the working-class home. Women needed to discover new institutions and media that would enable them to intervene on behalf of the poor without compromising their middle-class respectability. Reformist periodicals provided just the venue women needed to engage in this private form of public activism. Consequently, though discussions of the Condition-of-England Question were dominated by middle-class men throughout the 1840s, the assumption of male authority was increasingly undermined by the participation of women journalists in these debates.

It was within the reformist periodicals of the 1840s that the career of Elizabeth Gaskell (1810-65) first took shape. Recent scholarship has emphasized the important role of Gaskell's philanthropic activism in her career as a fiction writer.[2] However, none of these studies has explored Gaskell's career in reformist journalism and its role in shaping her authorial identity and early fiction. Like Christian Johnstone, Gaskell shaped her career within the context of middle-class reform movements, specifically the reformist periodical press. As a journalist, Gaskell came to define women's social activism as a form of inspired social observation. Like Harriet Martineau, she demonstrated how politically engaged acts of writing and seeing could be employed as consciousness raising activities both inside and outside of the domestic sphere. However, Gaskell defined her literary activism more narrowly than did Martineau, focusing much more specifically on the ways that fiction could promote understanding and reconciliation between class interests. Gaskell identified the degraded working-class home as a motivating cause for women's middle-class activism, and she located the solution to class strife within the moral and physical space of middle-class domesticity. The inter-dependent images of the radicalized middle-class home and the de-radicalized working-class home appear in much of Gaskell's work of the 1840s and can be traced to her engagement with the literature of urban investigation, especially the reformist periodical press.

The first part of this chapter will explore how reformist periodicals enabled Gaskell to find context for her literary activism. As a journalist, Gaskell contributed to the literature of urban investigation by writing about the domestic lives of the poor. As we will see, this experience had important implications for the development of her first social problem novel, *Mary Barton* (1848). At this early stage of her career, Gaskell, unlike Martineau and Johnstone, did not directly address the Woman Question in her writing. However, after her authorial identity was revealed in 1848, she indirectly served the purpose of promoting women's rights by embodying new stereotypes of the socially engaged woman that would later be re-employed in the cause of women's political self-advocacy.

The second part of this chapter will explore how the discourse on Gaskell's celebrity in the 1850s was part of a larger cultural debate over women's authorship in mid-Victorian culture. During the 1850s, the discourse on the liberation of the female author gained increasing autonomy from its roots within the middle-class literature of urban investigation and reform of the 1830s and '40s. This reflected the ongoing development of the women's movement during the 1850s and '60s as an independent field of middle-class political activity that privileged gender over class as its motivating cause. Gaskell's participation in the discourse on female authorship during the 1850s marks a shift in her career from a focus on social issues toward an examination of gender issues as an authorizing field of discourse. The publication of *The Life of Charlotte Brontë* (1857) was a key factor in bringing about this shift in Gaskell's career. Using the figure of Brontë as a focal point for investigating the 'abused woman author', Gaskell attempted to redefine notions of women's literary usefulness and value. While in her early industrial fiction Gaskell justified her entry into public discourse on the basis of her usefulness in promoting understanding between class interests, in *The Life of Charlotte Brontë,* she redefined her cause as the establishment of Brontë's critical reputation. The abused or neglected woman writer, for Gaskell, thus became a replacement for the oppressed worker: it was her living and working conditions that must be investigated and reformed in order to promote social progress. As we will see, Gaskell arrived at this ideological position through a long process of transformation which began in the reformist periodical press.

Gaskell as Journalist

Gaskell's first contribution to debates over the Condition-of-England Question was a poem she co-authored with her husband that appeared anonymously in *Blackwood's Magazine* in 1837. This poem, titled 'Sketches Among the Poor', demonstrates Gaskell's interest in the effects of urban poverty on industrial workers, a theme that would dominate her work in the 1840s. Written from the perspective of an adult reflecting on memories from childhood, the poem tells the story of a working-class woman who has been displaced from her rural home and now lives in a 'dark house behind an old elm-tree, / By gloomy streets surrounded' (2-3). All the while, she dreams of the day

> When she might leave the close and noisy street,
> And once again her childhood's home might greet,
> > It was a pleasant place that early home! (42-44)

As the woman regresses into senility and approaches death, she is cheered by 'sweet young memories' of her childhood in the country (128). Here and elsewhere in her early writings, Gaskell focuses on a generation of workers who grew up in the country but emigrated to industrial settings. There is a strong sense of grief over the degraded domestic life of the poor and a sense of nostalgia for a lost agrarian home.

Gaskell's fascination with working-class domesticity deepened as she became more closely associated with middle-class reformers, especially William and Mary Howitt. In the 1840s, the Howitts invited Gaskell to contribute short stories to two periodicals, *Howitt's Journal* and *Sartain's Union Magazine*. In *Howitt's*, Gaskell published three short stories: 'Life in Manchester: Libbie Marsh's Three Eras', 'The Sexton's Hero', and 'Christmas Storms and Sunshine'. She is also the probable author of a report on Emerson's Manchester lectures. In *Sartain's,* Gaskell published two stories: 'Martha Preston' and 'The Last Generation in England'. She also contributed a serialized story, 'Hand and Heart', to *The Sunday School Penny Magazine* edited by Travers Madge.[3] These periodicals were diverse in their aims and audiences: *Howitt's* was a magazine of popular progress, *Sartain's* was a middle-class American women's journal, and the *Sunday School Penny Magazine* was a cheap periodical intended for Sunday school teachers and their students. However, together these periodicals enabled Gaskell to deepen her interest in working-class domesticity. 'Martha Preston', for example, tells the story of a farm girl's trial of caring for her idiot brother, and 'Hand and Heart' tells the story of a working-class boy who learns that money will not bring happiness.

Gaskell's contributions to *Howitt's Journal* were especially important to her development as a fiction writer (Figure 4.1). More than any other periodical, *Howitt's* provided a context in which Gaskell could shape a public voice that would allow her to contribute powerfully to the discourse on urban investigation and social reform. It also enabled her experiment with a variety of narrative strategies that she would later employ in her first social problem novel, *Mary Barton*. An exploration of this journalistic context provides a foundation for an examination of Gaskell's fiction of the period.

Like many other magazines of popular progress published during the 1840s, *Howitt's Journal* (1847-48) was devoted to chronicling the efforts of middle-class philanthropists and reformers on behalf of the working classes.[4] Located within the discourse of urban investigation, *Howitt's* often included exposés of the harsh living conditions endured by laborers in industrial cities. For example, the journal's Weekly Record segment includes short reports on the 'Miseries of the Poor', 'Distress in the Manufacturing Districts', and 'Revelations of the Condition and Dwellings of the Poor in London'. Quasi-fictional tales, such as Mary Gillies' 'A Labourer's Home', provided dramatizations of how unsanitary living conditions promoted vice and misery in urban neighborhoods. In *Howitt's* the reformation of the degraded working-class home thus became the special focus of middle-class efforts to prevent the corrupting influence of revolutionary feeling among the laboring classes. As one report published in *Howitt's* noted, 'Whence it has happened that the classes in question have been compelled to spend their lives, from the moment of birth to that of death, in a poisoned atmosphere ... the deterioration of the body and the corruption of the mind have alike become inevitable' ('Health' 238).

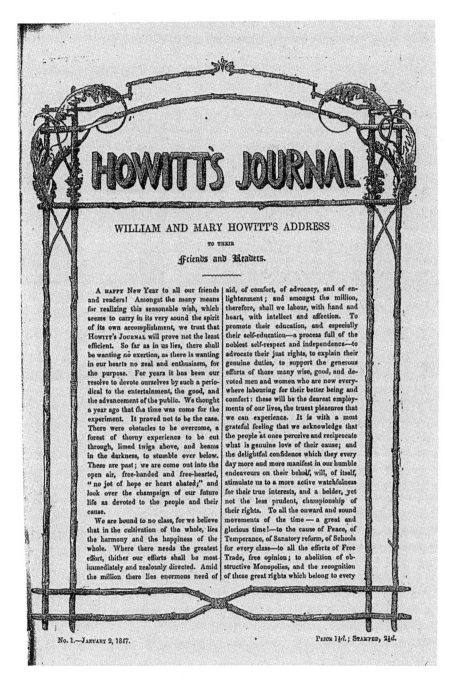

4.1 Title page, *Howitt's Journal.* Courtesy of Memorial Library, University of Wisconsin, Madison

86

FIRST-PERSON ANONYMOUS

Like may other reformist periodicals, *Howitt's Journal* assumed a contradictory stance on working-class rights. On one hand, William and Mary Howitt expressed a commitment to include readers and writers from all classes in their reformatory project. In an introductory preface to volume one, they make it clear that the journal is 'bound to no class, for we believe that in the cultivation of the whole, lies the harmony and happiness of the whole' ('Address' 1). At the head of their Weekly Record segment, they invite the 'opinions of others of all classes—be they rich or poor, be they masters or men, be they men or women' (1). The journal included contributions from working-class writers, most notably William Lovett and Ebenezer Elliott, and it addressed many issues that would be of concern to working-class readers, including the Corn Laws, educational reform, and sanitary legislation.

As much as *Howitt's* claimed to include working-class perspectives, it was still primarily a middle-class magazine. At 2 ½ pence per weekly issue, *Howitt's* probably would have been out of reach for all but the most prosperous of the working classes.[5] As an organ of middle-class values, it emphasized meliorist social change as an alternative to revolutionary action. The Howitts ask working-class readers to 'be at once firm and patient' as a process of peaceful social change moves forward ('Address' 2). In some respects, the Howitts' version of radical change seems to preclude working-class self-advocacy. In their introductory preface, the Howitts are careful to point out that those 'who would advocate the claims of one section of the community at the expense of those of the others, or of any other, would, so far from advancing the happiness of the section they appeared to patronize, inflict the severest blow on its progress' ('Address' 2). In this way, the Howitts aimed to activate middle-class readers, while simultaneously containing the revolutionary impulses of the lower classes.

Throughout their journal, William and Mary Howitt attempted to dramatize the possible effects of middle-class reform efforts on lower-class workers. In these dramatizations, the working-class reader is idealized as a receptive object of invasive middle-class investigations and philanthropic efforts. For example, in an article titled 'Visit to a Working Man', William Howitt sets out to answer those who 'doubt whether the working-classes are really benefited by all that has been attempted by education and other means' (242). He then provides the example of a reader of *Howitt's Journal* who works twelve hours per day to support his family and still finds time to read books in several languages after the children have gone to bed. Howitt ends the article with a specimen of the laborer's poetry and a call to arms: 'Go on, brave men, that teach, and braver ones that learn, till such scenes and such visits shall be every day things of life' (244). It is difficult to know whether Howitt was basing his article on an actual visit to a working man's home, but its intended effects are clear—to depict working men as the worthy objects of middle-class reform efforts.

Howitt's, unlike most middle-class periodicals of the 1840s, published its contributions with authorial signature. This policy was no doubt intended to increase the popularity of the periodical by highlighting the names of celebrity

ELIZABETH GASKELL

writers and social activists. Nevertheless, some writers, including Elizabeth Gaskell, chose not to identify themselves. As a contributor to *Howitt's*, Gaskell published her work under a pseudonym, Cotton Mather Mills, Esq. On one hand, Gaskell's choice of a male pseudonym seems odd considering that *Howitt's* was known for publishing women writers. The journal's second number, for example, lists the names of six celebrity women contributors, including Fredrika Bremer and Mary Russell Mitford. The names of William and Mary Howitt also headed each number of the journal, further reinforcing its identity as a periodical conducted by and addressed to members of both sexes. Within the pages of the journal, these women are depicted as having an important role to play as social investigators. For example, in one of their Weekly Record segments, the Howitts make reference to the reformist 'army' of 'soldiers' and 'Amazonian ones' who are needed to solve the nation's social problems (1). In some sense, Gaskell's use of a male pseudonym suggests her resistance to being included among these 'Amazonians'. Gaskell was no doubt anxious to avoid the negative publicity that might result from presenting herself as a female reformer or a celebrity writer. An even more likely explanation for Gaskell's choice of a male pseudonym was her desire to assume the identity of a male urban investigator—a middle-class man whose access to working-class neighborhoods and domestic spaces would not seem morally compromising.

An representative example Gaskell's journalistic fiction published in *Howitt's Journal* is 'Libbie Marsh's Three Eras' (1847). Published under the heading 'Life in Manchester', the story immediately locates itself within the discourse on urban investigation. It begins with a reference to the narrator's familiarity with life in the working-class districts of Manchester: 'Last November but one there was a flitting in our neighborhood' (310). While at first the reference to 'our neighborhood' and the colloquial 'a flitting' seems to suggest a working-class narrator, the 'Esq'. affixed to the authorial name suggests that the story will be narrated by a man who is familiar with the lives of the poor but belongs to a higher social class.

In addition to constructing the narrative perspective of a urban investigator, Gaskell explores a common theme in the literature of urban investigation: how the cultivation of domestic morality among the lower classes could ameliorate social unrest. Like the other reform-minded writers associated with *Howitt's Journal*, Gaskell aimed to construct an image of the lower classes that would justify (and in some sense reward) middle-class reform efforts. The heroine of the story, Libby Marsh, lives in poverty and misery as a seamstress in Manchester, but it is not social justice that she seeks. Her one desire is a home—a moral and physical space where she can find comfort and be of use to others. At the beginning of the story, Libby is described as a 'single person changing her place of abode, from one lodging to another' (310). She finds another house in which to lodge, but it is far from being a proper home. Since the entire family works in the factories, the house is empty and cheerless when she arrives. She is greeted only by 'dull-grey ashes' in the fireplace and an unattended child 'making dirt-pies at the entrance to the court' (310). She has no family and friends to care for her, and even more significantly, she has been deserted by 'her employers,—kind enough people in their way, but too

88   FIRST-PERSON ANONYMOUS

rapidly twirling round on this bustling earth to have leisure to think of the little work-woman, excepting when they wanted gowns turned, carpets mended, or household linen darned' (310).

Once Libbie is left alone in her bedroom, she looks out her window and sees a disabled child in a 'corresponding window', who writhes in pain while his mother soothes him (311). As an observer of this scene, Libby is represented as a forlorn orphan, staring longingly at an image of domestic tenderness, but for a moment she is also a stand-in for the urban investigator, whose invasive yet sympathetic gaze penetrates the privacy of a distressed working-class family. After engaging in daily watches out the bedroom window, she sends the boy an anonymous valentine—a canary in a cage. This marks the beginning of a close relationship between Libby and the boy's mother, Margaret Hall, who overcomes her initial bad humor and includes Libby in her family circle. Even though Libbie is overwhelmed with work, often 'drag[ging] herself along through the heated street', she is cheered by her sympathy with Margaret Hall and her son (334).

While Libbie is individualized as a sympathetic working-class heroine, she is also depicted as just one example of a larger class of individuals—the workers of Manchester. When Libbie takes Margaret and her son on a holiday to Denham Park, the narrator remarks on the moral benefits of fresh air and recreation on the working classes as a whole. It is described as

> the favorite resort of the Manchester work-people; for more years than I can tell; probably ever since 'The Duke', by his canals, opened out the system of cheap travelling. It is scenery, too, which presents such a complete contrast to the whirl and turmoil of Manchester; so thoroughly woodland, with its ancestral trees ... its 'verdurous walls', its grassy walks leading far away into some glade where you start at the rabbit, rustling among the last year's fern (335).

Written from the perspective of a urban investigator, this passage demonstrates how an aristocratic landscape, as an emblem of paternalism, is reconstituted as an ideal domestic space for laborers.[6] The 'grassy walks' that usually serve as the backdrop for aristocratic leisure become a pastoral retreat for the working classes, who utilize it—if only temporarily—for their domestic entertainments.

This idyll is interrupted by a vision of Manchester on the distant horizon with its 'motionless cloud of smoke' (336). Suddenly the workers realize that this is their true home 'where God had cast their lives, and told them to work out their destiny' (336). Such a vision, interestingly enough, does not bring a feeling of injustice or dissatisfaction to the workers; rather it causes them to exclaim, 'Hurrah for oud smoke-jack!' (336). However, just a few paragraphs later, we are told that the memory of the pastoral retreat would 'haunt in greenness and freshness many a loom, and workshop, and factory, with images of peace and beauty' (336). At once celebrating 'dear, busy, earnest, working, noble Manchester' and being 'haunted' by the possibility of a more peaceful life, the working classes are left in a state of ambivalence that precludes radical social change (336).

ELIZABETH GASKELL

The final installment of 'Libbie Marsh' begins with the death of Margaret Hall's son. Suddenly, there seems little possibility of a happy working-class home in dismal Manchester. The Halls' apartment, before the only site of domestic tenderness in the neighborhood, is now empty and desolate. The only one with a home is the dead child, who now resides in 'Father's House' (345). Resisting this hopelessness, Libbie begins to define her moral purpose:

> [Since] God has seen fit to keep me out o' woman's natural work, I should try and find work for myself. I mean ... that as I know I'm never like for to have a home of my own, or a husband, who would look to me to make all straight, or children to watch over and care for, all which I take to be woman's natural work, I must not lose time in fretting and fidgeting after marriage, but just look about me for somewhat else to do. I can see many a one misses it in this. They will hanker after what is ne'er likely to be theirs, instead of facing it out, and settling down to be old maids; and as old maids, just looking round for the odd jobs God leaves in the world for such as old maids to do,—there's plenty of such work,—and there's the blessing of God on them as does it (346).

In the end, Libbie moves into Margaret Hall's household and acts as ministering angel to the desolate mother. As a result of this union, Margaret is cured of her shrewish, 'unwomanly' ways, and Libbie is 'no longer the desolate, lonely orphan, a stranger on the earth' (347).

Ultimately, it is Libby's superior morality that enables her to create a home for herself, not her desire to alter the material conditions of working-class life in Manchester. Though the story suggests that the employment of women in factory work results in the moral degradation of the home, it offers no solution to this problem. Libby's home is thus more of a moral space than it is a physical one—an inner virtuousness that enables her to overcome the degradations of working-class domestic life. Such a home is de-politicized for the benefit of middle-class readers, who through their own philanthropic ministrations, sought moral rather than political solutions to working-class unrest. Thus, Gaskell's story, like so many other contributions to *Howitt's Journal,* created a consoling narrative intended to establish common ground between middle-class readers and the objects of their charity. By constructing ideal working-class readers in their texts, reformist writers attempted to dramatize the positive effects of middle-class activism on lower-class morals. This fiction undoubtedly played an important role in authorizing a variety of reform efforts, but it also performed the function of denying the material causes of working-class poverty.

If such periodicals were liberatory, it was most likely not through their creation of working-class heroes but through the creation of a new kind of women's social activism. At the same time reformist periodicals provided ways for middle-class women readers to re-imagine the intimate spaces of working-class life, they indirectly reconfigured the middle-class home as well. These periodicals aimed to purge the working-class home of politics and simultaneously to construct middle-class domesticity as the site of political activity. Though Gaskell was unwilling at

90 FIRST-PERSON ANONYMOUS

this stage of her career to identify herself as a woman writer, the reformist periodical press nevertheless provided her—and many other women—with the opportunity to participate in the discourse on working-class poverty and social reform.

The Politics of Domesticity in *Mary Barton*

Gaskell's experiences as a contributor to *Howitt's Journal* played an important role in the development of her first social problem novel, *Mary Barton* (1848). Written contemporaneously with 'Libbie Marsh's Three Eras' and other *Howitt's* stories, *Mary Barton* incorporates many of the narrative conventions and ideological concerns that characterize the literature of urban investigation within the reformist periodical press. By viewing *Mary Barton* as an extension of Elizabeth Gaskell's work in reformist journalism, we can begin to complicate readings of the novel that attempt to harmonize its class and gender politics.[7] Many recent studies conflate lower-class oppression with the struggles of middle-class women to speak out on issues of social and political concern.[8] While clearly issues of class and gender are connected in the novel, this relationship is more ideologically complex than has hitherto been allowed.[9] Although lower-class radicalism and the middle-class women's movement shared common roots in late eighteenth- and early nineteenth-century liberalism, they often operated at cross-purposes. As much as Gaskell insists on the common interests of middle-class industrialists and the laboring poor in *Mary Barton,* she does not encourage complete identification between these groups. To do so would be to locate her work within the rhetoric of ultra-radical working-class movements. Instead, Gaskell assumed the role of middle-class mediator that had become familiar to her as a contributor to *Howitt's.* As was the case in 'Libbie Marsh', Gaskell's task in *Mary Barton* was to activate middle-class reform efforts as a way of minimizing class conflict.

Such a task was of course complicated by Gaskell's sex, which to some extent stigmatized her participation in debates on the Condition-of-England Question. While the reformist periodical press had provided a forum for women to address these concerns, the social problem novel was a more controversial medium for women writers.[10] Women writers of social problem fiction, including Martineau, were often accused of having insufficient exposure to political and social issues to be able to create accurate depictions of lower-class life, let alone to propose solutions to social problems. In the minds of many Victorian reviewers, social problem novels by women were dangerous because they attempted to disrupt the boundary between masculine and feminine spheres of influence. As one critic put it, 'Fiction no longer limiting her range to the domesticities, boldly invades those realms of politics and economy, upon the confines of which she has hitherto stopped short with hesitating tread and averted eyes' ('A Triad' 574). In this way, social problem fiction was imaginatively associated with women's transgressions into the public sphere.

ELIZABETH GASKELL   91

In order to establish her authority as a social commentator, Gaskell needed to distance her novel not only from ultra-radicalism but also from conventionally feminine forms of fiction writing. After her experience as a contributor to *Howitt's Journal*, Gaskell's initial impulse was to publish *Mary Barton* under a male pseudonym, Cotton Mather Mills or Stephen Berwick (*Letters* 59; Uglow, *Gaskell* 183). She may have believed that a social problem novel published under a male name would have the greatest authority in debates over the Condition-of-England Question. Ultimately, however, the novel was published anonymously. It is difficult to know why Gaskell chose anonymity, but it is possible that she was persuaded to capitalize on the mystery and gender ambiguity associated with anonymous publication as a way of stimulating critical interest in the novel. Viewed from another perspective, Gaskell's decision to publish *Mary Barton* anonymously can be interpreted as important intermediate stage between her self-imposed male disguise as Cotton Mather Mills in *Howitt's Journal* and her later persona as Mrs. Gaskell, the high-profile woman of letters. When writing *Mary Barton*, Gaskell reconceived her own assumptions about the gendering of urban investigation and came to accept—however tentatively or temporarily—the model of high-profile women's authorship and activism proposed by *Howitt's Journal* and other reformist magazines.

Anonymous publication meant that neither the novel's narrative voice nor its audience was immediately classifiable in terms of conventionally masculine or feminine reading material. Gaskell reinforces the gender ambiguity of this narrative perspective in her preface, where she outlines the events that motivated her entry into public discourse:

> I bethought me how deep might be the romance in the lives of some of those who elbowed me daily in the busy streets of the town in which I resided. I had always felt a deep sympathy with the care-worn men, who looked as if doomed to struggle through their lives in strange alternations between work and want ... A little manifestation of this sympathy and a little attention to the expression of feelings on the part of some of the work-people with whom I was acquainted, had laid open to me the hearts of one or two of the more thoughtful among them (37).

At the same time that Gaskell locates herself in the masculine environment of the 'busy streets' of Manchester, she evokes the emotionality of a feminine domestic sphere with her interest in the 'feelings' and 'hearts' of the working men.

As in reformist journals, images of middle-class activism are paired with representations of the passive, yet potentially revolutionary, lower-class worker. After characterizing the state of the working classes, Gaskell implores readers to enact 'whatever public effort can do in the way of legislation, or private effort in the way of merciful deeds' in order to 'disabuse the work-people of so miserable a misapprehension' (38). Here the middle-class reader is defined as operating within either the 'public' or 'private' sphere, thus suggesting that the action of reform is an activity that encompasses conventionally masculine and feminine realms. The

92   FIRST-PERSON ANONYMOUS

passive object of these 'deeds' and 'efforts' is the undifferentiated mass of laborers, whose only source of agency, 'working', is nominalized as 'work-people'. Gaskell's preface suggests that if the middle classes do not take action, the working classes will assume a role of destructive agency, like 'a similar class on the Continent' (38).

In this way, Gaskell constructs a triangular relationship between middle-class reformers, laborers, and industrialists, with middle-class reformers performing an intermediary role. In a passage that might have been taken from the editorial page of *Howitt's Journal*, Gaskell emphasizes the interdependence of class-based perspectives, which are 'bound to each other by common interests, as the employers and the employed must ever be' (37). Likewise, she claims to 'know nothing of Political Economy, or the theories of trade. I have tried to write truthfully; and if my accounts agree or clash with any system, the agreement or disagreement is unintentional' (38). This claim to impartiality locates the novel within the context of middle-class reform efforts that claimed to mediate between the workers and their employers. Like the editors of *Howitt's*, Gaskell creates a contradictory role for middle-class readers, who must claim an active role in alleviating social problems while at the same time not harboring any strictly political motivations for these actions. Likewise, they must embrace the values of domesticity while at the same time disputing the boundary between political and domestic concerns.

In the text of the novel, the paradox of a depoliticized domestic politics is explored through a number of investigations of lower- and middle-class domestic spaces. Locating itself within the literature of urban investigation, the first chapters of the novel provide revealing comparisons between these domestic environments. The comparison between the luxurious home of the Carsons and the dismal atmosphere of Davenport's cellar has received much attention in Gaskell scholarship.[11] What has often been overlooked, however, is how these images of lower- and middle-class domesticity are transformed over the course of the novel. The reformation of domestic space is essential to Gaskell's vision of a mixed-gender middle-class politics, just as it is essential to her vision of a de-politicized lower-class idyll.

Mary Barton begins with an image of lower-class domesticity from the agrarian past: a farmhouse encountered by the Bartons and the Wilsons on their walk through Green Heys Fields. The picturesque farmhouse sits on the banks of a stream, its porch 'covered by a rose-tree' and bordered by a 'little garden ... crowded with a medley of old-fashioned herbs' (40). Like Dunham Park in 'Libbie Marsh's Three Eras', Green Heys Fields is historicized as a scene of working-class leisure, but it is also idealized as a pastoral setting located outside the boundaries of industrial reality. Presented as an unattainable dream throughout most of the novel, this ideal image haunts Alice Wilson, who is just as much an anachronism as the old farmhouse itself.[12] The pastoral home thus becomes an ideal moral and physical space that is incompatible with industrialism.[13] Throughout the novel, the pastoral home is contrasted to the real home of the working-class laborer in Manchester. In the beginning of the novel, working-class domesticity is depicted as a humble version of the middle-class home. Though it is far from luxurious, it is filled with cheerful sights and sounds: 'warm and glowing light' (49) and the 'merry chatter of cups and saucers' (50). Like a good middle-class woman, Mrs. Barton displays her 'crockery and glass' with pride and provides a decent supper for her guests (49). Though a few pages earlier John Barton expressed his frustration with the upper classes, this cheerful house does not seem likely to produce the kind of social instability suggested by the novel's preface.

At the same time that the novel allows readers to identify with the domestic values of the healthy lower-class home, it does not allow them complete identification. The middle-class reader is invited to assume the role of urban investigator—the sympathetic yet objective observer of domestic health and morals. Before entering the Barton household, the narrator tells readers that the 'half-finished streets, [are] all so like one another that you might have easily been bewildered and lost your way' (48). As alien visitor, the reader is then invited to follow 'our friends' into the Barton household (48). The windows are covered with drawn curtains and potted geraniums, designed as a 'defence from out-door pryers', but middle-class readers are not included among those who would invade the privacy of others out of prurient interest in their affairs (49). Collectively, they enact the role of sympathetic middle-class activist, whose surveillance produces knowledge that can be used to advance the cause of reform.

After the death of Mrs. Barton, these middle-class observers are witnesses to the disintegration of the Barton household: 'One of the good influences over John Barton's life had departed that night. One of the ties which bound him down to the gentle humanities of the earth was loosened, and henceforward the neighbors all remarked he was a changed man' (58). As the reader soon discovers, the replacement for these 'gentle humanities' of domesticity is political activism. At 'clubs' and the 'trades' union', Barton begins to connect his personal 'homelessness' to that of workers in general (59). The worker sees 'his employer removing from house to house, each one grander than the last ... while all the time the weaver, who thinks he and his fellows are the real makers of this wealth, is struggling on for bread for their children' (59). Lest readers become overly partisan, the narrator interrupts Barton's lamentations in order to remind readers that the proper middle-class reader must not only assume a stance of moral judgment but also one of political impartiality. 'I know that this is not really the case', she states, 'but what I wish to impress is what the workman feels and thinks' (60). As this description continues, the narrator inserts parenthetical remarks to assure readers that these are translations of the opinions of others. The worker is described as being able to 'understand (at least partially)' the laws of trade and as being '(to use his own word) "aggravated"' to see employers not sharing the burden of hard economic times (59). Yet, even with these parenthetical disclaimers, the narrator still identifies with the workers. 'The contrast is too great', the narrator exclaims and then asks rhetorically, 'Why should he alone suffer from bad times?' (60).

Throughout the first few chapters of the novel, the narrator continues this rhetorical dance, cleverly changing partners so as to mediate between the interests of laborers and industrialists. This distances the narrator and readers from 'those who, either in speech or in print, find it their interest to cherish such [revolutionary] feelings in the working classes; who know how and when to rouse the dangerous power at their command; and who use their knowledge with unrelenting purpose to either party' (61). This depiction of the reformist yet non-partisan middle-class narrator performs the function of foregrounding the middle-class *response* to class conflict rather than appearing to incite action on the part of either industrialists or laborers.

In chapter 6 of the novel, readers are asked to maintain their intermediary role by comparing industrialist and working-class domestic environments. Carson's house is depicted as a retreat from public life, one which is de-politicized in every way. After the factory fire, Mr. Carson takes advantage of some time off to 'lounge over breakfast' and to partake in 'domestic enjoyments' (96). His daughter Amy, with her 'pretty jokes, and her bird-like songs', takes away her father's newspaper and 'would not allow her brother Harry to go on with his review' (107-8). Even the servants, 'not feeling hunger themselves, forgot it was possible another might' (106). The intrusion of Wilson, who has come to request an infirmary order for Davenport, creates only a minor disruption in the apolitical privacy of the Carson household.

Meanwhile, on the other side of town, the lower-class household is far from being impervious to the outside world: Davenport's cellar is literally infiltrated by the 'stagnant, filthy moisture of the street' (98). The mother, ideally the active keeper of the hearth, is depicted as incapacitated by 'weak and passive despair' (100). As was the case with the Barton household, the misery and poverty of the Davenport household inevitably produces a radical consciousness: '[Barton] felt the contrast between the well-filled, well-lighted shops and the dim gloomy cellar, and it made him moody that such contrasts should exist' (101). As much as John Barton's reaction is meant to reveal the causes of a lower-class unrest, it even more importantly serves the purpose of warning readers of the disastrous consequences of middle-class passivity. Barton's reaction is depicted as being justifiable only to a point. As he walks to the druggist to obtain medicine for Davenport, his desire for justice is replaced 'by sin, by bitter hatred of the happy, whom he, for the time, confounded with the selfish' (102). Far from being just a victim, John Barton comes to represent a kind of blameworthy criminality that exists just below the surface of justifiable protest.

This criminal potential comes to fruition as conditions worsen in the impoverished working-class neighborhoods of Manchester. John Barton's revolutionary impulses are joined with those of other workmen in 'fierce terrible oaths', resulting in the murder of Harry Carson (241). We then return to the Carson household, which is now forced to deal with the violent effects of its negligence. The daughters of the household, engaged in idle chatter about balls and romance, are the first to be confronted with the murder. Sophy is elected to break the news to her father, waking him from sleep and symbolically from his own self-deception (259). Harry's body, the victim of a politically motivated crime, thus becomes a 'truth' that literally brings home the consequences of social inaction. This 'reality' finally violates the separation between Mr. Carson's public and private interests. At first this collision of spheres produces only a desire for vengeance; it is not until the end of the novel that Carson is able to fully comprehend the political and moral symbolism of his son's death.

At the same time the middle-class household is rudely awakened from its moral and political inertia, the lower-class household, though still destitute, also undergoes renovation. Essential to this remapping of working-class domesticity is the reformation of Mary Barton herself, who must assume her role as the head of a domestic household. Her work outside the home, far from providing her with domestic skills, has caused her to entertain vain hopes of rising beyond her sphere. At Mrs. Simmonds', she develops 'simple, foolish, unworldly ideas' from the pages of novels (121). Here Gaskell, like many other writers working within the middle-class literature of reform, identifies the lack of improving reading materials as one of the causes leading to the degradation of working-class domestic life. Instead of caring for her home, Mary gossips about 'fashions, and dress, and parties to be given' (140). Meanwhile, with the absence of her feminine influence, the Barton household becomes increasingly political—and dangerous reading material once again exerts a poisonous influence on the morality of the domestic sphere. We soon learn that John Barton reads a Chartist newspaper, *The Northern Star,* by the hearthside, and at night their domestic privacy is violated by

> strange faces of pale men, with dark glaring eyes, [who] peered into the inner darkness, and seemed desirous to ascertain if her father were at home. Or a hand and arm (the body hidden) was put within the door, and beckoned him away. He always went. And once or twice, when Mary was in bed, she heard men's voices below, in earnest, whispered talk (162).

The incursion of radical politics into the working-class home is a symptom of its diseased state. But it is not the oppressive circumstances outside the home that must be alleviated in order to restore domestic peace. The solution begins within the domestic sphere as a reformation of Mary's femininity.

The process of reformation begins when Mary first rejects and then acknowledges her love for Jem Wilson. In these scenes criminality is displaced from the political sphere onto the actions of the two lovers. When he is rejected by Mary, Jem claims that she is going to make him into 'a drunkard, and may be as a thief, and may be as a murderer' (175). Likewise, after Mary realizes her rejection of Jem is a mistake, she looks back on the 'vanity or the criminality of the bye-gone' (176). Of course, it is their alleged 'criminality'—his crime of murder, hers of coquettishness—that becomes the focus of public spectacle throughout the rest of the novel. The vindication of their moral virtue and the solidification of their romantic bond performs the function of displacing the 'truth' of John Barton's guilt, as well as the social circumstances that provoked his violent action. While the 'tremendous secret' of her father's guilt is 'imprisoned within her' (389), at the trial she triumphantly confesses the 'strength of her attachment' for Jem in front of the crowded courtroom (391). Even after the trial, John Barton's guilt becomes an 'awful forbidden ground of discourse' between the affianced lovers (419). This is reinforced by the physical disappearance of John Barton, who slinks 'like a thief by dead of night into his own dwelling' (413).

Many critics over the years have argued that the marriage plot in the second half of the novel acts so as to displace and suppress the industrialist plot centered on John Barton. Catherine Gallagher, for instance, sees the domestic and tragic plots as being 'mutually exclusive', resulting in formal incongruities (*Industrial* 81). While Gallagher sees these disjunctions as a function of Gaskell's conflicted Unitarianism, others, such as Raymond Williams, have seen them as a 'dramatization of the *fear of violence* which was widespread among the upper and middle classes' (*Culture* 90). When viewed within the context of the discourse on urban investigation within the reformist periodical press, these competing narratives do not seem as mutually exclusive as these critics might suggest. Industrialist and domestic plots are compatible to the extent that they support the interconnected projects of politicizing the middle-class home and depoliticizing lower-class domesticity. The suppression of the 'truth' of John Barton's guilt—if not his wasted body itself—is a prerequisite for the reconstitution of Mary's femininity and thus the reestablishment of a healthy working-class home.

In the final chapters, the restoration of Mary's domestic role is shown to result in the creation of an apolitical working-class domesticity. Putting aside her father's crime, Mary assumes the role of a nurse, 'and tenderly did she treat him, and fondly did she serve him in every way that heart could devise or hand execute' (422). John Barton, for his part, no longer battles with the industrialists but with the 'Destroyer, Conscience' (422). It is only through her father's death that Mary is able to extricate herself and her home from his crime and the radicalism that produced it. However, she soon realizes that the ideal of de-politicized domesticity can only be fully reestablished in a faraway land. In Canada she is able to realize what was formerly an unattainable ideal of pastoral innocence: 'a long low wooden house, with room enough, and to spare. The old primeval trees are felled and gone for many a mile around; one alone remains to overshadow the gable-end of the cottage. There is a garden around the dwelling, and far beyond that stretches an orchard' (465).

At the same time the ending of *Mary Barton* dramatizes the depoliticization of the lower-class home, it demonstrates a corresponding politicization of middle-class domesticity. Just as John Barton had been radicalized by his visit to Davenport's cellar, Mr. Carson returns from his first visit to the Barton household with a recognition of the contrast between the 'pompous sumptuousness' of his library and the 'grinding squalid misery' of the house he just left (439). With this realization, 'the foundations of his past life were razed to the ground, and the place they had once occupied was sown with salt, to be for ever rebuilt no more' (451).

The demolition metaphor in this passage suggests the need for domestic reconstruction, especially since Carson no longer desires 'riches, social distinction, a name among the merchant-princes' (451). Significantly, Carson invites Job and Jem into his *home* to discuss the political causes of John Barton's crime. This consciousness-raising experience becomes generalized to all who 'are lifted out of the contemplation of their individual case into a searching inquiry into the nature of their calamity, and the remedy (if remedy there be) which may prevent its recurrence to others as well as to themselves' (459). Thus, his personal tragedy, the death of his son, is translated into a change in industrialist practices. We are told that 'many of the improvements now in practice in the system of employment in Manchester, owe their origin to short earnest sentences spoken by Mr. Carson' (460).

We hear no more of the women of his domestic household—how they might have reworked their personal calamity into positive social action. But it is not middle-class femininity as much as it is middle-class *domesticity* that the novel aims to reform.[14] The novel's ending dramatizes the dangers inherent in the separation of public and private spheres as well as between morality and vocation. Just as the Carson household is activated by politics, so does the novel itself act to politicize the middle-class reading experience. Rather than encouraging escape or privacy, the social problem novel encourages a problematization of the boundaries between public and private time, just as it calls into question the assumption of conventionally masculine and feminine subject matter. The effect of these changes was to create a more respectable place for the social problem novel and novelists both within the home and within literary tradition. Even Carlyle, whose disapproval of novels was well known, claimed that *Mary Barton* was a 'Book which every intelligent person may read with entertainment, and which it will do everyone some good to read' (Easson, *Critical* 72). The most prestigious middle-class periodicals—liberal and conservative—praised the novel for its accurate depictions of lower-class life and its deep moral purpose.[15]

If *Mary Barton* argued for the politicization of middle-class domesticity, the revelation of Gaskell's identity in December of 1848 served to place the middle-class woman writer at the center of that moral and intellectual space. And it was at this point that Gaskell finally assumed—however reluctantly—the role of high-profile social reformer and woman of letters. In critical reviews of the period, Gaskell's femininity was often viewed as a positive attribute. The *Eclectic Review's* portrayal of Gaskell is typical:

> The authoress, a Manchester lady, is anxious to bring the parties at issue to regard themselves less as employers and employed, than as men. She flings aside technicalities, not because she is not wholly master of her subject, for that she evidently is, but because she would have her readers to forget them, and to follow her through the dwellings of the rich and poor, till they are impressed by what they see and hear (Easson, *Critical* 96).

98   FIRST-PERSON ANONYMOUS

Here Gaskell is depicted as a urban investigator who directs readers through forbidden urban spaces and also as a moral guide, whose 'sympathy' enables her to lead others with the 'hand of a clear, warm, and noble nature' (97). Because of her philanthropic role as a minister's wife, Gaskell is defined as one who observes the facts of urban poverty but is not contaminated by them. Likewise, since her knowledge is reproduced in texts written and consumed within the middle-class home, her urban wanderings are defined as a respectable form of social interventionism.

Gaskell's image of sympathetic middle-class femininity was reinforced by her public appearances in London during the spring of 1849. Though in some sense Gaskell's trip to London was motivated by her desire to escape the negative publicity generated by her novel in Manchester, it was in another sense a celebratory journey that enabled her to revel in her new status as a literary lion. As biographer Jenny Uglow points out, during this period 'Elizabeth rather enjoyed being spoilt' (225). Entertained by literary celebrities and lionized by the reading public, she came to be seen as a model of the useful middle-class woman author— the charming 'Mrs. Gaskell', whose domestic moralism could be converted into new forms of gendered literary activism. Critics, literary lions, and socialites— when recording their private impressions of Gaskell during her visit to London— remarked on her feminine, unaffected demeanor. Henry Crabb Robinson, for example, commented on her 'agreeable manners, with a hale florid complexion with nothing literary about her appearance' (qtd. in Uglow, *Gaskell* 227). Private characterizations such as this one helped to create the mystique surrounding Gaskell's narrative identity and served to solidify her 'respectability' as both middle-class matron and philanthropic author. After her return from London, she reinforced this image in letters to influential literary friends describing her philanthropic activities in Manchester.[16]

After the publication of Gaskell's second social problem novel, *Ruth* (1853), she came to be defined as a maternal sage, whose 'delicate womanly instincts, yet further refined by religion' made her an ideal instrument of social morality (Easson, *Critical* 228). While critics of earlier women's social fiction had viewed their treatment of social and political subject matter as a kind of literary transgression, critics of Gaskell's work were more likely to argue that she was ennobled by her treatment of 'coarse' subject matter. As George Henry Lewes put it, Gaskell treated controversial topics 'like a woman, and a truly delicate-minded woman; with a delicacy that is strong in truth, not influenced by conventions' ('Ruth' 476). Likewise, critic John Ludlow, writing for the *North British Review*, suggests that Gaskell's respectability as 'wife and mother' provides her with an 'exquisite purity of feeling in dealing with a subject which so many would shrink from' (151). He contrasts Gaskell's 'full, and wholesome, and most womanly perfection' to the 'harsh' genius of Charlotte Brontë, who lacks the maternal wisdom necessary to embody positive social values (169). Thus, ironically it is Gaskell's maternal femininity that authorizes her intervention in social debates over the state of the poor. Her choice of political subject matter is softened by her gender and class status, which place her achievement within the scope of domestic achievement and respectable philanthropic activity.

As much as these definitions of feminine activism facilitated Gaskell's career as a social problem novelist, they were also somewhat constraining. In one letter, Gaskell seems to object to the moral perfection readers responded to in her work. She writes, 'my books are so far better than I am that I often feel ashamed of having written them and as if I were a hypocrite' (*Letters* 228). In addition to having to contend with the difficulty of maintaining a sense of moral rectitude in her work, Gaskell also had to deal with more negative interpretations of her authorial role. After the publication of *Mary Barton,* Gaskell was criticized by factory owners in Manchester, who interpreted the novel as an attack against industrialist labor practices (Uglow, *Gaskell* 214). Likewise, some critics questioned the truthfulness of Gaskell's depictions of working-class life. One reviewer for the *British Quarterly Review,* for example, claims that the novel presents an 'exaggerated' and 'out of date' picture of class relationships in manufacturing districts (Beard 121). The reviewer further remarks, 'The distresses of the labouring poor are set forth in ample detail, and we cannot regard that as a fair picture of the state of society, which, at least by its omissions, would leave the readers to suppose that the wealthier classes were really as indifferent to the interests of those below them, as the writer says the poorer class believe them to be' (122). In response to reviews of this sort, Gaskell mourned the 'failure' of her novel, which proved to be more of a 'fire brand' than a 'tragic poem' (*Letters* 68).

After the publication of *Ruth,* Gaskell's work once again fell subject to negative criticism, but since her identity was now public knowledge, these critical attacks seemed more personal and damaging. In an 1853 letter to Anne Robson, she compares herself to 'St. Sebastian tied to a tree to be shot at with arrows ... what must be endured with as much quiet *seeming,* & as little inward pain as I can' (*Letters* 220-21). At the same time that some critics represented Gaskell as a maternal sage, others attacked her sense of domestic propriety. Gaskell heard tales of the novel being burnt by those who objected to its positive depiction of a fallen woman (*Letters* 227). Likewise, many critical reviewers that questioned the appropriateness and accuracy of her subject matter. One critic, for example, objected to 'such a book being received into families' because of its moral ambiguity (Easson, *Critical* 211).

The critical response to Gaskell's early novels thus constructs a contradictory image of her public persona: she is at once maternal sage and feminine transgressor, moral paragon and reckless social theorist. Gaskell to some extent legitimized the social problem novel as a medium for women's participation in political and social debates. At the same time that Gaskell's fiction identified the middle-class home as the proper location of social activism, the construction of her identity in the popular media functioned to authorize middle-class women as the source of new kinds of socially useful knowledge. However, the critical narratives surrounding the construction of Gaskell's authorial persona also reveal the kinds of cultural anxieties that accompanied the expansion of women's literary activism.

100 FIRST-PERSON ANONYMOUS

While on one hand the appearance of the socially engaged woman author seemed to promise increased social stability through more thorough moral policing of class boundaries, it also threatened the separation of conventionally masculine and feminine authorial and social roles.

The Woman Author and the Woman Question in the 1850s

The construction of 'Mrs. Gaskell' in periodical discourse of the 1850s reflected a broader critical obsession with the 'female author' as a cultural phenomenon. Throughout the early decades of the nineteenth century, the discourse on female authorship and the Woman Question played an important role in critical reviewing practices. But it wasn't until the 1850s that the project of defining and delimiting the role of the female author became a major critical preoccupation.[17] In hundreds of essays and reviews, critics debated women's proper role in the literary establishment. Was the increasing involvement of women in the profession a symptom of cultural progress or decline? Did women's literary achievements justify their increased participation in the public sphere? In what ways did the publishing industry facilitate or impede their literary efforts? Critical discussion of these questions was concentrated on literary texts that highlighted women's social and artistic roles, including Harriet Beecher Stowe's *Uncle Tom's Cabin* (1852), Elizabeth Gaskell's *Ruth* (1853), Charlotte Brontë's *Villette* (1853), and Elizabeth Barrett Browning's *Aurora Leigh* (1857). In reviewing these works and many other books published by women during the 1850s, periodical journalists attempted to theorize a feminine writing style and literary tradition.

As Elaine Showalter and others have pointed out, this often meant that women's texts fell subject to a critical double standard that devalued women's literary achievements.[18] In the minds of many Victorian reviewers, the question of what place women's literature should hold in the literary canon was conflated with the question of what place women should hold in contemporary political and social life. On one hand, reviewers often heralded women's novels as a superior form of art. As one writer for the *North British Review* remarks, 'We have to notice the fact, that at this particular period of the world's history, the very *best* novels in several great countries happen to have been written by women' (Ludlow 167). However, though reviewers often included this sort of laudatory rhetoric in their articles, they also attempted to construct the novel as an essentially feminine art form suited to women's natural emotionality and domesticity. The *North British Review* concludes it praise of women's novels with the following:

> Now, if we consider the novel to be the picture of human life in a pathetic, or as some might prefer the expression, in a sympathetic form, that is to say, as addressed to human feeling, rather than to human taste, judgment, or reason, there seems nothing paradoxical in the view, that women are called to the mastery of this peculiar field of literature (168).

ELIZABETH GASKELL

This review performs the function of redomesticating the visible, famous woman, locating her achievement within the domestic sphere. She expresses the 'human feeling' and sympathy associated with domesticity rather than the 'human taste' and 'reason' that characterize the masculine sphere of influence.

At the same time that some critics attempted to define gendered literary styles, other reviewers questioned the naturalness of these categories. An essay on Felicia Hemans, for example, addresses the critical preoccupation with gender in this way:

> There is still a practice in many critics to detect the style feminine from the style masculine. The sooner this is laid aside the better. There are styles which, speaking metaphorically, one may say have a feminine grace, or a feminine weakness. Such an observation has been made, by Sir James Mackintosh, on the style of Addison. But to pretend to say of a given page of composition whether a man or a woman has penned it, is absurd (Smith and Moir 643).

Here feminine writing is defined as a critical metaphor rather than as an essentialized gender marker. Hemans' style is feminine only in the sense that it appeals to the 'minds of her countrywomen' (644). The reviewer makes it clear that the woman writer has 'no monopoly in the lighter elegancies, and presume[s] nothing against her ability to excel in the graver qualities of authorship' (644).

The critical debate over masculine and feminine writing styles continued throughout the 1850s and '60s. Within the context of this debate, women were not merely the objects of this critical activity; as periodical reviewers and essayists, they played a key role in determining the terms by which women's texts would be read and discussed. During the period of 1850 to 1865, women contributed to the periodicals in unprecedented numbers, exerting influence in the most important political, social, and aesthetic debates. As Bessie Rayner Parkes noted in 1858,

> Literature again is followed, as a profession, by women, to an extent far greater than our readers are at all aware of. The Magazines of the day are filled by them ... Even the leaders of our newspapers are, in some instances, regularly written by women, and publishers avail themselves largely of their industry in all manner of translations and compilations. In the reading-room of the British Museum ... the roving eye may any day detect the bowed heads and black silk dresses of ladies who come there for references on every subject under heaven ('Profession' 8).

Indeed, it was during this period that Harriet Martineau published her most significant work in the *Westminster Review* and the *Daily News,* Elizabeth Gaskell contributed to *Household Words,* and George Eliot served as assistant editor of the *Westminster Review.*[19] Hundreds of other women writers—including Margaret Oliphant, Anne Mozley, Bessie Rayner Parkes, Elizabeth Rigby, and Dinah Mulock Craik—also contributed articles and reviews to periodicals during this period. These writers took part in the debate over the woman author by helping to redefine and reconsider women's authorial and social roles in mid-Victorian society. But it

102 FIRST-PERSON ANONYMOUS

is important to realize that these reviews were not feminist in the modern sense. Reviews of women's novels by Oliphant, Martineau, and Eliot were sometimes quite vituperative.[20] In these and many other reviews, women critics attempted to revise and reformulate existing models of women's authorship.

Throughout the 1850s, Gaskell became increasingly interested in the Woman Question. Though she was reluctant to associate herself with the emerging women's movement, she to some extent sympathized with its aims. At the instigation of Eliza Fox, Gaskell signed a petition in support of the Married Women's Property Act in 1856 even though she did not think it 'very definite, and *pointed*; or that it will do much good' (*Letters* 379). Other friends, including Fredrika Bremer, Charlotte Brontë, Harriet Martineau, Madame Mohl, Anna Jameson, and Elizabeth Barrett Browning, encouraged Gaskell's interest in women's issues.[21] Gaskell's interactions with these writers caused her to temper her conservatism on the Woman Question, but nevertheless her position in these debates was always conflicted. In an 1850 letter to Eliza Fox, for example, she argues that '*women*, must give up living an artist's life, if home duties are to be paramount', yet in the same letter she claims that all have some 'appointed work to do' (*Letters* 106, 107). In a subsequent letter to Fox, Gaskell describes her 'warring' selves and admits that she is sometimes 'coward enough to wish that we were back in the darkness where obedience was the only seen duty of women' (*Letters* 108, 109).

Beyond occasional comments on the Woman Question in her letters, Gaskell rarely treated women's issues explicitly in her writing. As I pointed out in the first part of this chapter, the construction of Gaskell's narrative persona in critical reviews of the 1840s and early 1850s had the effect of legitimizing the participation of middle-class women in the discourse over the state of the poor. However, the characters and plots of Gaskell's novels do not otherwise embody a consistent feminist position. It is only in Gaskell's non-fiction of the 1850s that her views on women's issues—especially her perspectives on the treatment of women authors— are more directly expressed. In her little-known satirical essay, 'A Fear for the Future', published anonymously in *Fraser's Magazine* in 1859,[22] Gaskell satirizes prejudicial attitudes toward women writers. In order to draw attention to the folly of conservative attitudes toward women's intellectual achievement, Gaskell writes in the voice of a 'respectable country gentleman', a 'staunch Conservative' from 'Slowington' who is distressed over the state of womanhood in the modern age (246). Like Rip Van Winkle, he has lived 'for the last five-and-twenty years ... altogether out of the "world",' that is, in rural England, where the 'experience of society [is] limited in extent and primitive in quality' (243). He travels to the city only to find 'nothing as it used to be', especially the manners and customs of social life (244). The narrator especially regrets that women are no longer a 'thoughtless, foolish, bewitching, loving, helpless, irresistible set of creatures' and instead gather 'under the brown banner of Matter of Fact, Stern Reality, and Common Sense' (245). He is especially shocked by their propensity for social work and writing:

ELIZABETH GASKELL 103

What modern young woman, of average ability and education, who is not at least 'a writer' in some magazine, or probably yet more ambitious, the author of a book, be it a novel in three volumes, travels in two, or poetry in one? As for the exceptionally clever among their sex, such light labours in literature no longer content them. They attack science, and produce authoritative tomes, books of reference (246).

These writerly activities make women 'public characters' who threaten to emasculate men, discouraging the expression of 'proper manly feeling' (248).

In order to illustrate all that is wrong with the modern woman, he tells an anecdote about a recent encounter at a London party. He approaches a group of young women 'with some conciliatory remark, at once suave, benignant, admiring, and jocose—in fact, couched after the usual manner of old gentlemen to young ladies' (247). He asks, 'And what breeze is stirring the flowers? ... what momentous subject is rippling over those rosy lips? Will you admit an old man to your conference? (247). One of the women satirically replies, 'we are talking about our dolls, of course', and then, laughing, admits that they are 'professional artists' (247). In another moment, the women are herded off into another room to discuss a pressing piece of parliamentary legislation, leaving the gentleman in 'very blank solitude' (247). While to some extent Gaskell may have been satirizing political women who had lost all vestiges of feminine delicacy, her main object seems to have been to poke fun at old-fashioned conservatives, especially those who foolishly value 'ignorance among women' (248). Such a message was well placed in *Fraser's Magazine*, which had once been known for its Toryism but was shifting in the 1850s toward a liberal political stance.[23] It had of course long been famous for its literary pranks and satirical essays. Working within this context, Gaskell created a caricature of conservative manhood sure to provoke laughter among readers of the magazine.

The 'Abused Woman Author' and *The Life of Charlotte Brontë*

The status of women within Victorian culture preoccupied Gaskell throughout the late 1850s. As many critics have noticed, Gaskell moved away from industrial subject matter after the publication of *The Life of Charlotte Brontë* (1857).[24] During this period, Gaskell directed her energy away from the Condition-of-England debate and became involved the discourse on the female author. While early in her career Gaskell demonstrated ways that middle-class women could help heal class divisions, in *The Life of Charlotte Brontë,* these class divisions become curiously blurred. Gaskell adapts the terms of the reformist debate over the plight of industrial workers to the discourse on the women author, figuring her as both initiator and object of middle-class reform efforts. Through her depiction of these separate yet interdependent images of the woman author, Gaskell not only attempted to generate deeper sympathy for women writers but also to authorize her own biographical practice as a politicized form of literary recovery. According to

104   FIRST-PERSON ANONYMOUS

this redefinition of women's activism, the issue of class-based oppression is marginalized and reappropriated; however, it still haunts the text in significant ways, re-emerging in Gaskell's contradictory reflections on gendered authorship and social responsibility.

In undertaking *The Life of Charlotte Brontë*, Gaskell was in some sense attempting to purify Brontë's public image—setting aside once and for all accusations of immodesty and impropriety generated in critical reviews of Brontë's novels. As Jenny Uglow puts it, since Gaskell was 'unable to save Charlotte in life, she would save her reputation in death' (*Gaskell* 389). One of the ways Gaskell attempted to reconstruct Brontë's public image was to emphasize the compatibility between intellectual activity and domestic virtue in her development as a writer. As Gaskell points out in a letter to Ellen Nussey, 'I am sure the more fully she— Charlotte Brontë—the *friend,* the *daughter,* the *sister,* the *wife,* is known, and known where need be in her own words—the more highly will she be appreciated' (*Letters* 370). Though at one point in the biography Gaskell suggests that the domestic and intellectual 'halves' of Brontë's life are separate (237-8), more often she demonstrates just how inextricably they are combined. In the opening chapters of the biography, she emphasizes the role of political and intellectual activities in Brontë's early domestic environment. From an early age, Brontë and her siblings demonstrate an interest in the political articles published in literary periodicals, especially *Blackwood's Magazine* (55). Gaskell tells us that 'politics were evidently their grand interest; the Duke of Wellington their demi-god' (58). As a reflection of their eccentric reading habits, their plays and stories are peopled with the heroes of newspapers and periodicals:

> Another noticeable fact is the intelligent partisanship with which they choose their great men, who are almost all staunch Tories of the time. Moreover, they do not confine themselves to local heroes; their range of choice has been widened by hearing much of what is not usually considered to interest children. Little Anne, aged scarcely eight, picks out the politicians of the day for her chief men (54).

Though Gaskell finds these habits rather odd, she still interprets them as evidence of the precociousness of the Brontë children rather than as a perversion of their proper gender roles. Domesticity and politics are depicted as having equally important roles to play in the development of their artistic genius.

Gaskell notes that when Charlotte Brontë enters Miss Woolner's school, she brings her love of politics along with her. She is fascinated with the debates over the Reform Bill and reports in a letter to her brother that she has not lost a 'penchant for politics' (67). In addition to taking part in conventionally domestic activities, Brontë participates in 'fierce discussions' of local politics in which all students express 'their opinions and their parties' (77). Once back at Haworth, Brontë maintains 'her childish interest in politics' (86) through letter writing and finds other ways to merge her intellectual interests and domestic responsibilities:

Books were, indeed, a very common sight in that kitchen; the girls were taught by their father theoretically, and by their aunt practically, that to take an active part in all household work was, in their position, woman's simple duty; but, in their careful employment of time, they found many an odd five minutes for reading while watching the cakes, and managed the union of two kinds of employment better than King Alfred (90-91).

Here Gaskell defines domestic responsibilities and intellectual activity as equally important forms of 'employment' that can be harmonized in such a way as to produce both domestic order and individual genius. Once Brontë begins writing fiction, she carefully balances her domestic and literary work responsibilities. Only after 'her household and filial duties' have been fulfilled does Brontë 'obtain leisure to sit down and write out the incidents and consequent thoughts', giving in to the 'possession' of literary activity (214). When Brontë finally confesses to her father that she is a published author, her announcement is met with calm approval, rather than censure: 'the existence of Currer Bell, the author, was like a piece of a dream to the quiet inhabitants of Haworth Parsonage, who went on with their uniform household life' (230).

While in many ways Gaskell's *Life* takes great pains to illustrate the compatibility between domestic and literary work, it also highlights the difficulties faced by women in attempting to balance the conflicting claims of home and professional responsibilities. In an aside, Gaskell writes, 'A woman's principal work in life is hardly left to her own choice; nor can she drop the domestic charges devolving on her as an individual, for the exercise of the most splendid talents that were ever bestowed' (238). In Charlotte Brontë's case, these 'domestic charges' are depicted as being at once morally elevating and physically debilitating.

The image of the isolated and disease-ridden Haworth Parsonage recurs throughout the biography as a signifier for the unhealthy effect of these domestic circumstances on Brontë's physical and psychological development (81, 243).[25] Like the distressed working-class household in *Mary Barton,* Haworth has no mother to protect its domestic hearth. Miss Branwell and Mr. Brontë are both incapable of assuming this duty, so the responsibility often falls on Charlotte, whose frequent absences from home disrupt domestic harmony. Though Gaskell points out that Charlotte is an exemplary housekeeper (4, 214), she does not believe these efforts are enough to combat unseen sources of moral and physical poison within the Brontë household. Similar to her description of Davenport's cellar in *Mary Barton,* Gaskell's graphic description of Haworth depicts a home that is permeable to degrading outside influences. Haworth is 'built with an utter disregard of all sanitary conditions' and haunts its inhabitants 'with all the sights and sounds connected with the last offices to the dead' (81-2). In this passage, Gaskell may have been making indirect reference to Benjamin Babbage's 1850 *Report to the General Board of Health*, which emphasized the unsanitary effects of the Haworth churchyard on public health. Babbage writes:

106   FIRST-PERSON ANONYMOUS

The churchyard is almost, if not quite, full of graves.... . Considering the present number of the inhabitants of Haworth, it would require the addition of at least an acre to the present churchyard, in order to meet the requirements of the population, and to allow of corpses being interred at proper intervals from each other, so as to prevent too great a collection in one place of decomposing matter' (19).

It is not known whether Gaskell read Babbage's report, but this and other references to sanitation in *Life* seem to suggest that it might have been a source. The similarities between the two texts suggest interesting ways that Gaskell may have been appropriating the discourse on urban investigation in *The Life of Charlotte Brontë*. In Gaskell's *Life*, the eye of the investigator is reconstituted as a gaze that penetrates the privacy of the middle-class home, measuring and judging its physical and moral health.[26]

The unhealthy moral influences of Haworth are further symbolized by Branwell Brontë, whose illicit affair with Lady Scott and frequent bouts of drinking become a constant worry for Charlotte, stealing her energies away from literary endeavor (198). The special treatment Branwell receives due to his sex is depicted as an especially degrading moral influence in the Brontë household. Even though all of the Brontë children show intellectual and artistic promise, the family's ambitions and educational resources are centered on Branwell: 'He is expected to act a part in life; to *do,* while they are only to *be*' (123). The result is that he becomes 'utterly selfish' and ultimately self-destructive (123). While Branwell is spoiled and indulged, Charlotte and her sisters teeter on the edge of middle-class respectability, taking positions as governesses and engaging in the sorts of household duties normally assigned to servants in the bourgeois household (345).

When describing these domestic inequities, Gaskell figures herself as a moralistic judge who interrupts the narrative in order to reinforce its moral message: 'These are not the first sisters who have laid their lives as a sacrifice before their brother's idolised wish. Would to God they might be the last who met with such a miserable return!'(89). Though such an interjection does not directly address readers, its intent is to stimulate their thinking in a way that encourages them to interpret Brontë's biography in universal terms. Like John Barton or Libbie Marsh, Charlotte Brontë is treated as an individual instance of a larger class of impoverished and oppressed laborers whose stories must be heard by middle-class readers in order to facilitate social reform.

Due to her unhealthy domestic circumstances, Brontë is not only an oppressed laborer but also a tortured genius who struggles against poverty and obscurity in her quest to produce great art.[27] This romanticized depiction of the struggling author was a distinct feature of mid-Victorian discourse. Many literary works foregrounded the vicissitudes of the literary life, including Dickens' *David Copperfield* (1849-50), Thackeray's *Pendennis* (1848-50), and Barrett Browning's *Aurora Leigh* (1857). In addition, scores of periodical essays chronicled the abuse of authors in debates over copyright and literary pensions.[28] In these periodical debates, the domestic instabilities endured by popular authors are often attributed to

ELIZABETH GASKELL 107

a lack of public appreciation. G. H. Lewes, for example, in an 1847 article in *Fraser's Magazine*, argues that improving the financial and social status of authors would prevent them from living 'from hand to mouth' and thus 'being forced to write down to the popular taste' ('Condition' 294). Ironically, literary critics such as Lewes most often blamed these abuses on their own critical establishment, which discouraged gifted writers with its harsh reviewing practices.

As a subset of the discourse on the 'abused author', critical discussions of the oppression of the female author intensified in the 1840s and '50s. An interesting example is an anonymous article entitled 'Female Authorship', published in *Fraser's Magazine* in 1846. This article recounts a conversation between a literary lady and a female friend over the trials of being a woman author. She complains about the literary establishment that insists on the 'unhappiness of literary women in their domestic life' and metes out 'condescending' praise (463). Though she often 'dwells on the lone position which a woman of genius occupies', she still clings to the 'earnestness of purpose' (465) that motivated her literary career and still finds time to cultivate a 'happy household' (466). In this way, the home of the female author becomes a replacement for the home of the laborer as a site of interest and investigation within the periodical press. Yet paradoxically, while the periodical press enables this investigatory discourse over the state of the woman author, it simultaneously acts as a contagion within this domestic space—the condescending praise that brings suffering.

In *The Life of Charlotte Brontë,* Gaskell enters fully into the discourse on the 'abused woman author', using Brontë's experience to illustrate the special difficulties faced by women whose works were reviewed in the periodical press. Gaskell cites many examples of institutional prejudice, beginning with Southey's discouraging response to Brontë's poems. She also quotes passages from Brontë's letters that express her feelings about the barriers faced by women in the literary establishment.[29] At other times Gaskell draws her own conclusions from the available evidence. She reports that after the publication of *Jane Eyre,* 'the press in general did little to promote the sale of the novel ... the power of fascination of the tale itself made its merits known to the public, without the kindly finger-posts of professional criticism' (226). When this critical neglect turns to 'cowardly insolence' in the *Quarterly Review* (259), Gaskell interrupts her narrative in order to defend Brontë from these critics:

> Not even the desire to write a 'smart article', which shall be talked about in London, when the faint mask of the anonymous can be dropped at pleasure if the cleverness of the review be admired—not even this temptation can excuse the stabbing cruelty of the judgment. Who is he that he should say of an unknown woman: 'She must be one who for some sufficient reason has long forfeited the society of her sex'? Is he one who has led a wild and struggling and isolated life,—seeing few but plain and outspoken Northerns, unskilled in the euphuisms which assist the polite world to skim over the mention of vice? Has he striven through long weeping years to find excuses for the

108   FIRST-PERSON ANONYMOUS

lapse of an only brother; and through daily contact with a poor lost profligate, been compelled into a certain familiarity with the vices that his soul abhors? (260)

What makes this passage remarkable is that it distinguishes between the rightful anonymity of the 'unknown woman' writer and the wrongful anonymity of the critic, who doffs his 'faint mask of the anonymous' as suits his pleasure. It is also interesting that Gaskell connects Brontë's critical victimization with the oppressive circumstances of her homelife. The coarseness of Brontë's writing comes not from contact with the poor but from interactions with the 'poor lost profligate', her brother. The critic's inability to sympathize with these domestic sources of oppression makes him incapable of appreciating Brontë's genius. But perhaps what is most remarkable about this passage is that Gaskell constructs the periodical reviewer as a man even though she knew that the article's anonymous author was a woman, Elizabeth Rigby (Lady Eastlake). It is impossible to know why Gaskell would intentionally suppress the female sex of the offending reviewer, but it may have been because she wanted to position Brontë as the victim of a masculine critical establishment in order to maximize public sympathy.[30]

At the end of *The Life of Charlotte Brontë,* Gaskell finally turns away from the harsh critical tradition, casting it aside as an unredeemable social element. Only non-professional readers, she claims, are capable of appreciating Brontë's achievement. She closes her biography with an appeal to this audience:

> But I turn from the critical, unsympathetic public,—inclined to judge harshly because they have only seen superficially and not thought deeply. I appeal to that larger and more solemn public, who know how to look with tender humility at faults and errors; how to admire generously extraordinary genius, and how to reverence with warm, full hearts all noble virtue. To that Public I commit the memory of Charlotte Brontë (402).

Here Gaskell removes the task of reading and judging from the harsh world of literary reviewing, constructing a reader who possesses both sympathetic domestic values and a politicized critical vocabulary. Elsewhere in the biography, Gaskell suggests that Brontë, through her own practice of private literary reviewing in her letters, demonstrated just the sort of sympathetic, yet critically rigorous, reviewing practices that are needed to encourage women's authorship (342-43, 355). To some extent Gaskell also includes her own biographical practice within the category of non-professional, sympathetic criticism. Of course, as a biographer and as an anonymous reviewer for *Fraser's Magazine* and the *Athenaeum,*[31] Gaskell was much more of an insider within the literary establishment than her comments would seem to imply. Somewhat hypocritically, she still aligns herself with non-professional readers in order to emphasize their common domestic values. The re-domestication and re-politicization of literary criticism, Gaskell implies, would reform those attitudes that impede women's careers in literary publishing. Thus in *The Life of Charlotte Brontë,* as in *Mary Barton,* Gaskell demonstrates how the act of reading at home can become a political activity. However, rather than proposing ways that politicized reading practices can heal class divisions, she suggests ways that they can address gender inequities within the middle-class home and within the male-dominated publishing industry. Gaskell attempts to rally women readers to the cause of the 'abused woman author' by constructing a monolithically patriarchal critical establishment and by intentionally downplaying the role of women within the field of literary reviewing—including her own professional activities as a biographer and critic.

At the same time that *The Life of Charlotte Brontë* enters into the debate over the 'abused woman author' in the 1850s, it also expresses cultural anxieties about the conflicts between women's social responsibilities and literary aspirations.[32] While the woman writer of the 1840s was authorized to claim a public role due to her advocacy of working-class interests, the woman writer of the 1850s was seen as being in danger of losing a socially useful mission in life.[33] Throughout her biography, Gaskell interrogates the depth of Brontë's commitment to social activism; inevitably, Brontë falls short of her expectations. Though Gaskell demonstrates that politics played a key role in Brontë's development as a writer, she seems disappointed that Brontë was such an unenthusiastic participant in philanthropic activities: 'Mr. Brontë was faithful in visiting the sick, and all those who sent for him, and diligent in attendance at the schools; and so was his daughter Charlotte too; but, cherishing and valuing privacy themselves, they were perhaps over-delicate in not intruding upon the privacy of others' (29).

At Miss Woolner's, Brontë is daily witness to the struggles of the poor during the Luddite riots; however, these social disturbances produce only distanced debate and observation, not direct social intervention (77). Gaskell points out that these early observations inform Brontë's treatment of working-class radicalism in *Shirley,* but she does not dwell on these influences. Instead, she highlights the gender issues associated with the novel's reception. After discussing G. H. Lewes' review of the novel, Gaskell reports that Brontë 'especially disliked the lowering of the standard by which to judge a work of fiction, if it proceeded from a feminine pen; and praise mingled with pseudo-gallant allusions to her sex, mortified her far more than actual blame' (284). By focusing on the novel's reception, Gaskell suggests that Brontë's personal and professional struggles in some sense serve as a replacement for a philanthropic role. Gaskell excerpts a passage from one of Brontë's letters that highlights her resistance to forms of political activism: 'You will see that *Villette* touches on no matter of public interest. I cannot write books handling the topics of the day; it is of no use trying. Nor can I write a book for its moral. Nor can I take up a philanthropic scheme' (364). Since Gaskell includes this remark without adding her own commentary, it is impossible to assess her moral stance in relation to Brontë's position. At various points in the biography, Gaskell seems to suggest that Brontë's lack of philanthropic zeal was justified due to her overwhelming personal and professional struggles. However, elsewhere the biography, she refers to the dangerous effects of Brontë's social isolation and self-absorption (169).[34]

Later in the biography, Gaskell suggests that Brontë might have been working on a social problem novel based on some visits she had made to prisons and hospitals in London: 'If she had lived, her deep heart would sooner or later have spoken out on these things' (373). She also notes that Brontë's funeral is attended by a 'village girl' who had been the grateful object of Brontë's past philanthropic acts (401). With these remarks Gaskell seems to be attempting to redeem Brontë from her self-absorption and political passivity. Yet this is a contradictory stance for Gaskell, who otherwise seems to sanction Brontë's social isolation and political inactivity as essential aspects of her romantic genius. The biography seems to ask: How can the object of charitable feeling also be the initiator of charitable acts? Yet how else can a woman authorize her entry into the realm of public discourse? Gaskell raises and then casts aside these questions in her own critical practice. By intervening on behalf of the woman author, Gaskell claims a morally active role for herself and middle-class readers, who must divert their philanthropic impulses to a new end—the reformation of those physical, moral, and critical conditions that impede the development and appreciation of a woman genius.

In such a configuration, gender usurps the role of class as a motivating cause for women's literary activism. That is, instead of middle-class women justifying their literary careers based on the necessity of philanthropic activism on behalf of the poor, they justify their careers based on the need for literary intervention on behalf of their fellow women writers. The 'abused woman author', rather than the oppressed worker, is defined as the appropriate object of reform efforts. This ideological shift corresponds to the general decline of working-class radicalism and the development of an organized women's movement during the 1850s.[35] In its early stages, the women's movement was focused on improving vocational opportunities and working conditions for middle-class women. Within these debates, Gaskell's *Life of Charlotte Brontë* soon became a contested narrative. An 1857 review published in *Blackwood's Magazine* discusses Gaskell's *Life of Charlotte Brontë* as 'evidence of what hundreds of young women have to undergo, who have no proper outlet for their mental activities' (Dallas, 'Currer' 78). In contrast, Margaret Oliphant, citing Branwell Brontë's tragic fall, interprets the *Life* as evidence that circumstances are 'not harder upon the daughters of the race than upon its sons' ('Condition' 143). In response to Oliphant's interpretation of the Brontë story, Bessie Rayner Parkes remarks in the first issue of the *English Woman's Journal* that 'destitution is for them [women] a more awful thing; that there are depths of horror, of degradation, into which men cannot fall' ('Profession' 13).

Gaskell's investigation of the domestic life of the 'abused woman author' in *The Life of Charlotte Brontë* was a powerful narrative that was replicated in various forms in the periodical press. For example, in an article titled, 'A Woman's Pen', published in the *Englishwoman's Journal* in 1858, Eliza Meteyard illuminates the travails of neglected woman author. Like Gaskell, Meteyard employs narrative strategies associated with the literature of social investigation in order to draw attention to the critical institutions and domestic practices that oppress women. The story is written from the perspective of a middle-class man who wanders into a rural neighborhood. Like the social investigator, the visitor sympathetically views the cottages of the poor and fastens on one that warrants his particular attention: the home of a retired authoress who supports herself by selling tea and other sundries. He is appalled that this great woman has been reduced to a state of poverty and begs to speak with her. She tells him that her life is indeed difficult but that 'the majority of literary women could tell as sad a tale as I can in this respect; and thus many of us, though the world knows it not, have a thorny path to tread, though such is hallowed by the dignity annexed to our work' (255). She tells the stranger that she will accept charity neither from his hands nor from the state. Instead, following the model of the self-sufficient lower-class worker, she advocates only 'some plan of self-assistance' so that literary women might organize themselves (256). She proposes they establish a 'fund on the principle of the Friendly Societies,—a few of the Manchester Unions affording admirable examples' (256). This would promote a work ethic among women authors, rather than compromising their morals with 'an endowment like a poor-law' (257). In the end, the stranger helps the authoress by arranging for her works to be republished and secretly adding to her royalties a 'fitting sum' of his own (258). As a consequence, the shop is closed and the authoress regains her independence. Meteyard's story follows in the same vein as narratives within the literature of urban investigation in the 1830s and '40s: the middle-class stranger provides assistance to the worker that enables her to be a righteous, self-supporting member of society.[36] Like the figure of Charlotte Brontë in Gaskell's *Life,* the authoress in this story must be recovered from obscurity and degradation, and the source of her oppression must be exposed and reformed. The woman author comes to be defined as the initiator of investigatory practices—and their object.

However much critical fascination with the 'abused woman author' facilitated the discourse on women's rights and employment opportunities, it also posed some significant barriers to the development of their literary careers. Though *The Life of Charlotte Brontë* and other texts in the 'abused woman author' genre had the effect of rescuing women writers from obscurity, they also had the effect of mythologizing and sentimentalizing their life stories. Even though Gaskell for the most part succeeded in dispelling cultural beliefs about Brontë's coarseness and impropriety,[37] she replaced them with new stereotypes about the tortured female genius, whose personal travails and private life were inseparable from her work.[38] Likewise, though Gaskell enhanced her own literary reputation by publishing *The Life of Charlotte Brontë,* she did so by using the details of Brontë's private life as ammunition for her own war with the critical establishment.[39]

Gaskell's exposure of Brontë's life and career made many women sympathize even more deeply with the plight of their fellow women writers. Even the obscure Marian Evans, having just published her first stories in *Blackwood's Magazine,* found *The Life of Charlotte Brontë* 'deeply affecting throughout' (*Letters* 2: 319). Yet on another level women authors such as Eliot—who clung to journalistic anonymity in the same way that 'Currer Bell' assiduously maintained her

112 FIRST-PERSON ANONYMOUS

pseudonymity—must have feared the kind of personal exposure that Gaskell's biography enacted, regardless of its literary or liberatory intent. As Eliot well knew, to have the details of one's life and career exposed to the reading public was to lose a certain amount of narrative and professional flexibility. The next chapter will demonstrate how anonymous and pseudonymous publication enabled Eliot to distance her work from the discourse on feminine writing and the female author. Rather than emphasizing the connection between her private life and public selves, she demonstrated how obscurity and gender ambiguity could be converted into literary power.

Notes

1   For example, Edwin Chadwick includes the names of male inspectors from various districts of Great Britain. See Nord (1-15) and Poovey (*Making* 55-97) for a discussion of the gendering of urban investigation.
2   See, for example, Parker's 'Fictional Philanthropy' and D'Albertis' *Dissembling Fictions* (45-71).
3   Uglow provides a partial bibliography of Gaskell's periodical publications (*Gaskell* 617-19). Easson ('Elizabeth Gaskell and the *Athenaeum*') and Unsworth & Morton tentatively identify other articles as Gaskell's. In addition to these publications, Gaskell may have written a number of other pieces intended for the periodicals. In an 1849 letter, Mary Howitt writes to Gaskell, 'Perhaps you can send me the article—for I presume it is already written and is one of the many manuscripts which lie in a certain desk drawer, & may have lain there for years' (qtd. in Uglow, *Gaskell* 173).
4   Other reformist periodicals included *Tait's Edinburgh Magazine* (1832-61), *The People's Journal* (1846-49), *Eliza Cook's Journal* (1849-54), *Jerrold's Shilling Magazine* (1845-48), and *Household Words* (1850-59).
5   It is difficult to theorize the relationship between the intended and actual audience of reformist periodicals. As Maidment points out, the 'price, format, and tone of most the magazines' would not have excluded artisan-class readers (88). However, they were probably less accessible to the poorest members of the working class, especially those who were the targets of middle-class philanthropic efforts. Weekly middle-class journals were more expensive than the penny weeklies and did not contain the news that attracted lower-class readers to Sunday papers such as the *Weekly Dispatch,* the *Sunday Times,* and *Bell's Life in London* (Altick, *English* 342).
6   Here Gaskell appropriates the conventions of Chartist journalism, which used the picturesque to symbolize an idealized working-class cultural history. See Anne Janowitz, who argues that the Chartist press used the picturesque as a means of 'link[ing] the contemporary struggle to a communitarian past located in the countryside' (278).
7   See, for example, Stoneman (68-86), Krueger (*Reader's Repentance* 169-86), Robin Colby (33-46), and Warhol (47-71), all of whom contend that Gaskell constructs models of women's social activism as an alternative to male models of interventionism in *Mary*

ELIZABETH GASKELL 113

Barton. Others, such as Nord (142-57) and Schor (13-44), argue that the middle-class woman author identifies with her working class characters.

8 Robin Colby, for example, argues that the novel presents a 'persuasive argument for female vocation' through its depictions of lower-class women (45). Colby conflates the experiences of working-class women characters in the novel with the experiences of all 'Victorian women', whose 'labor was not fully recognized or sanctioned' (34). Mary's increasing sense of agency and social responsibility in the novel thus 'help[s] Gaskell make her case for integrating women within the public sphere' (37).

9 In this respect, I agree with Rosemarie Bodenheimer, who treats women's social fiction as a genre that 'represent[s] the range of interconnected social dilemmas that constitute their [women's] own ideological membership in the Victorian middle class' (*Politics* 17).

10 Important early examples include Harriet Martineau's *The Rioters* (1827) and 'A Manchester Strike' (1832), Charlotte Tonna's *Helen Fleetwood* (1841), Frances Trollope's *Michael Armstrong, the Factory Boy* (1840), and Elizabeth Stone's *William Langshawe* (1842). See Kestner and Fryckstedt for further background on the tradition of women's social problem fiction in England.

11 See, for example, Krueger (*Reader's Repentance* 172-3) and Lansbury (17-19).

12 Other references include Alice's description of her childhood home (69-70) and her delirious return to this space (309).

13 This motif is also used in Elizabeth and William Gaskell's poem, 'Sketches Among the Poor'.

14 In this regard, I agree with Jenkins, who argues that Gaskell's Unitarianism leads her to view 'sentimental' interventionism 'as a model of behavior to be neither limited to women nor restricted to the domestic sphere' (96).

15 The *Athenaeum*, for example, proclaims, 'we have met with few pictures of life among the working classes at once so forcible and so fair' (Chorley, 'Mary Barton' 1050). See also Charles Kingsley's review of *Mary Barton* in *Fraser's Magazine* (429-32) and John Forster's review in the *Examiner*.

16 See especially Gaskell's letters to Dickens (*Letters* 98-100).

17 For further discussion of the literary and sociological factors that contributed to the discourse on the female author in periodicals during the 1850s, see Helsinger, Lauterbach, Sheets and Veeder's *The Woman Question*.

18 Showalter (73-99), Thompson (*Reviewing* 8-24), Tuchman and Fortin (175-202).

19 Martineau was a contributor to the *Westminster Review*, the *Edinburgh Review* and many other periodicals during the 1850s. She was also a leader writer for the *Daily News* from 1852 to 1866. Gaskell contributed fiction and articles to *Household Words* from 1850 to 1858. She also contributed to *Fraser's Magazine* during the 1850s. George Eliot contributed to the *Westminster Review* from 1851 to 1857 and to the *Leader* from 1851 to 1856. Most of these writers' contributions were anonymously published. However, some articles appeared with initials (e.g., Martineau's 'Miss Sedgwick's Works' and Gaskell's 'Shams'). Only rarely did these authors include their names, and usually only

because it was a requirement for a particular periodical (e.g., Gaskell's 'Robert Gould Shaw', published in *Macmillan's Magazine*).

20 Oliphant, 'Modern Novelists, Great and Small' (1855), Eliot, 'Silly Novels by Lady Novelists' (1856), Martineau, 'Villette' (1853).

21 See Rubenius (38-56). Gaskell was also connected to the Langham Place Group through her association with Eliza Fox (Uglow, *Gaskell* 311).

22 The *Wellesley Index to Victorian Periodicals* suggests that there is some doubt as to whether this article was written by Gaskell. However, since the article is published with the initials 'E. C. G'. and Gaskell is known to have contributed to *Fraser's Magazine* during this period, I am assuming that she was the author of the article. See also Unsworth & Morton's findings.

23 A brief history of *Fraser's Magazine* is included in the *Wellesley Index to Victorian Periodicals*, Vol. 2.

24 See, for example, Krueger ('Female Paternalist') and Rubenius (60-61).

25 An etching of Haworth is also used as a frontispiece in the biography. Many readers, including George Henry Lewes and Virginia Woolf, responded as much to the biography's depiction of Haworth as they did its representation of Charlotte Brontë (Uglow, *Gaskell* 429).

26 The eye of the urban investigator is also trained on social institutions that produce unsanitary living conditions. In Gaskell's *Life*, Cowan Bridge School is described as an especially unhealthy institutional environment. Descriptions of the food (42) and punishments (45) at the school are graphic examples of this investigatory perspective. Of course, Gaskell's exposure of the failures of middle-class institutions in *The Life of Charlotte Brontë* was just as controversial as her analysis of lower-class domestic life in her social fiction. See Gérin for a discussion of the controversy surrounding the publication of *The Life of Charlotte Brontë* (189-201). This controversy reflects larger critical concerns about the tendency of literary biography to intrude too far into the realm of domestic privacy. See Henry Brougham's review of the *Memoirs of Lady Hester Stanhope* and R. A. Willmott's review of *Homes and Haunts of the British Poets*. For a general discussion of contradictory Victorian attitudes toward middle-class domestic privacy, see Trodd, who argues that Victorians were torn by the 'desire to raise the roofs and examine the secret crimes which may be festering beyond the reach of public opinion ... [and] the need to keep the home as a sacred space, inviolable by the external world and under no external surveillance' (4).

27 See Easson's 'Domestic Romanticism' for a discussion of the Romantic elements of Gaskell's characterization of Brontë. See also D'Albertis for a feminist interpretation of this romanticization ('Bookmaking').

28 Articles on the 'abused author' are too numerous to cite, but see, for example, 'Public Patronage of Men of Letters' (1846), 'English Journalism' (1846), and 'Appreciation of Literary Merit' (1852).

29 Gaskell includes many excerpts from Brontë's correspondence that address this issue, for example Brontë's explanation of her pseudonym (199) and her letters to G. H. Lewes (*Letters* 283, 293).

30 See Uglow for further discussion of Gaskell's treatment of Rigby's review (*Gaskell* 404).

31 Gaskell published 'The Golden Legend' and 'Spiritual Alchemy' in the *Athenaeum* in 1851 as well as 'Sermons and Sermonizers' in *Fraser's Magazine* in 1857.

32 See ('Bookmaking') and Bick for alternative interpretations of Gaskell's contradictory stance toward Brontë.

33 This theme appears elsewhere in women's writing of the 1850s, especially Elizabeth Barrett Browning's *Aurora Leigh* (1857), which foregrounds the conflict between women's artistic aspirations and social duties. In book 6, Aurora contemplates the conflict between 'Philosopher against philanthropist, / Academician against poet, man / Against woman, against the living, the dead,— / Then home, with a bad headache and worse jest!' (207). Gaskell reinforces the connection between her biography and *Aurora Leigh* by including a stanza from the poem on her title page.

34 See D'Albertis for further discussion of Gaskell's preoccupation with Brontë's 'morbidity' ('Bookmaking' 7-11).

35 Barbara Taylor (275-87) provides a useful overview of the development of the women's movement in the late 1850s and '60s. See also Tholfsen (197-242) for an examination of the decline in working-class radicalism during this period.

36 Harriet Martineau's *The Rioters* (1827) follows this general pattern.

37 See, for example, Charles Kingsley's statements about his misjudgment of Brontë and his subsequent conversion after reading Gaskell's *Life*. 'How I misjudged her!' he exclaims. 'Well you have done your work; & given us the picture of a valiant woman made perfect by sufferings' (Easson, *Critical* 398).

38 As Coral Lansbury points out, Gaskell's *Life* made Brontë 'as much a character of fiction as Jane Eyre. There are few areas of scholarship where the writer and her works are so conflated as with Charlotte Brontë ... The *Life of Charlotte Brontë* established a mode of critical procedure that continues to the present day. It is difficult to know when the Brontëan critic is speaking of Jane Eyre or Charlotte Brontë' (83).

39 See Ira Nadel (121-30) and Robin Colby (75-87) for discussion of Gaskell's strategies of self-representation in *The Life of Charlotte Brontë*.

CHAPTER 5

Gender and Representation: George Eliot in the 1850s and 60s

If for Elizabeth Gaskell obscurity was an obstacle women writers must overcome in order to be accepted by the literary establishment, for George Eliot it was a means to an end. Throughout her career, Eliot used anonymity and pseudonymity to distance her identity from her work. By creating 'George Eliot' as an intermediary persona between herself and her readers, Eliot was able to resist being defined according to cultural stereotypes of feminine writing and the 'abused woman author'. Eliot's early work emerged from within the narrative conventions of anonymous periodical journalism and the critical discourse on female authorship. Eliot employed pseudonymity in her early novels as a means of capitalizing on the public's desire to know and to gender authorial identity. Instead of providing the details of her life as a pathetic or scandalous answer to public inquiries, she presented the public with the unknowable 'George Eliot', who expressed a cultured rather than essentially gendered perspective on moral questions.

In redefining the woman author, Eliot, like Gaskell, turned away from the politics of class that had authorized women's writing careers in the 1830s and '40s. Instead of premising her entry into public discourse on the necessity of public activism on behalf of the poor, Eliot justified her participation on the basis of her role in improving middle-class self-culture and literary taste. In doing so, she was anticipating the work of Matthew Arnold, who in the 1860s would lead the campaign for reforming middle-class culture and education. At the same time, she was continuing the work of Johnstone, Martineau, and Gaskell, who had defined women's literacy practices as appropriate objects of middle-class reform. However, Eliot was less interested in attacking the critical establishment for its abuse of women authors than she was interested in drawing attention to the inadequacy of contemporary models of female authorship.

As a reviewer and assistant editor for the *Westminster Review* during the 1850s, George Eliot had a vital role to play in shaping debates over women's authorial careers. The first part of this chapter will examine Eliot's 'Silly Novels by Lady Novelists' (1856), demonstrating ways that it contributed to the debate over the status of women authors in Victorian society. The definitions of cultured authorship theorized and embodied in the 'Silly Novels' essay had important implications for the development of George Eliot's first work of fiction, *Scenes of Clerical Life*, serially published in *Blackwood's Magazine* in 1857. The second part of this chapter will examine Eliot's career in the 1860s, demonstrating ways that her authorial identity was shaped within the context of debates over authorial signature and controversies over female suffrage. The final part of this chapter will explore

118   FIRST-PERSON ANONYMOUS

how Eliot's novel *Felix Holt* (1866) emerges from within this context, emphasizing self-culture as a prerequisite for political representation. In *Felix Holt*, Eliot evokes the social problem novel and the reformist periodical as genres associated with the rise of the Victorian woman author only to point to their ineffectuality as vehicles for women's writing in the modern age. Eliot ensures her place in the canon of English letters by defining a model of authorship that is premised on culture rather than on notions of essential femininity or feminist self-advocacy.

George Eliot and Periodical Journalism in the 1850s

In 1846, Eliot began her career in journalism as a contributor to the *Coventry Herald and Observer*. In 1851, she became a writer for the *Westminster Review* and served as a sub-editor for the periodical from 1852 to 1854. She also contributed to the *Leader* and *Fraser's Magazine* during the 1850s (Pinney 4: 452-55). Eliot's work in periodical journalism played an important role in shaping her identity as a cultural critic and reader of contemporary literature. Her experiences as a contributor to the *Westminster Review* were especially influential in the development of her thinking about issues of gender and authorship. Writing anonymously for the *Westminster*, Eliot, like Gaskell, entered into debates over the role and status of the female author. Eliot's most important contribution to this debate was 'Silly Novels by Lady Novelists', an article published in the *Westminster Review* in 1856. In this article, Eliot criticizes women's novels in order to make an argument for more cultured models of women's authorship. At several points 'Silly Novels By Lady Novelists' seems to fit within the mid-Victorian discourse aimed at defining gendered styles of writing.[1] In typical fashion, Eliot's essay applauds the accomplishments of the best women writers, praising the 'precious specialty, lying quite apart from masculine aptitudes and experience' that distinguishes women's literary craft (162). Employing the vituperative rhetoric of contemporary criticism, Eliot chastises those women who write on subjects outside their proper realm of experience:

> There seems to be a notion abroad among women, rather akin to the superstition that the speech and actions of idiots are inspired, and that the human being most entirely exhausted of common sense is the fittest vehicle of revelation. To judge from their writings, there are certain ladies who think that an amazing ignorance, both of science and of life, is the best possible qualification for forming an opinion on the knottiest moral and speculative questions (148-49).

This passage suggests that the limited education and experience of the lady novelist make her incapable of comprehending the 'knottiest moral and speculative questions', which presumably are more accessible to the narrator. However, the essay does not merely focus on satirizing women's writing; it also aims to improve and reform their literary efforts. In pursuing this end, Eliot defines the ideal woman author in this way:

> A really cultured woman, like a really cultured man, is all the simpler and the less obtrusive for her knowledge; it has made her see herself and her opinions in something like just proportions; she does not make it a pedestal from which she flatters herself that she commands a complete view of men and things, but makes it a point of observation from which to form a right estimate of herself (155-56).

Eliot's carefully balanced phrases, 'a really cultured woman, like a really cultured man', suggest that self-cultivation brings an equality that is beyond conventional gender categories. She implies that successful authorship is less a matter of gender than of self-culture. Rather than seeking an all-encompassing perspective, the woman writer must turn her investigative gaze inward, thus developing the kind of self-knowledge that will enable her to communicate effectively with others.

By defining culture as a characteristic that is located outside gender-defined literary genres, Eliot establishes a role for the woman author that is similar to the authorial role of the anonymous woman journalist: she is not limited by confining definitions of appropriate feminine subject matter but by her own level of self-cultivation. She does not display knowledge as a way of gaining greater personal attention but as the means by which she can develop taste in herself and her readers. Such a definition fits well within the editorial guidelines of the *Westminster Review*—partly written by Eliot—that promise to 'elevate the standard of the public taste, in relation both to artistic perfection and moral purity' (Eliot & Chapman, 'Prospectus' 7). As a woman journalist constructing and working within these guidelines, Eliot tried to create a narrative voice that presented a cultured point of view. Instead of communicating 'information, which is the raw material of culture', the woman author must provide 'sympathy, which is its subtlest essence' (156). In other words, rather than displaying her knowledge, she enters into sympathetic union with her readers, enabling them to gain a broader moral perspective. She is able to establish this sympathetic relationship with others by exercising 'self-criticism', which enables her to judge her own abilities and limitations (161).

In her attempt to reform women's authorship, Eliot places the onus not only on women writers but on the critical establishment, which encourages women's mediocrity. She criticizes the misplaced chivalry of reviewers, who 'tell one lady novelist after another that they "hail" her productions "with delight"' and thereby give an inflated estimation of literary value (161). When blaming the critical establishment for the low quality of women's fiction, Eliot makes it clear that she is not attacking it for its abuse of poor and neglected women writers. The average lady novelist, Eliot claims, is not a woman who writes in order to stave off poverty; rather, she writes in order to relieve her 'busy idleness' and to satisfy her literary pretensions (162).

120   FIRST-PERSON ANONYMOUS

Following in this same vein, Eliot constructs the lady novelist as an upper-class woman who writes about aristocratic life. As reviewer, Eliot aligns herself with the middle-class liberal readers of the *Westminster Review,* who would object to the typical woman writer's aristocratic bias:

> The fair writers have evidently never talked to a tradesman except from a carriage window; they have no notion of the working classes except as 'dependants'; they think £500 a year a miserable pittance; Belgravia and 'baronial halls' are their primary truths; and they have no idea of feeling interest in any man who is not at least a great landed proprietor, if not a prime minister. It is clear that they write in elegant boudoirs, with violet-coloured ink and a ruby pen (142).

As many critics have noticed, the narrative voice in passages such as this one seems to construct a male authorial persona. The narrator seems offended that liberal middle-class men, such as those who read the *Westminster Review,* are excluded from 'feeling interest' in novels by lady writers. After all, most liberal readers of and contributors to the *Westminster* are not likely to fit the mold of a Tory 'great landed proprietor'.

However much Eliot's narrative voice in 'Silly Novels' seems to conform to a middle-class masculine ideal, it is difficult to classify in strictly gendered terms. Though the essay might seem patriarchal in tone, it does not contain a single passage where the 'editorial we' is directly associated with masculine gender markers. For the most part, Eliot's objection to lady novelists seems to be based more on class than on gender. While she brutally satirizes upper-class women writers, she singles out middle-class women as examples of the very best contemporary authors. Eliot makes positive mention of Gaskell, Brontë, Martineau, and Stowe, pointing out that 'fiction is a department of literature in which women can, after their kind, fully equal men' (162). By including the hedge 'after their kind', Eliot implies that women's writing is essentially different than men's writing, though potentially equal in terms of quality and accomplishment. This implication is of course contradicted by the fact that Eliot's own journalistic voice is difficult to classify in essentializing terms.

Eliot emphasizes the gender ambiguity of her editorial perspective through shifts in point of view. For example, she takes on the voice of the average man in a long passage in quotation marks meant to personify the 'popular prejudice' against women novelists: 'After a few hours' conversation with an oracular literary woman, or a few hours' reading of her books, [men] are likely enough to say, "After all, when a woman gets some knowledge, see what use she makes of it! Her knowledge remains an acquisition, instead of passing into culture . . "'. (154, 155). After another half of a page written in the voice of the average man, the editorial persona re-enters the narrative, remarking that 'it is true that the men who come to such a decision on such very superficial and imperfect observation may not be among the wisest in the world' (155). Such masculine attitudes are 'unconsciously encouraged by many women who have volunteered themselves as representatives of the feminine intellect' (155). In this way, the 'editorial we' defines itself in opposition to both the average man and the typical female author.

The gender ambiguity of Eliot's narrative voice in 'Silly Novels' reflects the instability of gender identifications in the editorial voice of periodical journalism during the 1850s. The *Westminster* not only employed a woman—George Eliot herself—as its assistant editor during this period but also employed some prominent women as contributors, most notably Jane Sinnett and Harriet Martineau. Given the fact that many literary women of the period mention the *Westminster* in their letters, it is also likely that the periodical had a mixed-gender readership. One quality most of the readers and writers of the *Westminster* had in common was their middle-class social status. Consequently, though the narrative voice of the *Westminster* inscribes gender ambiguities when defining the cultured writer and reader, its class loyalties are more clearly defined. Working within the ideological parameters and editorial guidelines of the *Westminster Review,* Eliot participated in the critical project of redefining of the author in terms of class and self-culture rather than strictly in terms of gender. Self-culture, for Eliot, comes to stand for the moral virtue and educated wisdom inherent within middle-class notions of individuality. Through self-improvement and self-cultivation, middle-class authors define their work less in terms of essential gender than in terms of moral and aesthetic value.

The narrative voice of Eliot's *Westminster* essays is an important precursor to the narrative voice in her early fiction. Eliot's experience as an anonymous reviewer and editor undoubtedly made her sensitive to the travails that could face the woman journalist who went on to publish book-length works under her own name. By publishing her first stories anonymously in *Blackwood's Magazine* in 1857, Eliot avoided public exposure—that mixture of adulation and censure that plagued high-profile women writers such as Harriet Martineau and Elizabeth Gaskell. *Blackwood's,* like the *Westminster Review,* catered to a middle-class audience, but because it was a magazine rather than a review, it was more self-consciously gender-balanced in its tone and contents. In addition to including reviews of contemporary literature, *Blackwood's* included serialized fiction, essays, poetry, and humor. *Blackwood's* employed some women writers during the 1850s, most notably Margaret Oliphant. As gender-inclusive as the audience and contributors list of *Blackwood's* might have been, its editorial voice sometimes took on a masculine gendering. It was well known that the magazine was directed by the men of the Blackwood family—and that its contributors included some of the most well known male writers of the age. The personification of *Blackwood's* editor as 'Christopher North', a middle-class Tory gentleman, also contributed to the magazine's conservative, masculine tone in its early years. However, by the 1850s most articles in *Blackwood's* were not written in masculine personae. Thus, the narrative voice of the periodical as a whole was ambiguously gendered. This complex point of view provided Eliot with model for her own form of narration that alternately reinforced and challenged the assumption of a male narrator.

122   FIRST-PERSON ANONYMOUS

With this journalistic context in mind, we can begin to understand the complex narrative structures and gender relationships in 'Amos Barton', the first story in the series that would later be known as *Scenes of Clerical Life*. Over the years most critics have interpreted the narrator of 'Amos Barton' as a masculine voice Eliot used to mask her feminine identity.[2] While it is impossible to deny that the narrator is sometimes personified as a man, a closer reading reveals that the narrative voice is much more complex in terms of class and gender than has commonly been assumed.

Early on in the story, the narrator situates herself in terms of political affiliation and class status. In the second paragraph, she makes it clear that she is not one of the earnest reformers who 'rejoices in the New Police, the Tithe Commutation Act, the penny-post, and all guarantees of human advancement' (41). Rather, her imagination 'does a little Toryism by the sly' and 'has an occasional tenderness for old abuses' (41). Following the politics of the periodical as a whole, the narrator thus defines herself as a middle-class Tory who is wary of reformist ideology. Throughout the story she demonstrates her skepticism of philanthropy, especially Barton's humorous attempts to preach to the pauper classes (59-66). As in *The Life of Charlotte Brontë,* the narrator of 'Amos Barton' defines herself as an investigator of middle-class domestic life. She voyeuristically observes the conversations and actions of others, inviting the reader to 'accompany' her in her investigations (44). The narrator and reader are often figured as invisible visitors in middle-class domestic spaces: 'And now that we are snug and warm with this little tea-party, while it is freezing with February bitterness outside, we will listen to what they are talking about' (46). However, unlike Gaskell's investigatory narrators, Eliot's narrator has no social abuses to expose. Though Milly Barton's death due to domestic overwork is presented as sentimentally tragic, it is not meant to exemplify a larger social problem that must be addressed in fictional form. Though the poverty of rural curates at first seems to be the cause the novel is addressing, this interest is soon replaced by moral concerns, especially the town's harsh judgment of the Bartons based on circumstantial evidence. The narrator's incursions into the domestic privacy of the middle classes are thus justified by the promise of improving readers' moral culture.

Like the middle-class inhabitants of Shepperton, readers must learn to develop moral sympathy for 'fellow-countrymen' of the middle classes (81). The narrator remarks that her desire is 'to stir your sympathy with commonplace troubles—to win your tears for real sorrow: sorrow such as may live next door to you—such as walks neither in rags nor in velvet, but in very ordinary decent apparel' (97). Positioning the reader between the upper and lower classes, the narrator seems at once to be lowering and raising the taste of readers so as to produce sympathetic communion among members of the middle class. The narrator hopes that her text will produce mutual sympathy not only in the extra-literary world of those who 'may live next door to you' but also within the context of the reading process. Following in the same vein as 'Silly Novels', the narrator of 'Amos Barton' suggests ways that reading habits can be reformed in order to make way for more cultured literacy practices. Instead of focusing on the critical establishment, she singles out 'lady readers' of novels as the special objects of her reformatory efforts (80). At the beginning of chapter five, she personifies the typical female reader as 'Mrs. Farthingdale ... who prefers the ideal in fiction; to whom tragedy means ermine tippets, adultery, and murder; and comedy, the adventures of some personage who is quite a "character"' (80). She goes on to spell out her prescription for reforming the taste of the female reader: 'Depend upon it, you would gain unspeakably if you would learn with me to see some of the poetry and the pathos, the tragedy and the comedy, lying in the experience of a human soul that looks out through dull grey eyes, and that speaks in a voice of quite ordinary tones' (81). In this way, she distinguishes her work from the silly novels produced by lady novelists and at the same time defines her reformatory project as the improvement of women's literary taste.

As much as Eliot identifies women readers as objects of reform in 'Amos Barton', she doesn't otherwise present her work as an alternative model of feminine or feminist literary practice. As in 'Silly Novels', class allegiances are more easily discernable than gender identifications. On one hand, 'Amos Barton' posits a masculine narrative voice, usually identified by the pronoun 'I', which takes on many of the same characteristics as the masculine editorial voice of *Blackwood's Magazine*. Light-hearted and droll, the narrator establishes his masculinity by making reference to heterosexual impulses shared with a male reader: 'You and I, too, reader, have our weakness, have we not? ... Perhaps it may lie in an excessive admiration for small hands and feet, a tall lithe figure, large dark eyes, and dark silken braided hair' (69). This is of course the same persona that constructs Milly as a domestic angel and the Countess Czerlaski as a flat stereotype of the vain and insensitive upper-class woman. In addition to objectifying and stereotyping women characters, the male narrator often reinforces the separation between his own knowledge and those areas of knowledge associated with women's culture. For example, chapter three concludes with the following: 'Chess is a silent game; and the Countess's chat with Milly is in quite an under-tone— probably relating to women's matters that it would be impertinent for us to listen to; so we will leave Camp Villa, and proceed to Milby Vicarage ...' (74). Here the narrator is depicted as a male listener who defines himself in opposition to the discourse of female culture—the 'women's matters' that are beyond the reach and interest of a coterie male readership.

However, as was the case in 'Silly Novels', 'Amos Barton' also encodes more gender-neutral narrative perspectives, usually signaled by the 'editorial we'. When describing Countess Czerlaski's plans to depart from Milby, the editorial voice of 'Amos Barton' seems to be inclusive of the Countess's female perspective: 'The thing we look forward to often comes to pass, but never precisely in the way we have imagined to ourselves. The Countess did actually leave Camp Villa before many months were past, but under circumstances which had not at all entered into her contemplation' (80). Here the 'editorial we' is presented as a universalized voice that includes the Countess' point of view rather than being narrowly defined in gendered terms.

Elsewhere in the story, the narrator claims to have an insider's knowledge of the same female matters that previously had been beyond the reach of her interest or understanding. Chapter seven begins in the voice of a male persona, saying, 'I can hardly bear to think of all the rough work she did with those lovely hands—all by the sly, without letting her husband know anything about it, and husbands are not clairvoyant' (99). However, as the passage continues, it becomes increasingly focused on representing those forms of knowledge that male readers—like Amos Barton himself—are incapable of accessing due to their insensitivity or obliviousness. Eliot continues, describing how Milly

> salted the bacon, ironed shirts and cravats, put patches on patches, and re-darned darns. Then there was the task of mending and eking out baby-linen in prospect, and the problem perpetually suggesting itself how she and Nanny *should* manage when there was another baby, as there would be before very many months were past (99).

The accumulation of this detail, quickly shifting into Milly's close third-person point of view, departs from the implied male point of view of other sections of the story. Once again, the narrator's perspective expands to include both masculine and feminine realms of knowledge. The death of Milly not only enables the citizens of Shepperton to sympathize with Amos Barton but also allows Amos Barton—and male readers—to enter into Milly's perspective, finally understanding the effects of over-work within the domestic sphere. By making diverse forms of gendered knowledge accessible to readers, the narrator attempts to help them develop a sympathy that crosses gender lines.

This universalizing stance is demonstrated in another passage in the story where the narrator reflects on the gendering of the creative process. Reflecting on Milly's superior skills as a seamstress, the narrator remarks, 'She was even trying to persuade her husband to leave off tight pantaloons, because if he would wear the ordinary gun-cases, she knew she could make them so well that no one would suspect the sex of the tailor' (58).[3] Read as a satirical analogy for the role of the female author in Victorian society, this passage pokes fun at the gendering of the author position. Just as Milly's tailoring would most likely be considered professional just as long as it weren't associated with her gendered persona, Eliot's writing would be considered serious just as long as she weren't identified as a female author. As a kind of inside joke played on readers, this passage begins to suggest the pleasure associated with playfully satirizing the public's desire for a gendered authorial persona.

Eliot's ambiguously gendered narrative voice in 'Amos Barton', like the narrative voice in 'Silly Novels', both constructs and subverts notions of essential gender and gendered writing. By publishing her stories in *Blackwood's* Eliot aligned her work with its class and gender identifications. In addition, she used its policy of anonymity to draw attention to the constructedness of her own literary persona. Because the 'I' and 'we' of *Scenes of Clerical Life* did not connect to an authorial name, they called into question the notion of referentiality between author and narrator. The gender and identity of the narrator thus became an unknowable puzzle that drew readers into the extra-literary world on a search for the real author. Consequently, the narrative voice of Eliot's early fiction was less of a disguise for her gender than it was an enticement to more complete understanding.

When Eliot made the decision to publish her stories in book form, she was no doubt aware that public fascination with its mysterious author would only increase. In order to create an additional barrier between herself and the public, she constructed the pseudonym 'George Eliot' to shield her from the prying inquiries of readers. As many critics have noted, such a strategy was a necessary defense given the irregularities of Eliot's private life and the essentializing discourse on women's writing in the periodicals.[4] But Eliot's pseudonymity was far from being strictly a device for defending herself against criticism. As Rosemarie Bodenheimer points out, pseudonymity enabled her to express a sense of 'play between genders' and multiple identities that had characterized even her earliest literary endeavors (*Real Life* 125). By adopting a pseudonym, Eliot attempted to reinforce the gender ambiguity of her authorial persona and to fuel the debate over gendered authorship. The pseudonym was different than Gaskell's 'Cotton Mather Mills' in some important respects. Gaskell used her pseudonym to establish her authority as a urban investigator within the specific context of *Howitt's Journal*. George Eliot, on the other hand, used her pseudonym not only as an authorizing gesture within the male dominated field of professional writing but also as a marketing device that enabled her to establish herself as a literary celebrity.

Early in her career, Eliot discovered that the gender ambiguity of her pseudonym could be used as a marketing strategy—both for increasing the sale of her books and for establishing her work within the high-culture literary canon.[5] Indeed, the pseudonymous publication of *Scenes* in 1858 ignited an unprecedented furor as critics publicly and privately attempted to reconstitute the gender and identity behind the mysterious pseudonym 'George Eliot'. Members of the reading public searched the society rolls of midlands England, uncovering suspects from among the country clergy. After the publication of *Adam Bede,* letters to the editor of *The Times* identified a Mr. Liggins as the probable George Eliot, and to the real George Eliot's amusement—and later annoyance—Mr. Liggins did not deny the honor.

In response to this critical frenzy, many prominent authors added their own speculations. Martineau and Gaskell, for example, engaged in a protracted correspondence over the identity of the author of *Scenes of Clerical Life*. At first Gaskell was persuaded by evidence that Liggins was the author, but later she changed her opinion based on the accumulation of evidence in support of Marian Evans' authorship (Gaskell, *Letters* 583-86). Martineau played a key role in convincing Gaskell and others that Evans was the real author behind the George Eliot persona (Martineau, 'Letter to Bracebridge'). As Sara Hennell writes to Martineau in 1859, 'It is very kind of you to bother yourself in the extinguishing of the multitude of false reports [about Liggins' authorship]—& I am particularly glad that you should set

Mrs. Gaskell right' ('Letter'). Martineau's packet of evidence was passed around privately, eventually falling into Gaskell's possession (Gaskell, *Letters* 594).

Such attempts to reconstitute the authorial gender and identity of anonymous and pseudonymous authors have a rich history in nineteenth-century critical writing, beginning with the critical fury over the anonymous publication of Scott's Waverley novels. Other examples include the critical discourse surrounding the anonymous publication of Elizabeth Gaskell's *Mary Barton* (1848) and the pseudonymous publication of Charlotte Brontë's *Jane Eyre* (1849). Well aware of this history, Eliot and Lewes made an effort to capitalize on the critical interest in Eliot's identity. In a letter to Blackwood about the delayed publication of *Adam Bede,* Lewes writes,

> G. E. is very uncomfortable about the delay in printing. He thinks—and I agree with him—that *mystery* as to authorship will have a great effect in determining critical opinion ... When Jane Eyre was finally known to be a woman's book the tone noticeably changed. Not that I believe in the possibility of anything adventitious permanently hurting a *good* book, but there is always something temporary in the success of a novel, and one may as well secure all adventitious aids (qtd. in Haight 268).

As one of many 'adventitious aids' that could be used to secure critical—and financial—success for an author, the pseudonymous publication of *Adam Bede* created just the kind of 'mystery' that would stimulate favorable reviews and sales.[6] Of course the driving force behind this mysteriousness was the notion of gender itself. Because the gendering of the author position was of such cultural and ideological importance in mid-Victorian print culture, its suppression generated just the kind of critical furor that could be the springboard to blockbuster literary status. Indeed, soon after its publication, *Adam Bede* was a critical and financial success. Most periodical reviews were favorable and included speculations on the sex of the mysterious George Eliot.

When the name 'Marian Evans' came to be inextricably connected to the pseudonym 'George Eliot' in the summer of 1859, Eliot worried that her financial and literary status would be imperiled. But this anxiety was soon replaced by the desire to further capitalize on the success associated with the 'George Eliot' name. After completing the 'Lifted Veil' in 1859, Eliot hoped that John Blackwood would make an exception to his usual practice of anonymous publication so that the story would appear in *Blackwood's Magazine* under her pseudonym. Blackwood responded by suggesting that he 'thought it better not to fritter away the prestige' that would accompany the publication of her next major work of fiction (qtd. in Haight 297).

However, as Eliot soon found out, Blackwood was less concerned with the loss of prestige associated with employing her pseudonym than he was concerned about the negative connotations associated with the 'George Eliot' name. When it became time to negotiate the publication of *The Mill on the Floss,* Blackwood was steadfast in his opposition to pseudonymous publication, proposing instead to serialize the novel anonymously in *Blackwood's Magazine:*

> In the Magazine we would not put any author's name, and it would be great fun to watch the speculations as to the author's life. The style would be to me easily recognizable, but no one, especially of the puffing writing and publishing order, would suppose that we would throw away such an advantage as putting the magic words 'George Eliot' at the head of a series of papers (qtd. in Haight 307).

Craftily written as it was, Blackwood's rationale for anonymous publication was not enough to convince George Eliot. She argued that 'publication in Maga [*Blackwood's*], in the case of a new writer concerning whose works there is some expectation and curiosity, would inevitably reduce what would otherwise be the certain demand for three-volumed copies' (*Letters* 3: 151). Finally, after a rather protracted and somewhat contentious correspondence with Eliot, Blackwood finally admitted that he objected to the 'withdrawal of the incognito' because it might 'prove a disadvantage' to Eliot's reputation (qtd. in Haight 315). In her response to this letter, Eliot criticized Blackwood's 'depreciatory view' of her proposal and proceeded to investigate other possible venues for publishing *The Mill on the Floss* (3: 218). But in the end she managed to convince Blackwood to publish her novel just as she liked—in three volumes with her pseudonym on the fly page.

What this interchange demonstrates is that for George Eliot pseudonymity and anonymity were not interchangeable narrative devices. If *The Mill on the Floss* had been published anonymously, Eliot would have lost any prestige associated with its success. In order to fashion a career as a literary sage, Eliot knew that she must offer readers and critics a signifier for the authorial source of the text, even if it were just the name of a fictional persona. To choose anonymity would be to assume a safer course, but not a more profitable one. Eliot's pseudonym enabled her to capitalize on her growing fame while still complicating authorial gender.[7] While at first she feared the association between the names 'Marian Evans' and 'George Eliot', she soon learned that a pseudonym could take on its own complex significations that were at once both dependent on and independent of those attached to the name of the historical author.

Even with the financial success brought on by the use of her pseudonym, Eliot still seemed to feel uncomfortable about her new status as a high-profile authorial identity. Like Martineau, she feared being constructed by the popular media as the latest literary lion, whose personal life was fair game in public interpretations of her novels. Such literary lionism in Eliot's view was a form of egotism that could have devastating effects on her work (*Letters* 3: 99). In order to recapture the privacy and freedom from essentialized gender definitions she had experienced as an anonymous author—while still capitalizing on the marketability of her pseudonym—Eliot needed to complicate the relationship between the names 'Marian Evans' and 'George Eliot' in a way that would free her from both

128   FIRST-PERSON ANONYMOUS

essentializing discourses on female authorship and unwanted intrusions into her personal life.

One of the most important means Eliot used to re-establish this indeterminacy in her authorial identity was to continue to use her pseudonym even after her identity became known to the public. As Edward Dowden would later remark, Eliot's pseudonym became a 'second self' that 'stands at some distance from the primary self ... [and that] utters secrets, but secrets which all men of all ages are to catch; while, behind it, lurks well pleased the veritable historical self secure from impertinent observation and criticism' (403).[8] In this respect, Eliot's approach to authorial self-naming can be usefully contrasted to that of Elizabeth Gaskell. While both authors published anonymously in the periodicals throughout the 1850s, they differed in their approach to authorial signature when publishing book-length texts. As the author of *The Life of Charlotte Brontë*, Gaskell used her own name as a signifier for a new kind of female subjectivity—the middle-class woman whose advanced literacy practices could expose the oppressive conditions faced by women writers in the middle-class home and within the critical establishment. Eliot, on the other hand, used a pseudonym into problematize notions of stable authorial identity based on gender.

By the end of the 1850s, periodical reviews were beginning to respond to the gender complexity of Eliot's literary identity. In their reviews of *The Mill on the Floss,* many journalists seem genuinely confused about how to treat Eliot's authorial gender and name. Though reviewers knew that 'George Eliot' was Marian Evans, they still often had difficulty reconciling these separate identities with the complex narrative voice they saw displayed in her fiction. E. S. Dallas, a reviewer for *The Times,* places quotation marks around George Eliot's name throughout his review. '"George Eliot" is as great as ever', he begins his article. 'She has produced a second novel, equal to her first in power, although not in interest' (Carroll, *Critical* 131). His use of quotation marks—especially when followed by feminine pronouns—calls attention to the difficulty of establishing direct referentiality between the historical, gendered author and the fictionalized author of the work in question. Though Dallas' intent most likely was to emphasize the fact that 'George Eliot' was a pseudonym for a female author, the net effect is an ambiguity in terms of authorial gender and identity. In this way, Eliot's work began to take on the same complex gendering that had been characteristic of her periodical writing and early fiction.

The gender ambiguity of the narrator in *The Mill on the Floss* made some critics question its sexual identification. While many reviews objected to the sensuality of Eliot's treatment of the romantic magnetism between Maggie Tulliver and Stephen Guest, the *Saturday Review* seemed especially uncomfortable with the same-sex eroticism implied by Eliot's narrative gaze. Referring to the scene where Stephen kisses Maggie's arm in a fit of passion, the reviewer writes,

> There is nothing wrong in writing about such an act, and it is the sort of thing that does sometimes happen in real life; but we cannot think that the conflict of sensation and

principle raised in a man's mind by gazing at a woman's arm is a theme that a female novelist can touch on without leaving behind a feeling of hesitation, if not repulsion, in the reader ('The Mill' 471).

The 'conflict of sensation' this anonymous reviewer describes seems to be a response not only to the gender indeterminacy of the George Eliot persona but more importantly to the sexual ambiguity of the narrative gaze, which seems to be male and yet belongs to the female identity behind the masculine persona. Here Eliot's complexly gendered narrative perspective becomes a kind of dangerously roving gaze that does not know the proper bounds of gender-defined passionate impulse.

While Eliot's complexly gendered narrative voice in *The Mill on the Floss* caused a crisis of representation in literary reviews, it provided an opportunity for other reviewers, such as Dinah Mulock Craik, to theorize androgyny as an alternative to feminine authorial identity. In her review of *The Mill on the Floss* written for *Macmillan's Magazine*, Craik, like Dallas, places the name 'George Eliot' in quotation marks. However, unlike Dallas, she insists on using male pronouns as referents to the authorial name: 'Another impression made strongly by the first work of "George Eliot", and repeated by "his" (we prefer to respect the pseudonym) second, is the earnestness, sincerity, and heart-nobility of the author' ('To Novelists' 444). Insisting later in the article that the novel displays 'sexless intelligence', Craik further questions the referentiality of the authorial name—both in terms of gender and identity (446). This treatment of Eliot's pseudonymous status was most likely influenced by Craik's own experience as an author[9] and by her stance on women's emancipation. In her series of essays, 'A Woman's Thoughts About Women', published serially in *Chambers' Edinburgh Journal,* Craik defines authorship as an ideal profession for women because it allows them to express their artistry while still maintaining domestic privacy, thereby avoiding the 'corporeality', of public performance (87). With their sexed identities separated from their 'genius', women writers could publish their work widely and still 'sit as quiet by our chimney-corner, live a life as simple and peaceful as any happy "common woman" of them all' (87). In this way, Craik suggests that a correspondence between historical and fictional identities is secondary to the quality and meaning of the literary work itself.

What these critical responses to *The Mill on the Floss* demonstrate is an instability in the gender definitions that had motivated reviews of women's novels throughout the 1850s. Unable (or unwilling) to attach the authorial name to a historical identity, critics struggled to find the language to describe Eliot's narrative voice. This conflict of interpretation was in many ways produced by the narrative conventions that Eliot adapted from the periodical press and re-employed in her fiction writing. These narrative techniques enabled Eliot to capitalize on the desire for knowledge of authorial gender and identity and also enabled her to place her work within the category of sexless literary achievement.[10] Of course, what this really meant to Eliot was that she could begin to construct herself as a professional

130 FIRST-PERSON ANONYMOUS

writer, who as N. N. Feltes has remarked, was in a position to control the 'conditions, terms, and content' of her work (219).[11] In this way, she could begin to locate her work within the realm of high-culture literary production—a domain of professional writing which was increasingly defined as a masculine preserve (Tuchman & Fortin).

Eliot's construction of a complexly gendered authorial identity enabled her to establish herself as a moral instructor, who, like Matthew Arnold, was capable of elevating the standard of public taste. In composing *Romola,* she writes that her

> predominant feeling is,—not that I have achieved anything, but—that great, great facts have struggled to find a voice through me, and have only been able to speak brokenly. That consciousness makes me cherish the more any proof that my work has been seen to have some true significance by minds prepared not simply by instruction, but by that religious and moral sympathy with the historical life of man which is the larger half of culture (*Letters* 4: 97).

In this way, Eliot constructs writing and reading as processes that allow both writer and reader to overcome the limitations of individual identity and enter into the realm of culture. As a replacement for identity, culture enables writers and readers to enter into sympathetic union with others. Of course such a separation from individuality could only be partial or temporary, as Eliot demonstrated in her own career as a pseudonymous writer. In order to establish herself as a Victorian sage, Eliot could not disown individuality completely; in order to establish an *oeuvre* and a healthy bank account, she needed an authorial stand-in that would help readers to categorize and interpret her work. But as we have seen, Eliot was careful to make sure that this categorization was not strictly carried out on gendered terms.

The construction of Eliot's complex literary persona and her sympathetic reader can be seen as a form of resistance to the essentializing discourses on gender and authorship circulating within literary culture during the 1850s. Like Gaskell, Eliot was interested in exploring the ways that middle-class women's writing could be liberated from confining definitions of feminine writing and reading practices. In attempting to fashion more sympathetic yet rigorous readers for women's fiction, Eliot had much in common with Gaskell, whose *Life of Charlotte Brontë* aimed to reform the critical practices that impeded women's writing careers. In the careers of both writers during the 1850s, the cause of the woman writer came to be defined as an alternative but still politicized motivation for women's writing that would replace the evangelical and reformist models of earlier days. Yet Gaskell's and Eliot's contributions to the debate over the woman author during the 1850s differed in significant respects. Unlike Gaskell, Eliot did not believe that championing the case of the 'abused woman author' or embracing a high-profile gendered identity would lead to the elevation of women's literary reputations. While Gaskell believed that new forms of politicized literary recovery would improve the working conditions and critical reception of women authors, Eliot believed that only through the creation of new forms of narration would women be able to enter the realm of high-culture literary discourse. Further, Eliot believed that by defining a cultured and ambiguously gendered narrative personae, women writers enhance their status within the critical establishment.

Eliot's resistance to stereotypes of gendered authorship was dependent on the conventions of anonymous and pseudonymous publication associated with mid-Victorian print media—conventions that were for the most part abandoned as old-fashioned by the late 1860s. The next part of this chapter will explore how Eliot negotiated this epistemological shift within the publishing industry and within the context of her own career as a high-culture novelist. The discourse on authorial signature was connected to debates over literary canonicity and women's enfranchisement—controversies that shaped her social problem novel, *Felix Holt, the Radical* (1866).

Signature Wars: Anonymity and Political Representation in the 1860s

The ethics of anonymous journalism became a major critical preoccupation during the late 1850s and 1860s.[12] Some journalists claimed that anonymity was an essential component a free press because it enabled writers to express controversial political viewpoints without as much fear of personal exposure and liability.[13] In order for the press to speak truth, some journalists argued, it must be separated from the opinions and interests of the individual. This position is perhaps most clearly articulated by E. S. Dallas in his articles on journalism published in *Blackwood's Magazine* in 1859. Dallas argues that anonymous journalism functions as a 'reflection of public feeling, a representation of popular opinion' ('Popular' 181-82). Within the broader category of political representation, the press promised to act as a 'fourth estate' that would exert influence on public affairs. With the diversity of periodicals and newspapers, Dallas claims, 'every class has its organ; every topic finds a journal; every interest has a friend in the press' (181). Though Dallas does not explicitly refer to the indirect political representation offered to women by anonymous publication, he does discuss the importance of domestic privacy in maintaining a free press. Including the signatures of authors in periodicals and newspapers would subject private individuals to undue 'publicity' that would compromise the sanctity of the home and 'surrender to the vulgar gaze all our inmost thoughts and all our hidden life' (185). Such publicity would act as a deterrent to those authors who—like women—found it a personal necessity to 'draw the line between what ought to be public and what ought to be private' (185).

Despite the support of critics such as E. S. Dallas, the convention of anonymous publication was quickly becoming a relic of the past. Though periodicals such as *Blackwood's Magazine* clung to journalistic anonymity, the policy of signed publication became increasingly common in literary periodicals founded in the late 1850s and 1860s, including *Macmillan's Magazine* (1859-1900), the *Fortnightly Review* (1865-1900), and the *Contemporary Review* (1866-1900). The gradual movement away from anonymous publication had important implications for the development of women's literary careers in the late Victorian period. By requiring signature, editors made it increasingly difficult for women to engage in low-profile literary careers. While the celebrity associated with signed publication was attractive to many women who wanted to make names for themselves, it was a barrier to those who relied upon anonymity as a means of separating their private and public identities. The personal exposure associated with signed publication also made it more difficult for women to exert political influence since as female writers they might have a more difficult time treating conventionally masculine subject matter in their work.

As argued in previous chapters, Victorian women had a great deal at stake in maintaining a separation between their private lives and public careers. Anonymous publication allowed them to influence the direction of debates over social and political issues without exhibiting themselves as high-profile political celebrities and to engage in professional careers without being labeled 'public women'. During the 1850s and '60s, the importance of their anonymous contributions to periodical journalism was just beginning to gain recognition. In *Essays on Women's Work* (1865), Bessie Rayner Parkes observes that 'as periodicals have waxed numerous, so has female authorship waxed strong' (120). She then goes on to describe the role of journalism in providing middle-class women with employment and political influence:

> The magazines demanded short graphic papers, observation, wit, and moderate learning—women demanded work such as they could perform at home, and ready pay upon performance; the two wants met, and the female sex has become a very important element in the fourth estate (120-21).

Parkes points out that one of the main reasons women were so successful in adapting their talents to the periodical press was that it permitted them to maintain a sense of domestic privacy while still pursuing public careers. It is the 'easiest of all' careers for educated women, she contends, because 'its successful exercise demands little or none of that moral courage which more public avocations require' (121).

Parkes does not go so far as to predict the potential consequences of the gradual movement away from anonymous publication on women's writing careers. Indeed, though most journalists were aware of the vast contributions of women to periodical journalism, few acknowledged this fact when advocating for signature in a reformed periodical press. In his argument against anonymous publication in the *Fortnightly Review* (1865), Anthony Trollope points out that there are times when books must be published anonymously or pseudonymously in order to allow for the 'timidity' of female authors, but he allows no such exception for the women authors of periodical literature (492). According to Trollope, whenever journalists attempted subjects such as science, theology, social matters, and politics—those subjects coded 'masculine' within literary culture—the publication of the author's name was necessary to establish his credibility. To the extent that such articles are written by 'men who have studied such subjects with minds capable of comprehending them', they could be trusted as authoritative sources of information (495). This definition of authorship would of course exclude those women authors who had little access to the educational opportunities that would provide them with the kind of qualifications Trollope demands.

Another article in defense of signature published by Thomas Hughes in *Macmillan's Magazine* defines the desired masculinity not so much in terms of subject matter and qualifications but in terms of overall sensibility. He suggests that those who insist on hiding behind the anonymous 'editorial we' are guilty of transgressing the essential masculinity of the English author. Hughes writes, 'the habit of open dealing in all matters has been always acknowledged and reverenced as a manly—one may almost say, *the* manly—virtue, ever since there was a man on the earth' (his italics; 166). Hughes argues that anonymous publication is akin to speaking from 'behind a veil'—in other words, to adopt the trappings of femininity, using subterfuge and indirection as a way of gaining influence (166). Hughes thus suggests that signature would create a more 'manly' style of writing in the periodical press.[14]

At the same time that the convention of signed publication in periodicals such as *Macmillan's Magazine* and the *Fortnightly Review* encouraged women's visibility within print culture, the suffrage movement involved women in more high-profile forms of public activism, including public demonstrations, petition campaigns, and women-only pressure group journalism. Though the campaign for women's enfranchisement did not succeed until 1918, the success of other legislation aimed at improving women's legal status—the Matrimonial Causes Acts (1857, 1878) and the Married Women's Property Acts (1870, 1882)—proved that women's political activism could produce social change. As the debates over the Woman Question took shape around specific legislative campaigns, middle-class women intellectuals were increasingly called upon to use their names in service of the cause, both as signatories on petitions and as the authors of signed periodical essays.

During this period there arose the first women's pressure-group periodicals. The most significant of these was the *English Woman's Journal,* which provided a forum for discussions that would lead to the development of the middle-class women's movement in England. With its focus on issues of women's employment and education, the *English Woman's Journal* provided a model of how women could use pressure-group tactics to influence public policy.[15] However, because these periodicals were directed to a limited audience comprised mainly of like-minded readers, this influence was probably somewhat limited. It should not therefore surprise us that some of the most important documents in support of women's enfranchisement came from anonymous periodicals and newspapers.[16]

One of the most influential of these anonymous texts was Harriet Taylor's 'The Enfranchisement of Women', published in the *Westminster Review* in 1851. In this essay, Taylor argues that enfranchisement and improved educational opportunities would make women more forthright in their interactions with men, instead of resorting to 'indirectness' and 'artifice' to exert political influence (306). By developing a 'public spirit', women would become the equal companions of men and would be less likely to be motivated by self-interest and vanity in their relationships with others (307). Enfranchisement would not only improve the moral character of the middle-class household but would also liberate women's writing from the 'servilities of toadyism' required by their subordinate position within the literary establishment (310). Taylor argues that women 'depend on men's opinion for their literary as well as for their feminine successes', and consequently rarely have the courage to challenge conventional notions of 'correct' feminine behavior (310). Of course, by publishing her article anonymously, Harriet Taylor could not escape the conflict between her private identity and her public writing. Just as 'literary women' must force a separation between their domestic and professional lives, so does Taylor necessarily operate from within this same dilemma. Taylor suggests that enfranchisement can heal such public and private flaws in women's characters. Rather than engaging in covertly political forms of literary self-representation or domestic display, women would express their political viewpoints openly and with their names plainly in view.

The debate over the enfranchisement of women had much in common with debates over anonymous publication: anonymity and indirection are marked as feminine character flaws that can only be corrected if individuals are given the opportunity to merge their private and public identities. Just as advocates of signature believed that writers would become more honest and socially responsible if they were forced to attach their names to their work so did advocates of female enfranchisement believe that the vote would enable their constituencies to express their political viewpoints in more socially responsible ways. The debate over anonymity was not just about individual responsibility but also about individual social value. Many felt that journalism could only be considered a high-culture medium if it began paying more attention to the quality of its editors and contributors. In the most prestigious mainstream literary and political periodicals, especially those that advocated signature, 'quality' names usually meant masculine ones.[17]

Of course, questions of value also were a major point of contention in the debate over the enfranchisement of women and the lower classes. The debates over women's legal status during the 1860s were connected to debates over political representation associated with the second Reform Act (1867), which enfranchised thousands of working-class citizens. In 1867, John Stuart Mill proposed an amendment to the Reform Bill that substituted 'person' for 'man' in the language defining eligible voters (Helsinger et al. 2: 41-47). Though Mill's proposal was defeated in parliament, it still succeeded in inflaming the debate over women's enfranchisement in the periodical press. Consequently, at the same time that journalists debated whether workers were sufficiently cultured and disinterested to become responsible members of the electorate, they also debated whether women could embody these same social values. Were the subordinate political positions occupied by women expressions of their essential class and gender identity? Or was this subordinacy a result of imperfect social, educational, and political institutional arrangements? Put another way, to what extent was quality work—whether it was a periodical essay or a parliamentary vote—dependent on the identity of its 'author'?

Debates over these questions during the 1860s played an important role in further delineating a new kind of subjectivity for the middle-class woman: she must have political viewpoints separate from those of the men in her life, perspectives that were developed and refined through education and purposeful reading.[18] Yet the cultivation of her individual political standpoints must not devolve into the pursuit of separate class and gender interests.[19] Rather, her acts of self-cultivation must enable her to develop an Arnoldian sense of culture that would enable her to act disinterestedly for the public good.[20] In this sense, the role of the ideal political woman was similar to the image of the new woman author in the 1860s: she would represent certain gender and class interests by signing her name to her work while at the same time expressing a cultured, disinterested viewpoint on political, social, and literary questions.

Slippage between the debates over literary and political representation during the 1860s had important implications for the novel. For decades the social problem novel had provided an alternative medium for women to participate in debates on class and gender issues. However, with the decline of middle- and lower-class radicalism in the 1850s, the social problem novel fell into critical disfavor.[21] The movement toward the higher journalism in the 1860s corresponded with a movement toward the high-culture novel during this same period.[22] As the novel gradually came to be accepted as an art form, it also came to be associated with authorial signature. The realistic novel was thus disassociated from its roots in social activism and came to be understood as a medium for instilling timeless cultural values. Consequently, the anonymous, philanthropic author was seen as a relic of the past. When defining the kind of novel likely to cultivate culture in readers, critics theorized a form of realism located somewhere between gritty depictions of lower-class life and sentimentalized representations of upper-class manners.[23] For many critics, there was only one woman author whose work epitomized the new high-culture realism: George Eliot. John Morley, for example, praised Eliot's ability to '[steer] clear of the Charybdis of depraved realism, without falling into the Scylla of sentimentalism' ('George Eliot' 276). This middle-ground position enabled her to express a 'very rare natural temper fertilised by an uncommon culture' (277).

For Eliot the 1860s represented a decade of transition—from a career as an anonymous periodical essayist and pseudonymous novelist to a career as a high-culture literary icon. In the '60s, Eliot gradually gave up periodical journalism, devoting herself exclusively to fiction writing. In some sense, this shift also marked her movement away from the kind of direct intervention in debates over authorship, class, and gender that had characterized her career as a reviewer during the 1850s. However, though in her later career Eliot treated issues of gender and authorship more indirectly, her work was still deeply connected to critical debates over the gendering of literary and political authority in the 1860s.

Gender and Political Representation in *Felix Holt*

Was it unethical for women to attempt to influence politics indirectly through anonymous and pseudonymous authorship? Though Eliot never directly poses this question, it informs and complicates her writing throughout the 1860s. Eliot had for the most part given up anonymous journalism by the mid-1860s, but she was still closely connected to the periodical press by virtue of her association with George Henry Lewes. When Lewes assumed the editorship of the *Fortnightly Review* in 1865, Eliot expressed approval of its policy of signed publication: 'the principle of signature, never before thoroughly carried out in England, has given it an exceptional dignity, and drawn valuable writers' (*Letters* 4: 211). Of course, she was counting herself among these 'valuable writers' since her essay, 'The Influence of Rationalism', was published in the *Fortnightly's* first number. Eliot's article was one of only twelve contributions by women published in the *Fortnightly Review* during the 1860s.[24] Like many of her fellow women reviewers, Eliot did not publish her article under a recognizably feminine signature: the name 'George Eliot', not 'Marian Evans', appears on the periodical's table of contents.

Given Eliot's approval of the *Fortnightly's* policy of signed publication, it is difficult to explain her reluctance to publish her own signature. By publishing her essay pseudonymously, Eliot seemed to be implying that a feminine signature would not necessarily produce 'quality' in the same way that a masculine signature would. Though for men signature might give their work an aura of 'dignity', for women it was likely to give the impression of vanity and egotism. The implied double-standard in Eliot's position on authorial signature reveals her own contradictory stance regarding issues of gender and representation in the political realm. Indeed, Eliot was just as contradictory in her position on women's literary representation in the periodicals as she was on the issue of women's political representation. Though Eliot expressed support for women's education and property rights, she was more reluctant to back the movement toward women's enfranchisement.[25] In a letter to John Morley, she attributes this reluctance to the 'peculiarities of my own lot which have caused me to have idiosyncrasies rather than an average judgment' (*Letters* 4: 364).

Eliot's contradictory, 'idiosyncratic' views on women's political representation informed her choice of subject matter for *Felix Holt* (1866). Though during the 1860s Eliot's novels were historical in focus, they also foregrounded contemporary issues of political and literary representation. As Catherine Gallagher points out, it was in the 1860s that Eliot began to reconsider the goals of a descriptive literary realism in response to debates over the viability of descriptive systems of political representation (*Industrial* 219-67). Just as John Stuart Mill and Matthew Arnold questioned whether universal suffrage would promote social development, Eliot questioned the ability of descriptive realism to promote the right kind of social change. Only through self-culture and education would members of the disenfranchised classes be qualified to participate as equal contributors to the political realm. Likewise, only by depicting culture as a realm of value separated from social reality would literature be able to promote a more progressive national politics.

If, as Gallagher suggests, this movement 'ended what we call the Condition of England Debate', what did this mean for the woman writer (265)? The movement toward the 'politics of culture' had an important impact on the definition of the woman author in Victorian society. While women of the 1830s and '40s justified their participation in political discourse on the basis of immediate social necessity—the threat of class warfare—by the 1860s the role of the political middle-class woman author had become more complex. As discussed in chapter four, the discourse on women's rights emerged as an autonomous field of activity beginning in the 1850s. Instead of justifying their writing as a means of intervening in political debates on behalf of the poor, women began to envision their literary practice as a means of interceding in political debates on behalf of their own sex. This conceptual shift explains why the industrial novel for the most part disappeared in the 1860s, gradually being replaced by the new woman novel as an alternative form of politically engaged fiction.

The development of the Woman Question as an autonomous realm of intellectual activity in the 1850s and '60s thus corresponds with the 'politics of culture' in some significant ways. Rather than using the realistic novel or the anonymous periodical as a way of indirectly influencing political affairs, the social problem novel and the women's periodical came to be associated with various forms of political self-advocacy and self-representation. Working within the context of these print media, the woman author justified her contributions to the political realm by virtue of her own disenfranchisement. In essence, she became her own cause.

Of course, it was just this sort of self-advocacy based on gender that Eliot so objected to in her own literary practice. As demonstrated in the first part of this chapter, Eliot attempted to problematize the connection between her private and authorial identities as a way of resisting socially imposed definitions of feminine writing. Such a separation of identities was difficult to achieve in the 1860s, when women's political invisibility was such a contentious public issue. In deciding to write a social problem novel, Eliot was entering a field of discourse that traditionally had foregrounded questions about the proper role for women in the public sphere. Eliot highlighted the changing circumstances surrounding women's participation in political discourse by drawing attention to the difficulties faced by women who had no access to political representation. But she did not propose self-advocacy as a solution to the problem of women's disenfranchisement. Rather, she proposed self-culture as an alternative to the kind of middle-class political activism constructed in social problem novels of an earlier age. While, as many feminist critics have noted, Eliot's depiction of the apolitical middle-class woman in *Felix Holt* in many ways demonstrates conservatism on the Woman Question,[26] it also subtly critiques the social conditions that placed women in a position of political dependency. As Alison Booth points out, the novel's treatment of gender politics suggests that there are 'irreconcilable differences between men and women and

138 FIRST-PERSON ANONYMOUS

their respective fields of power and influence in English society' ('Not All Men' 147). In addition, the novel indirectly expresses Eliot's concerns about the role of women in establishing a national literature and culture—and her desire to make a place for her own work within the increasingly narrow canon of high-culture novels.

By setting *Felix Holt* in the 1830s, Eliot was not only recalling the political struggles that defined the Victorian era but also the specific, gender-laden forms of discourse and models of feminine authorship that had emerged during the same time period. The same era that had expanded the franchise to thousands of middle-class male voters had also produced the middle-class woman writer, whose access to reformist journalism and social problem fiction had opened up new realms of influence in the public sphere. As Eliot well knew, the 1830s had also produced some of the first organized attempts to extend the franchise to women. Writing in the late 1860s—when the journalistic anonymity that had facilitated women's participation in public discourse was under attack and when the debates over the second Reform Bill once again brought the issue of women's enfranchisement to public attention—Eliot was bringing together the two historical time periods as a way of comparing and contrasting the issues of class, gender, and representation that characterized each age. To write a social problem novel was to evoke a very specific set of generic conventions that had been defined as old-fashioned and obsolete within literary culture. Eliot self-consciously employed these generic conventions in order to point to their obsolescence and to propose a new model of women's literary practice. Eliot's reconstruction of the social problem novel thus reinforces cultural instabilities about the status of the popular media—and women—in shaping social reality.

Felix Holt employs many of the conventions associated with earlier social problem novels: it integrates domestic and political subject matter and suggests ways that class divisions can be healed through the dissemination of middle-class values and culture. But *Felix Holt* departs from the conventions of social fiction in some significant ways. While earlier social problem novels stressed the immediacy of the social crises they depicted, *Felix Holt* is set thirty-four years in the past. Though certainly contemporary debates over gender and political representation in the press would have provided sufficient motivation for a social problem novel, *Felix Holt* addresses these issues in the context of the 1830s. Like many other contemporary writers, Eliot looked back on the era of the first Reform Bill with a sense of nostalgia—and conservative hindsight.[27]

Another way that *Felix Holt* appropriates and transforms the narrative conventions of earlier social fiction is through its depiction of a middle-class 'stranger' in its opening pages. In the conventional social problem novel, the visitor wanders into an unfamiliar working-class neighborhood as a prelude to acts of urban investigation and philanthropic activism on behalf of the poor. But Eliot's narrator has a more wide-ranging and philosophical perspective than the narrators of earlier social problem novels. Riding on the outside of a stagecoach, the stranger watches the scenery pass by, metaphorically viewing the stages of modern English

GEORGE ELIOT 139

history, as he 'passed rapidly from one phase of English life to another' (4). Early on in his journey the stranger sees the 'trim cheerful villages' of the agrarian past (3). However, the scene soon changes:

> the land would begin to be blackened with coal-pits, the rattle of handlooms to be heard in hamlets and villages. Here were powerful men walking queerly with knees bent outward from squatting in the mine, going home to throw themselves down in their blackened flannel and sleep through the daylight, then rise and spend much of their high wages at the ale-house with their fellows of the Benefit Club (4).

Unlike the narrators in earlier social problem novels, the traveler does not stop in the industrial town in order to investigate its horrors; rather, he continues on his journey into the rural community of Treby Magna and proceeds to learn about its middle-class inhabitants. In this way, the narrator literally and metaphorically leaves behind the problems associated with industrialism, instead focusing on domestic conflicts and electoral politics in a small town. Sympathy is turned away from the suffering poor and toward the struggles of the Transome family and its private 'inherited sorrow' (8).

Throughout the novel, the connection between private affairs and political conflicts is equally remote. As many critics have noted, *Felix Holt* is far from radical in its class politics.[28] Though the narrator comments at one point that 'there is no private life which has not been determined by a wider public life', she still claims that the novel 'is chiefly concerned with the private lot of a few men and women' (45). Whenever characters do become involved in politics in the novel, it is usually with disastrous consequences. The radicalism of Felix Holt is shown to produce dangerous results—social instability, rioting, and death. As a result, by the end of the novel, Felix Holt has less desire for political activism than when he started. As Henry James points out, at the beginning of the novel, 'we find [Felix] a Radical and we leave him what?—only "utterly married"' (Carroll, *Critical* 275).

As I pointed out in the previous chapter, this depoliticization of working-class characters was a key component of reformist discourse in the 1840s. *Felix Holt* differs from these reformist texts by calling into question not only the aims of lower-class radicalism but of middle-class radicalism as well. Harold Transome's attempt to represent the interests of the lower classes results in electioneering activities that provide the underlying cause of the election day riot. Thus, instead of dramatizing the ways in which radical activism on behalf of the poor could empower the middle classes, Eliot seems to use the conventions of social problem fiction ironically to dramatize the necessity of their disempowerment. At the end of the novel, one can only be relieved that Harold Transome has returned safely to his life of leisured ineffectuality.

Through its criticism of middle-class interventionism, *Felix Holt* indirectly critiques the goals of the social problem novel as a literary genre. It suggests that middle-class writers cannot 'represent' the interests of the working classes any more than Harold Transome can 'represent' them. Any attempt at lower-class

140 FIRST-PERSON ANONYMOUS

representation is really a form of self-advocacy or naïve idealism. Certainly earlier social problem novels had expressed cultural fears about the ways in which radical politics and print culture could result in social chaos. But they usually presented middle-class radicalism as an alternative to more dangerous forms of lower-class activism. Likewise, they represented the female radical—epitomized by the interventionist narrator—as the facilitator of improved class relations.

Felix Holt offers no such representation of the middle-class feminine radicalism. The female characters, like the narrator herself, are distanced from the novel's political events. Without a motivating political 'cause', the women of Treby Magna have no reason to become involved in local politics. They prepare to attend Harold Transome's nomination speech with little concern over its political content:

> Places at convenient windows had been secured beforehand for a few best bonnets; but, in general, a Radical candidate excited no ardent feminine partisanship, even among the Dissenters in Treby, if they were of the prosperous and long-resident class. Some chapel-going ladies were fond of remembering that 'their family had been Church'; others objected to politics altogether as having spoiled old neighbourliness, and sundered friends who had kindred views as to cowslip wine and Michaelmas cleaning; others, of the melancholy sort, said it would be well if people would think less of reforming parliament and more of pleasing God (181).

Due to their ignorance of political affairs, most women of the community are easily manipulated by the electioneering activities of Jermyn and Johnson. Like the disenfranchised working class, women can be 'managed' in order to influence the voting of enfranchised males (175). Commenting on a recent election campaign, Johnson remarks, 'if you'll believe me, sir, one fourth of the men would never have voted if their wives hadn't driven them to it for the good of their families' (175).

For many women, the theatrics of religious turmoil act as a replacement for political activity. The high church acts so as to 'rally feminine instinct and affection to reinforce the decisions of masculine thought' (214). Without an opportunity to exert direct influence in politics, women turn to religion as a way of participating in a public forum. When it is announced that Rufus Lyon will be engaging the high-church curate, Theodore Sherlock, in a public debate, 'the feminine world of Treby Magna was much more agitated by the prospect than by that of any candidate's speech' (220). Of course, the agitation surrounding this debate dissipates when the curate fails to make his appearance in the public pageant. The 'church people' depart calmly, acknowledging that the 'adjournment was not altogether disagreeable', while the 'more acrid Dissenters, whose temper was not controlled by the habits of retail business, had begun to hiss' (226). But in the end the event closes with no change in the status quo; participation in religious controversy thus proves to be a poor replacement for direct political representation.

Throughout the novel, women's disengagement from the political realm is defined in opposition to the political activism of their masculine counterparts. When Harold Transome returns home from abroad, he proceeds to construct a middle-class home in which his mother must assume a role of powerlessness. While before his return Arabella Transome had acted as 'chief bailiff, and to sit in the saddle two or three hours every day', now she must perform the role of 'grandmamma on satin cushions' (17). When Harold announces his switch to the Radical party, she is unable to influence him to return to the Tory fold. In this sense, Mrs. Transome's situation might seem to serve as an argument against those anti-suffragists who believed that a women's political interests were always included and represented by those of the men in their lives.[29] In a bitter dispute, Harold tells his mother that women's political viewpoints are irrelevant because 'it doesn't signify what they think—they are not called upon to judge or act' (35). Angered by her son's remark, Mrs. Transome nevertheless realizes that her only choice is to assume the conventional feminine role in political dispute, to 'repress the speech they know to be useless; nay, the speech they have resolved not to utter' (35).

After Harold puts his mother in her place, the narrator often intrudes into the narrative to point out the injustice of this domestic confinement. She tells us that Mrs. Transome's only outlet is the 'occupation of taking stitches to produce what neither she nor any one else wanted' (85). This useless activity becomes a metaphor for her entrapment in a conventional feminine role:

> The finest threads, such as no eye sees, if bound cunningly about the sensitive flesh, so that the movement to break them would bring torture, may make a worse bondage than any fetters. Mrs. Transome felt the fatal threads about her, and the bitterness of this helpless bondage mingled itself with the new elegancies of the dining and drawing rooms, and all the household changes which Harold had ordered to be brought about with magical quickness (103).

In this way, the oppressive 'elegancies' of middle-class domestic space reinforce Mrs. Transome's political powerlessness. The domestic sphere offers no consolations for women who have a 'self larger than their maternity' (102). After the election, she cannot '[resist] the temptation to say something bitter about Harold's failure to get returned as a Radical' (304). But this only results in 'feminine self-defeat', because it results in her being shut out 'more completely from any consultation by him' (304). Her exclusion and failure, the narrator points out, demonstrate how 'poor women, whose power lies solely in their influence, make themselves like music out of tune, and only move men to run away' (304). Excluded from direct political representation, women become bitter and self-defeating.

Mrs. Transome's misery is a function of her class status as an upper middle-class woman, whose silken bondage does not allow her any power beyond that of influence. Having been brought up in a dissenting radical household, Esther Lyon would seem to have a better chance of exerting some influence beyond conventional definitions of idle womanhood. After all, it was in the dissenting radical press that modern conceptions of the political and philanthropic woman had first taken shape. However, whether it is by virtue of her in-born gentility or her desire for social mobility, Esther does not act as a politically active foil to Mrs. Transome. She self-consciously removes herself from any political activity conventionally associated with the philanthropic female. Instead of Hannah More she reads Byron; instead of becoming active in the Sunday schools, she teaches French. For Esther, being an upwardly-mobile middle-class woman means following a set of prescribed rules: 'A real fine-lady does not wear clothes that flare in people's eyes, or use importunate scents, or make noise as she moves: she is something refined, and graceful, and charming, and never obtrusive' (65). Being a 'fine-lady' also means that she must not intrude in men's political discussions. When Harold flatters her by asking to take part in a conversation on 'election affairs', she declines by saying, 'I have no interest with any one who is not already on the right side' (162). And when he flirtatiously remarks that she is wearing Liberal colors, she responds, 'I fear I must confess that it is more from love of blue than from love of Liberalism. Yellow opinions could only have brunettes on their side' (162).

Self-consciously apolitical, Esther does not seek any cause outside of her own self-contained world until she meets Felix Holt. His criticism of her 'fine-ladyism' causes her to view her own life as a 'heap of fragments' that lacked 'some great energy ... to bind them together' (160). Even though Esther yearns for a cause that will bring together her own fragmented self-image, it is romantic, not political, motivation she seeks: 'there was the sense, that if Felix Holt were to love her, her life would be exalted into something quite new—into a sort of difficult blessedness, such as one may imagine in beings who are conscious of painfully growing into the possession of higher powers' (213). She thus defines her own personal growth as an acknowledgment of her own inferiority. Stung by his continual criticism, she imagines him as a 'rock, and she was no more to him than the white clinging mist-cloud' (287). Such characterizations of Esther's relationship to Felix Holt are jarring to many modern readers, who find themselves wishing that Esther would develop a more independent sense of self.[30] Indeed, by predicating the development of women's selfhood on masculine approval, the novel seems to suggest that romantic love provides the only means by which women can cultivate moral depth. When Esther finally learns of her true parentage, she is able to respond with maturity and compassion only because her relationship with Felix 'had taught her to doubt the infallibility of her own standard, and raised a presentiment of moral depths that were hidden from her' (235). Thus the narrative suggests that romantic love is what enables a woman to overcome her own vanity and enter into sympathy with others.

At the same time that Esther begins to develop morally, she also gains a sense of self-awareness about the reasons behind her own political inactivity. When Felix tells her of his plans for a life of poverty and social activism, she responds, 'A woman can hardly ever choose in that way; she is dependent on what happens to her. She must take meaner things, because only meaner things are within her reach' (245-46). Through Felix, she experiences 'the first self-questioning, the first

GEORGE ELIOT

voluntary subjection, the first longing to acquire the strength of greater motives and obey the more strenuous rule' (247). She is of course dependent on Felix to provide the marker by which to judge her own worthiness, and as a result, it is only her love for him that would enable her to reach outside her own circumscribed femininity and imagine a better, more cultured self. Presumably, all of the qualities that will make her a better wife for Felix will also make her a better citizen: a sense of self-development, moral responsibility, and sympathetic devotion. Yet she pursues this program of self-development without political ambition or philanthropic objects.

In this way, Eliot proposes the cultured woman as an alternative to the political one. Rather than empowering herself through forms of philanthropic activism, the cultured woman improves herself through self-cultivation. Eliot suggests that even though Esther's expanded sense of self does not enable her to change political reality, it still enables her to develop a greater sense of agency in determining her own future.[31] Faced with the seemingly unalterable reality of a union with Harold, Esther suddenly realizes that 'her life was a book which she seemed herself to be constructing—trying to make character clear before her, and looking into the ways of destiny' (353). Here individual agency is defined as a form of self-authorship, where the meanings of 'character' and 'destiny' are partially self-constructed. Fatherless and motherless, Esther seems to have no 'author' inside or outside of the text. She is thus able to view her own identity as a self-referring cluster of signs that can be altered at will. Suddenly she is able to see design and purpose in her life. When Harold points out the mistakes in her netting, she responds, 'Those blunders have a design in them' (357). While for Mrs. Transome the threads of her work were symbols of her entrapment, for Esther these same threads symbolically represent her own destiny as an self-constructed, though unintentional, plan.[32]

Of course Esther's destiny does have another 'author'—George Eliot herself. However, since this pseudonym is a construct and thus problematizes a direct homology between author and narrator, the text in some sense becomes self-enclosed and self-authoring. By drawing attention to the constructedness of character, author, and text, Eliot questions the ability of a social problem novel to represent or to change reality. Further, she calls into question the ability of the author to succeed in carrying out any interventionist plan of action. The novel then becomes an exploration of how individuals can improve their own moral quality in a way that will make them more productive members of the community. The novel never promotes women's suffrage; instead, it suggests ways that women—like the disenfranchised working classes—can develop into the kind of citizens who have the potential for becoming equal partners in marriage and society.

Esther demonstrates this potential in the novel's trial scene, where she becomes heroic by virtue of her ability to represent another. Though she has no opportunity to sway the jury with factual evidence, she is able to use her only political weapon—sympathetic influence:

When a woman feels purely and nobly, that ardour of hers which breaks through formulas too rigorously urged on men by daily practical needs, makes one of her most

144   FIRST-PERSON ANONYMOUS

> precious influences: she is the added impulse that shatters the stiffening crust of cautious experience. Her inspired ignorance gives a sublimity to actions so incongruously simple, that otherwise they would make men smile (414).

As a form of 'inspired ignorance', the quality of her testimony is limited by her own status as a poorly educated woman who is ignorant of the factual evidence that forms the basis of a court decision. As Rita Bode has argued, Esther is in a sense the 'author' of Felix's public identity, reconstituting his public image from the fragments presented at the trial (780). Esther tells the court that Felix's 'nature is very noble; he is tender-hearted; he could never have had any intention that was not brave and good' (415). But it is more her own cultured persona that captures the attention of the court: 'There was something so naïve and beautiful in this action of Esther's that it conquered every low or petty suggestion even in the commonest minds. The three men in that assembly who knew her best ... felt a thrill of surprise mingling with their admiration' (415). In the end, it is the testimony of the 'generous-hearted woman' that sways the judge toward leniency in his sentencing of Felix (416). Thus, at the same time that Esther constructs Felix as a cultured man, she constructs herself as a cultured woman, thereby simultaneously influencing the outcome of the trial and her own destiny. Esther's representations, like Eliot's, reveal her own culture at the same time that they are identifying these qualities in others. Literary representation and self-representation become mutually reinforcing, sympathetic activities that exist outside the realm of social and political reality.

In the end, Esther's slowly developing social consciousness does not motivate her to become politically active or to advocate for her own rights in a society that has mandated her political inactivity. She, like Felix, ends the novel only 'utterly married'. However, the last chapter holds out the promise of a larger moral or social purpose for Esther. When Felix once again reviews his reformist plans for the future, Esther's response is, 'You think you are to do everything. You don't know how clever I am. I mean to go on teaching a great many things' (440). While these 'many things' might be left undefined in the novel, the concept of an equal marriage is less vague. When Esther remarks that her 'husband must be greater and nobler than I am', Felix responds, 'If you take me in that way I shall be forced to be a much better fellow than I ever thought of being' (440-41). Though on one level this interchange is just clever repartee, it is nonetheless the most equal communication which has yet occurred between Felix and Esther. Esther is no longer Felix's student, who must be chastised and guided by her superior; she is an individual who has the potential to do a 'great many things'. In this way, Eliot, like Harriet Taylor before her, suggests the ways in which marriage can be mutually improving—making both members of the relationship more socially responsible. However, unlike Taylor, Eliot does not go so far as to suggest that marriage would be improved by women's enfranchisement. Rather, she suggests that the institution of equal marriage creates the conditions under which women can take on a more responsible public role.

Eliot thus proposes the activity of mutual cultivation and self-improvement as a replacement for selfish acts of self-advocacy based on class or gender. In an 1868 letter to Barbara Bodichon, she argues that gender alone is not a valid criterion for determining the right for vocational opportunity:

> No good can come to women, more than to any class of male mortals, while each aims at doing the highest kind of work, which ought rather to be held in sanctity as what only the few can do well... . The deepest disgrace is to insist on doing work for which we are unfit—to do work of any sort badly (*Letters* 4: 425).

Here Eliot suggests that it is the characteristics of individuals, not their gender or class identifications, which enable them to produce the 'highest kind of work'. Rather than pursuing her own self-interest in the guise of philanthropy, the cultured woman represents herself through apolitical, self-consciously literary textual representations. As a result, her influence on political affairs is always mediated, always distant from direct forms of political activism. By the last chapter of *Felix Holt,* the political status quo has not changed: electioneering is destined to continue and artisans such as Felix Holt are destined to remain unrepresented in parliament for many years to come. Likewise, Arabella Transome remains ensconced in her gilded cage, powerless and politically redundant. And, as Alison Booth points out, 'in spite of the plot of reconciliation, the sexes seem to glare at each other unappeased' ('Not All Men' 157).

But the story doesn't end there. In 1868, just after the passage of the second Reform Act, Felix Holt once again addresses the workmen, this time in an anonymous article published in *Blackwood's Magazine.* The publication of an essay outside the boundaries of the fictional text in some sense promises to express the author's 'real' political viewpoints on the current crisis over the passage of the second Reform Act. However, what we receive instead is a series of narrative snares. In the essay, Felix Holt once again expounds upon about the necessity of self-cultivation for working men: 'Whether our political power will be any good to us now we have got it, must depend entirely on the means and materials—the knowledge, ability, and honesty, we have at command' (340). The success of enfranchisement depends on the extent to which working men are able to 'put knowledge in the place of ignorance, and fellow-feeling in the place of selfishness' (345). This sense of social responsibility will enable gradual political change, 'so that the public order may not be destroyed' (345).

By claiming to speak by and for the working classes, this 'speech' at first seems to conform to the conventions of middle-class reformist journalism of the 1840s, which constructed fictional representations of working-class readers and contributors as a way of dramatizing the effects of middle-class reform efforts on the objects of their charity. However, unlike the working-class characters represented in reformist periodicals of an earlier age, Felix Holt does not speak to the middle-class audience of the periodical itself (in this case, *Blackwood's*); rather, he speaks to 'fellow-workmen' (338). The middle-class audience is thus depicted as

146 FIRST-PERSON ANONYMOUS

eavesdropping on a speech intended for an entirely different set of listeners. Yet it is impossible to imagine this intended audience as anything but a fiction since Felix Holt is a character from a novel. Even though most readers knew the real author of the speech was George Eliot, they knew that this name was also a fiction. These narrative devices make it impossible to read the speech as any direct statement of Eliot's political beliefs. While they comment directly on current political events, they are self-consciously fictional. By drawing attention to the fictionality of audience and author, the speech comments ironically on the role of the politically engaged author and the periodical press. Instead of directly expressing her political viewpoints with her own signature to an audience of concerned peers, Eliot constructs multiple layers of narrative voice between herself, her readers, and the political content of her writing: a pseudonymous author writing anonymously to her peers in the guise of a fictional character addressing a fictional audience.

At the end of the essay and at the end of the novel, Eliot's cultured woman remains mysterious and unknowable. Her femininity has no direct political use any more than her novels have any clear social purpose. Her narrative identity, like her texts, is a cluster of signs without reliable referents in the social world. Contained in the world of literary representation, she becomes a self-constructed enigma: the woman author representing herself representing others. This definition of the cultured woman is formed in stark contrast to emerging definitions of the 'political woman' in the popular press of the 1860s. Increasingly visible, the politically engaged woman made no separation between her public and private identities: her feet were firmly planted on the platform and her eye was on the ballot box. By the end of the 1860s, women were increasingly taking on high-profile roles in the debate over political issues including the Contagious Diseases Acts (1864, 1866, 1869) and women's suffrage.

The increasing visibility of the movement was made apparent in a single act of public protest—the 1866 petition to parliament in support of women's enfranchisement. This petition, sponsored by John Stuart Mill, was signed by 1,499 of the most important women writers and activists of the day, including Harriet Martineau, Frances Power Cobbe, Helen Taylor, and Barbara Bodichon (Helsinger et al. 2: 40-41). Though the petition failed to win the vote for women, it served as a moment of mass self-exposure for women writers, who were beginning to define a more politically visible role for the woman writer. Signature and identity thus came together in one crystallizing historical moment.

Of course, there was one key name missing from this petition—George Eliot's. Eliot's refusal to stand up and be counted with her fellow women writers and intellectuals demonstrates her unwillingness to abandon anonymous and pseudonymous models of women's authorship. At the same time, it demonstrates her conservatism on issues of gender and political representation. By proposing women's self-improvement through marriage as an alternative to enfranchisement, Eliot in many ways added weight to the argument against women's suffrage.[33] Such a meliorist position on the issue of women's political representation is indeed surprising considering that she counted the most ardent women radicals among her closest friends. Yet as I have pointed out, Eliot's representations of women in *Felix Holt* suggest that her views were on the issue of women's political representation were far from stable. At the same time that Eliot seemed to be defining an apolitical role for middle-class women, she also drew attention to the inadequacies of educational and political institutions for providing women with the skills they needed to be more active, responsible members of society.

Eliot's definition of the 'cultured woman' also had important implications for the future of her career and for the canonization of women's writing in general. At the same time that Arnold and other practitioners of the 'higher journalism' constructed the high-culture novel as a distinctly masculine domain, Eliot reconfigured this category to be inclusive of her own literary practice. Eliot invaded the realm of the male-dominated publishing industry by leaving behind the interventionist agendas and gender-based activism that historically had been associated with the development of women's entry into political discourse. In addition, by maintaining her pseudonymity, Eliot reinforced the gender complexity of her own identity enough to allow her to achieve status as a cultured, rather than feminine, woman writer. Ironically, while high-culture fiction in general came to be associated with the celebrated names of famous male authors, the women's high-culture novel came to be associated with the pseudonym of a single woman author—George Eliot. As Eliot no doubt realized, a woman's signature and a man's carried different values within the literary establishment during the 1860s. While signed publication and enfranchisement promised women an expanded public role and a higher status within literary culture, this promise would not be fulfilled for many years to come. Located in the historical gap between Victorian and modern definitions of the woman author, Eliot constructed herself as a self-conscious anachronism, who maintained the old-fashioned convention of pseudonymous authorship regardless of popular convention. This narrative practice undoubtedly made Eliot's later work conservative but also ensured its canonicity. While the works of most of Eliot's high-profile contemporaries disappeared from the canon, her own work came to epitomize high-culture literary production.

The construction of George Eliot as a literary icon was inseparable from the movement toward high-culture, signed publication in Victorian print media during the 1850s and '60s. For the woman poet, these developments presented unique challenges since poetry, even more than fiction, often fell subject to biographical criticism. The next chapter will focus on the career of Christina Rossetti, exploring ways that she was able to work within and against the stereotypes associated with the Victorian 'poetess'. Writing anonymously and pseudonymously for literary periodicals in the 1850s, Rossetti expressed anxiety over her conflicted desire for obscurity and literary fame. In the 1860s, she temporarily resolved this dilemma by publishing her poetry in *Macmillan's Magazine*, one of the first literary periodicals to adhere to a policy of signed publication. This enabled her to establish a name for herself as a devotional poet and cultural sage. Yet, as we will see, Rossetti still found ways to recapture the indeterminacy of anonymous publication as a way resisting constraining definitions of female authorship.

148 FIRST-PERSON ANONYMOUS

Notes

1 For this reason, 'Silly Novels' has for many years held a controversial place in the study of Victorian women's literature. Some feminist critics such as Shirley Foster have read the essay as an anti-feminist diatribe against women's novels, pointing out that Eliot's assumption of a 'masculine' editorial voice demonstrates her internalization of patriarchal values and critical stance (189). Others, such as Susan Tush, have argued that the essay is feminist in its attempt to formulate a higher critical standard for women's writing. My intent is not to resolve this controversy but to point out ways that 'Silly Novels' contributed to the discourse on the woman author during the 1850s—and how it formulated new definitions of women's authorship from within this context.

2 See, for example, Hardy (126-30) and Beer (52-55).

3 This passage may also be a reference to Carlyle's *Sartor Resartus,* which uses tailoring as a metaphor for the creative process (218-20).

4 For example, see Swindells (51), Showalter (58), Gilbert and Gubar (452), and Tuchman and Fortin (180).

5 See Welsh (123) and Ina Taylor (164).

6 Lewes and Eliot felt that this strategy followed the precedent set by Sir Walter Scott, whose anonymity had created a critical sensation decades earlier (Eliot, *Letters* 2: 505).

7 Recent feminist analyses by Boumelha and Judd emphasize that pseudonymity was a choice for women writers rather than a requirement for their participation in public discourse. Judd argues that the masculine pseudonym was intended to shelter an essential female creator located behind the mask. I am more likely to agree with Boumelha, who argues that pseudonymous publication de-essentialized the authorial voice. She points out that Eliot's pseudonym challenges the notion 'that the author (a coherent historical, biographical, psychological entity) precedes, originates—if you like, authorises—the fiction of the text' ('George Eliot' 15). See also Ginsburg and Welsh (113-31) for fascinating discussion of issues of identity and pseudonymity.

8 It is important to note that this could not be a complete separation after the summer of 1859 since by that time most readers were aware of the existence of Marian Evans behind the pseudonym. Bodenheimer points out that Eliot's 'instinct to hide was created by an equally powerful desire to see herself reflected favorably in the glass of public opinion' (*Real Life* 146). See also Booth for a discussion of the conflicting claims of individuality and impersonality, fame and reticence, femininity and androgyny, in Eliot's career (*Greatness*).

9 Craik was a prolific journalist, writing essays and reviews for *Fraser's Magazine* and many other periodicals. She also published several works of fiction, including *Olive* (1850), *John Halifax, Gentleman* (1856), and *A Life for a Life* (1859).

10 Hardy (126-46) and Doody provide further discussion of the specific narrative strategies Eliot used to establish a sexless or universalized narrative persona in her novels. In embracing a sexless model of authorship, Eliot was following in the tradition of George Sand, Madam de Staël, Margaret Fuller, and Harriet Martineau. Like Eliot, they all had fallen subject to discourses on the female author and consequently strove to define themselves outside these conventional definitions. Of course, the construction of Eliot as

a sexless literary identity has a long history in twentieth-century criticism (David 173; Booth, *Greatness* 16). Deirdre David views this trend toward constructing George Eliot into a 'de-sexed, degendered presence' as a expression of patriarchal control (175). However, in light of Eliot's views women's authorship, we might wonder whether the creation of a sexless identity wasn't just what Eliot was trying to accomplish. Rather than viewing Eliot strictly as a product of patriarchal definitions of the authorial role, we might instead view her as an example of a woman writer who—at least partially—was able to fashion her own public image in a way that defied the gender stereotyping associated with mid-Victorian authorship.

11 See also Redinger, who argues that Eliot 'grew into' her professional name, 'endowing it with a personality all its own' (334). She argues that the name 'George Eliot' acted as a 'synthesizing agent' in her life and work, enabling her to establish a public image as a Victorian sage (335).

12 Brake (*Subjugated Knowledges* 19-26) and Hiller (123-26) provide useful commentary on the historical development of the debate over authorial signature. For contemporary views, see Trollope, 'On Anonymous Literature' (1865); Hughes, 'Anonymous Journalism' (1861); Morley, 'Anonymous Journalism' (1867); Kinnear, 'Anonymous Journalism' (1867); 'Anonymous Journalism' (1858), and 'The Identity of Journalism' (1856).

13 See 'The British Press: Its Growth, Liberty, and Power' (1859) and 'Anonymous Journalism' (1858).

14 In response, advocates of journalistic anonymity stressed the 'manliness' of unsigned publication. The *North British Review*, for example, argues that to require signature would be to 'emasculate and tame our manly and independent press' ('The British Press' 398).

15 See B. Harrison (282), Herstein (61), and Parkes, 'Review of the Last Six Years'.

16 For example, see anonymously published articles by F. W. Newman ('Capacities of Women') and Harriet Martineau ('Middle-Class Education') in the 1860s.

17 For example, the *Fortnightly Review*, one of the most prominent of the new periodicals to require signature, published only twelve contributions by women during the 1860s (or 1.8 percent). Even periodicals that remained anonymous, such as *St. Paul's Magazine*, often highlighted the names of a male editors and attempted to give the impression of a masculine textual community (Turner).

18 Lydia Becker's article in the *Contemporary Review* (1867) discusses how the reading of periodicals and newspapers facilitated the development of women's self-culture and political awareness (310-11).

19 Riley discusses the cultural anxieties surrounding the development of the suffragist movement as a political interest group (67-95). These anxieties were centered on the 'belief that women are distinct from men in what they want, that they would therefore vote as a class or mass, and that sex hostility would thus be formalised' (70).

20 The term 'culture' took on many meanings in the 1860s as intellectuals debated role of literature and education in establishing a national identity and facilitating social progress. In an 1866 address to the House of Commons, Radical MP John Bright

attacked the 'culture' of newspaper writers, who pretentiously displayed their knowledge of the classics (see 'Culture' 711). In response, Arnold began publishing a series of essays on culture in the *Cornhill Magazine* (1867-68), which were later republished as *Culture and Anarchy* (1869). In these essays, Arnold famously defined culture as a 'study of perfection' (31) that produces 'sweetness and light' (37). In debates over working-class and female suffrage, journalists emphasized the importance of self-culture as a prerequisite to enfranchisement. In her famous essay, 'What Shall We Do with Our Old Maids?' (1862), Frances Power Cobbe encourages women writers to devote 'special study and careful cultivation' as part of their overall professional development (609). See Brantlinger (237-58), Eagleton (45-67), Heyck (190-220), and Williams (*Culture and Society*) for a discussion of how conceptions of 'culture' shaped intellectual practice in England, gradually resulting in the aesthetic movement and the institutionalization of English studies. See Tuchman and Fortin for a discussion of the gender implications of these changes.

21 See, for example, Buchanan, 'Immorality in Authorship' (1866), Lewes, '*Ruth* and *Villette*' (1853), and McCarthy, 'Novels with a Purpose' (1864). The decline in the status of 'novels with a purpose' was undoubtedly connected to a general cynicism about the benefits of philanthropic activism that emerged in the 1860s (see 'The Philanthropy of the Age', 1869). Inevitably, both philanthropy and social problem fiction became feminized in the minds of many critics (e.g., 'Authoresses', 1865). See Brantlinger for a general discussion of the movement away from radicalism in politics and fiction during the 1850s and '60s (205-35). See also Kestner (142-43) for a discussion of the economic and political forces leading to the gradual disappearance of the social problem novel as a narrative genre.

22 For discussion of the establishment of high-culture journalism and criticism, see Woolford and Kent. Heyck (190-217) and Tuchman & Fortin (65-92) provide discussion of the development of the high-culture novel. For a contemporary view of the canonicity of high-culture fiction, see 'Present Aspects and Tendencies of Literature' which distinguishes between a masculine 'true or high literature', which expresses national culture, and 'wholesome popular literature', which aims to instruct and entertain the masses (158, 165).

23 See Brantlinger, who argues that realism at mid-century, especially in the work of Eliot, Thackeray, and Trollope, demonstrates a 'rejection of reform idealism' and the desire to 'maintain a balance or stalemate between radicalism and conservatism' (207).

24 According to the *Wellesley Index to Victorian Periodicals,* only seven of these articles were published with recognizably feminine bylines (Houghton).

25 In 1867, at the suggestion of her friends, Barbara Bodichon and Emily Davies, Eliot contributed a small sum toward the establishment of Girton College. But she refused to sign the famous 1867 petition to parliament for the enfranchisement of women. See Haight (396).

26 See, for example, Uglow (*George Eliot* 190-92), Brady (135-48), and Zimmerman.

GEORGE ELIOT

27 James Moncreiff's 'Secret Voting and Parliamentary Reform' (1860), for example, looks back on the agitation surrounding first Reform Bill as 'the entrancing rapture of our boyhood' that can 'raise the pulse and stir the blood no longer' (293).

28 See, for example, Ruth Yeazell, who views the novel's domestic plot as a strategy for 'covering and containing' the class issues raised by the novel (144). Likewise, Lyn Pykett argues that the novel's shifting, distanced narrative perspective is an expression of the Arnoldian project of depoliticizing class politics. See also Craig, Bamber, Gallagher (*Industrial*), and Williams (*Culture* 102-109) for further analysis of the conservative class politics of *Felix Holt*.

29 For example, in her review of Mill's *Subjection of Women* published in the *Edinburgh Review* (1869), Oliphant argues and man and a woman represent a 'composite being' politically and as such should be represented by a single vote (588-89).

30 See, for example, Kristin Brady, who argues that Esther 'succeeds . . . merely by pleasing the men who exercise power' (142). See also Zimmerman and Uglow (*George* 175-92).

31 Rita Bode provides an examination of Esther's agency in the novel. Bode argues that Esther's choice of a husband 'is something of a "political" decision, for whether consciously or instinctively, she chooses the person over whom she can exercise some authority' (770). See also Carroll (*Conflict* 225-33) and Uglow (*George Eliot* 180-81) for a discussion of the element of choice as it relates to Esther's development.

32 See Bode for a full analysis of sewing and netting as tropes in the novel (782-83).

33 Zimmerman discusses the relationship between Eliot's conservatism on women's enfranchisement and the novel's representation of marriage as a substitute for political activism.

CHAPTER SIX

Christina Rossetti and the Problem of Literary Fame

During the 1850s and '60s, to publish as a woman and a writer was to evoke a complex array of gender stereotypes. This was especially true for women poets, whose work often fell subject to biographical readings. As Angela Leighton and Margaret Reynolds have pointed out, Victorian critics often relied on the 'assumption that women's poetry was always about personal experience and that its true subjects were home and the heart' (xxviii).[1] Critics thus viewed the woman poet as a domestic angel, whose self-disclosures illuminated the pleasures of the home. Alternatively, critics associated the woman poet with Romantic notions of passion, desire, and tortured self-renunciation. Women's poetry was mined for information that would reveal the secret passions and struggles of the 'poetess'. As Margaret Linley has demonstrated, during the Victorian period the word 'poetess' was an unstable, contested term, which relied on the construction of the 'erotically charged glorified figure of the abandoned woman writer', who is 'always on the verge of extinction, in danger of being left out or forgotten by literary history' (291). Debates over the roles and identities of the Victorian 'poetess' thus intersected with the discourse on the 'abused woman author' in some interesting ways. As discussed in chapter four, the 'abused woman author' served as a focal point for periodical discourse on the Woman Question during the 1850s. The woman writer came to represent a new kind of oppressed intellectual laborer whose liberation depended on the reformation of social and domestic practices that maintained separate spheres ideology and privileged male genius.

It is within the context of conflicts over the gender and authorship during the 1850s and '60s that the career of Christina Rossetti took shape. Like George Eliot, Rossetti was faced with the dilemma of how to make a name for herself without evoking constraining stereotypes associated with female authorship. In the early years of her career, she published anonymously and pseudonymously in literary periodicals as a way of resisting biographical readings of her work and maintaining a sense of domestic privacy. However, at the same time she capitalized on the stereotype of the 'abused woman author' through her own pseudonymously published poems and through the mediating influence of her brothers. Like many other women poets of the period, Rossetti was well aware of the conflicted stereotypes and conventions associated with the 'poetess' and to some extent was able to exploit these conventions for her own ends (Linley 291).[2]

During the 1850s Rossetti interrogated and to some extent appropriated stereotypes associated with female authorship; however, she did not otherwise become actively involved in promoting women's rights. Though she was associated

154   FIRST-PERSON ANONYMOUS

with the Langham Place Group during the 1850s, her poetry did not function so as to popularize women's causes.[3] Likewise, though she was associated with a variety of philanthropic organizations,[4] she did not shape her work within the context of reformist journalism or the Condition-of-England Question. Certainly there were models of women poets who premised their careers on social activism during the 1850s. Both Eliza Cook and Elizabeth Barrett Browning to some extent embraced the role of poetry in shaping public opinion on women's issues and the state of the urban poor. However, Rossetti aimed for a more self-consciously literary role for her work. As she writes to her brother Gabriel in 1870, 'It is not in me, and therefore it will never come out of me, to turn to politics or philanthropy with Mrs. Browning' (*Letters* 1: 348).

Early in her career, Rossetti chose a distinctly high-culture medium for her poetry: the Pre-Raphaelite periodical, *The Germ* (1850). *The Germ*, like many other periodicals of the period, focused on women as a source of fascination and controversy. However, unlike many mainstream literary periodicals that published essays and reviews that directly addressed women's issues, *The Germ* provided a self-consciously literary response to the Woman Question. By publishing poetry, fiction, literary essays, and illustrations, *The Germ* provided only indirect, coded references to debates over the political role of women and the treatment of women authors in Victorian society. Within the context of early Pre-Raphaelitism, women became romanticized figures—both as geniuses and objects of desire—whose abjection was represented as both gorgeous and pathetic. The debate over the Woman Question and the 'abused woman author' was thus co-opted and re-fashioned by the Pre-Raphaelite Brotherhood, leading to the development of an array of new forms of literary representation that both marginalized and facilitated the development of Christina Rossetti's career. The first part of this chapter examines Rossetti's contributions to *The Germ,* investigating the extent to which she was involved in editing the periodical and contributed to its artistic goals. It also explores how her image as a tortured woman genius was constructed through her poetry and mediated through her brothers' editorial activities. The second part of this chapter explores how conflicts between Rossetti's desire for authorial notoriety and her fear of self-display inform her fiction of the 1850s, especially *Maude* (1850) and *Corrispondenza Famigliare* (1852). The final section of this chapter investigates the legacy of Rossetti's early conflicts over name and fame, demonstrating how these dilemmas influenced her decision to pursue signed publication in *Macmillan's Magazine* in the 1860s and at the same time to employ poetic strategies that problematized direct correspondence between her life and work.

Christina Rossetti and *The Germ*

The chronology of events leading to the publication of *The Germ* in 1850 is familiar to most scholars of Victorian literature. In 1849, soon after the formation of the Pre-Raphaelite Brotherhood (PRB), Dante Gabriel Rossetti persuaded the group to found a journal that would promote their aesthetic principles and establish their literary reputation. After much discussion, the brethren decided to title their periodical *The Germ* and appointed William Michael Rossetti its editor. In addition to involving members of the PRB, other like-minded writers were invited to contribute, including Coventry Patmore and William Bell Scott. In the first number of the periodical all contributions were published anonymously; however, most contributors elected to include their names in subsequent issues of the periodical, perhaps hoping the change would boost circulation. But this strategy was not enough to rescue *The Germ* from financial disaster. After only four issues, it ceased publication in May of 1850. Though William Rossetti reports that it was the initial desire of the PRB to avoid 'politics' in their journal, such a goal was of course unattainable, especially where gender politics were concerned (*PRB Journal* 23). In fact, *The Germ* was very much a part of the debate over the Woman Question during the 1850s, reinscribing cultural anxieties about women's authorial careers. While *The Germ,* like many other literary periodicals of its day, was undoubtedly complicit in the construction of gender stereotypes, it also reflected certain instabilities and disruptions in the Victorian sex-gender system. Many of these disruptions were due to the participation of Christina Rossetti in the otherwise masculine literary project.

Though some contemporary biographers and critics referred to Christina Rossetti as the 'Queen of the Pre-Raphaelites',[5] it is probably more accurate to say that Rossetti's connection to the PRB was always somewhat tenuous. Although Rossetti had a close literary relationship with both brothers, she was not admitted as a full-fledged member of the PRB. Indeed, when Gabriel suggested that Christina be included as a member of the Brotherhood in September 1848, both John Everett Millais and William Holman Hunt rejected his proposal. In response, Dante Gabriel Rossetti wrote to Holman Hunt,

> When I proposed that my sister should join, I never meant that she should attend the meetings, to which I know it would be impossible to persuade her ... . I merely intended that she should entrust her productions to my reading; but must give up the idea, as I find she objects to this also, under the impression that it would seem like display, I believe,—a sort of thing she abhors (*Letters* 1: 45).

While in this passage Dante Gabriel Rossetti may have been accurately characterizing his sister's fear of public exposure, he was probably also attempting to construct her as a stereotypical female writer for the benefit of his Pre-Raphaelite brothers, reassuring them that she was not the kind of woman who would actively seek literary notoriety.

William Rossetti's retrospective accounts of his sister's contributions to *The Germ* represent her as a passive, shy, and somewhat delicate woman writer who had to be coaxed into participating in the project. According to William, Christina did not offer her poems for publication in *The Germ*; rather, he would select and

156   FIRST-PERSON ANONYMOUS

copy them from the family album whenever the need arose. In his introduction to the reprint of *The Germ* in 1899, William is careful to note, 'my sister's contributions to this magazine were produced without any reference to publication in that or in any particular form' (17). Likewise, William points out that it was his brother Gabriel who selected the pseudonym 'Ellen Alleyn' for Christina to use in the second number of *The Germ* (*PRB Journal* 47). In their letters and memoirs, the Rossetti brothers offer no explanation for what they see as their sister's reticence as a contributor to *The Germ*. Rather, they attempt to construct an image of her as a self-effacing authoress who like all truly feminine women would never intentionally publish or seek literary fame.

This image of Christina Rossetti is also constructed in the *Pre-Raphaelite Brotherhood Journal* written by William Rossetti from 1849 to 1853. In this *Journal*, a daily diary intended to chronicle the activities of the PRB, including their work on *The Germ,* Christina Rossetti is rarely mentioned. Many passages which originally referred to Rossetti were later excised by William as he prepared the *Journal* for publication.[6] In passages where her poetry *is* mentioned, it is often referred to as filler used to round out each number of *The Germ.* William writes that when preparing the second number, he 'copied out ... another poem of our Sister's, 'Sweet Death', as it seems doubtful whether there will be an odd corner adapted to either of the little things I had before selected' (*PRB Journal* 44). Later, in preparing the third number, William uses the same kind of deprecatory language when referring to his sister's poems: 'In default of any adequate poem', he writes, 'I looked up my Sister's old thing named 'An Argument', which is at least long enough and in a narrative form. Tupper, to whom I read it, is very much delighted with it; but the fact is it is not quite up to the mark' (56). By referring to Rossetti's poems in this way, William constructed her as a 'poetess' rather than a 'real' poet, whose writings would do in a pinch. Such a message and tone fit William's immediate audience—members of the PRB who might peruse his chronicle of their masculine community.

These representations of Christina Rossetti as a passive and somewhat reluctant contributor to *The Germ* do not quite fit with what we know about her early ambitiousness as a poet. At the time of the publication of her poems in *The Germ*, Rossetti was no literary novice: though only 19, she had already published two poems in *The Athenaeum* and a collection titled *Verses* (1847). This publishing experience—and the kind of professional seriousness that it implies—makes it doubtful that Rossetti played a strictly passive role in determining which of her poems would appear in *The Germ*. Indeed, her letters of the period show that she was to some extent actively involved in the project. In January of 1850, she remarks, 'Do not think the *Germ* fails to interest me: indeed the forthcoming number is continually in my thoughts' (*Letters* 1: 34). In a subsequent letter, she writes to William, 'Do you know, I seriously urge on your consideration the increase of prose and decrease of poetry in the *Germ*, the present state of things strikes me as most alarming' (1: 37). In the same letter she questions whether her *Athenaeum* poems should be republished in *The Germ* (1: 37). Since these poems were originally published under the initials 'C. G. R'., Rossetti may have been concerned that their publication in *The Germ* might enable readers to uncover the real identity of 'Ellen Alleyn'. She writes to William, 'my *nom de guerre* is worthy of Gabriel', perhaps implying that she has internalized her brother's desire that she remain anonymous (1: 37). Yet she seems to retain the right to veto her brothers' editorial decisions; after all, her *Athenaeum* poems did not appear in *The Germ*. Thus, although Rossetti in some ways ceded artistic control as a contributor to *The Germ*, she was probably not as passive as her brothers made her out to be in their letters, diaries, and memoirs.[7]

Indeed, in her letters to her brothers, Rossetti was careful to distance herself from the stereotype of the sentimentalized female author. In a letter to William, for example, she sarcastically suggests that he publish her letters in *The Germ*:

> Should all other articles fail, boldly publish my letters; they would doubtless produce an immense sensation. By hinting that I occupy a high situation in B-ck-m P-l-e, being in fact no other than the celebrated lady—, and by substituting initials and asterisks for all names, and adding a few titles, my correspondence might have quite a success (*Letters* 1: 37).

In this passage, Rossetti makes it clear that she is not the kind of female author who would expose her personal life to public view. In a later letter, she emphasizes that she does not want her work to fall subject to the kind of biographical/gendered readings that the female author was often forced to endure in contemporary reviews. Upon hearing that Thomas Woolner was interested in reading some of her poems, for example, Rossetti wrote to her brother William:

> Mr. Woolner is welcome to any of my things which you may have energy to copy. Only I must beg that you will not fix upon any which the most imaginative person could construe into love personals; you will feel how more than ever intolerable it would *now* be to have my verses regarded as outpourings of a wounded spirit (1: 16).

Wishing for her work to be appreciated on its own terms rather than as the production of a sentimentalized female author, Rossetti had good reason to be protective of how her gendered identity and poetry were received and represented by her brothers.

Rossetti's letters suggest that she was to some extent involved in selecting which of her poems would appear in *The Germ* and how her literary identity would be represented. It is much more difficult, however, to determine the extent of her editorial control once she released the poems. Those Rossetti initially published in *The Germ* were, like all other contributions to the first number of journal, printed anonymously, thereby effectively masking the gender of the contributors and suggesting a unified voice and artistic perspective.[8] Rossetti's 'Dream Land', with its sensual depiction of a dying woman, fits well with the other art and poetry published in the journal's first number. Thomas Woolner's 'My Beautiful Lady', a

158   FIRST-PERSON ANONYMOUS

poem depicting the love affair between a man and a woman, opens the first issue of the magazine. It is followed by 'Of My Beautiful Lady in Death', which depicts a woman's demise and the misery of her grief-striken lover. The pair of poems is accompanied by William Holman Hunt's illustrations, which further emphasize the journal's emphasis on women as the gorgeous objects of male desire and grief (Figure 6.1).

Like other representations of women in the first number of *The Germ*, Rossetti's 'Dream Land' depicts an ailing, repining lady who is destined to die. Having come 'from very far' (6), she now lies by the sea:

> Rest, rest, a perfect rest,
> Shed over brow and breast;
> Her face is toward the west,
>   The purple land.
> She cannot see the grain
> Ripening on hill and plain;
> She cannot feel the rain
>   Upon her hand. (17-24)[9]

Rossetti's representation of melancholy womanhood in this poem may be attributed to her own early interest in Gothic fiction, which often sensationalized the imprisonment and suffering of female protagonists.[10] Though Rossetti evokes Gothic motifs, she provides no specific historical setting or context for the woman's suffering. Separated from a context or social identity, the woman simply becomes a gorgeous object of contemplation. While the object of the poetic gaze is specifically defined as female, the gender of the speaker's voice is more ambiguous. Though readers might presume that the poem's author was male, its anonymity prevents them from identifying a definitively masculine response in the speaker's attitude toward the dying woman. After the PRB began publishing the signatures of contributors in the second number of *The Germ*, the gender of Rossetti's poetic voice became much less ambiguous. When published under the pseudonym 'Ellen Alleyn', Rossetti's lyric 'I' became more explicitly feminine in its associations. Her anxieties about the incongruity of her pseudonym and her desire to establish a name for herself are reflected in three poems published in the second number of the journal: 'A Pause of Thought', 'A Testimony', and 'Song'. For example, in 'A Pause of Thought', she writes,

> I looked for that which is not, nor can be,
>   And hope deferred made my heart sick, in truth;
>   But years must pass before a hope of youth
>   Is resigned utterly.

6.1 Frontispiece to *The Germ* by William Holman Hunt. Courtesy of Ashmolean Museum, Oxford

160 FIRST-PERSON ANONYMOUS

> I watched and waited with a steadfast will:
>> And, tho' the object seemed to flee away
>> That I so longed for, ever, day by day,
>>> I watched and waited still. (1-8)

At first the poem seems to suggest that marriage is the 'object' of the speaker's desire, but a later stanza identifies this ambition more specifically as establishing a 'name' for herself:

> Sometimes I said,—'It is an empty name
>> I long for; to a name why should I give
>> The peace of all the days I have to live?'—
>>> Yet gave it all the same.

> Alas! thou foolish one,—alike unfit
>> For healthy joy and salutary pain,
>> Thou knowest the chase useless, and again
>>> Turnest to follow it. (13-20)

The speaker's desire for a 'name' may be interpreted as Rossetti's desire to be known as an author and as a participant in the PRB. This ambition is perhaps curbed by the speaker's fear that this name would be just as 'empty' as the pseudonym she has adopted. Will fame bring the fulfillment and happiness she desires? Instead of providing an answer to this question, the poem refers to the 'chase' the speaker cannot resist—the poems that must be written.

Did William or Dante Gabriel Rossetti select this poem for *The Germ* because of the way that it constructed 'Ellen Alleyn' as a mysterious and somewhat tortured authoress? Or did Christina Rossetti select this poem for the periodical because it expressed her anxieties as a woman writer? In either case, it is hard to believe that Rossetti's meditations on literary fame would have coincidentally been selected by William Rossetti as he sought filler for the second number of *The Germ*. Most likely the decision to publish 'A Pause of Thought' was made collaboratively between Rossetti and her brothers as they selected poetry which would fulfill the journal's specific artistic goals.[11] However, by highlighting and sentimentalizing the trials of a female author in their journal, the Rossetti brothers were also contributing to the discourse on female authorship that preoccupied literary criticism of the period. It may have been the journal's preoccupation with this subject matter that caused Christina to remark in a letter to Amelia Barnard Heimann that the tone of the journal might 'be somewhat heavy' (*Letters* 1: 33). 'If an amusing tale could regularly come out in each number', she writes, 'it seems to me its prospects might improve' (1: 33). Perhaps what she was unwilling to admit to Heimann was that she had contributed to this 'heavy' tone through the subject matter of her own poetry.

CHRISTINA ROSSETTI

Not all of Rossetti's poems published in the second number of *The Germ*, however, present the image of a woman author tortured by her desire for fame. 'A Testimony' represents writing not so much as an expression of vain ambition than as a means of testifying to the limitations of human vanity. The poem begins,

> I said of laughter: It is vain;—
>   Of mirth I said: What profits it?—
>   Therefore I found a book, and writ
> Therein, how ease and also pain,
> How health and sickness, every one
> Is vanity beneath the sun. (1-6)

The rest of the poem provides the text which the speaker has written in her book — observations on the various forms of human vanity. Only once does the speaker interrupt her discourse with a reminder that the poem is a testimonial by the persona identified in stanza one:

> All things are vanity, I said:
>   Yea vanity of vanities.
>   The rich man dies; and the poor dies:
> The worm feeds sweetly on the dead.
> Whatso thou lackest, keep this trust:—
> All in the end shall have but dust. (25-30)

When attached to the name 'Ellen Alleyn', this 'I' becomes a moralist or sage, who through writing is able to see beyond the vanity of everyday living. Such a sage voice is more morally confident than the speaker in 'A Pause of Thought'. In 'A Testimony', writing is viewed not as an instrument of vanity but as a means of testifying against its immoral influence.

The second number of *The Germ* also included Rossetti's famous 'Song' ('Oh! roses for the flush of youth'). While 'A Pause of Thought' and 'A Testimony' represent writing as a moral and artistic compulsion, 'Song' communicates a sense of resignation to artistic invisibility. The poem reads,

> Oh! roses for the flush of youth,
>   And laurel for the perfect prime;
> But pluck an ivy-branch for me,
>   Grown old before my time.
>
> Oh! violets for the grave of youth,
>   And bay for those dead in their prime;
> Give me the withered leaves I chose
>   Before in the olden time. (1-8)

162   FIRST-PERSON ANONYMOUS

Though Rossetti was only eighteen when she wrote this poem, she does not allow herself the 'roses' associated with youth and love. Likewise, though she is a published poet, she does not allow herself the 'laurels' associated with artistic achievement. Instead, she chooses 'ivy' as a symbol of her fidelity, perhaps to God but most likely also to her family attachments, including the PRB.[12] The poem emphasizes that she has 'chosen' these attachments as an expression of her own will. Read within the context of her pseudonymous status as a contributor to *The Germ*, the poem can be interpreted as a meditation on her *choice* to suppress her name and desire for artistic notoriety.

When considered in conjunction with Rossetti's other poems published in the second number of *The Germ*, 'Song' creates a portrait of a woman author in conflict. Was her desire for literary fame hopeless and vain? Or was writing an instrument that would allow her to dispense sage wisdom on important moral questions? This image of the woman author in conflict was most likely created not only by Rossetti but also by her brothers, who selected her pseudonym and edited her work. The revisions of 'Song' illustrate particularly well the ways in which the editorial process worked to create a specifically feminine persona for 'Ellen Alleyn'. When the poem was published, it appeared without the first three stanzas which are to be found in the manuscript version. These omitted stanzas alter the gender configurations of the poem significantly:

> They told me that she would not live,
> > But how could I believe their word?
> Her cheeks were redder than a rose,
> > And smoother than a curd.
>
> Her eyes were full of a deep light,
> > Steady, unmoved by hope and fear:
> And though indeed her voice was low,
> > It was so sweet and clear.
>
> But now that she is gone before,
> > I trust I too shall follow fast:
> And so I sit and sing her song,
> > And muse upon the past.[13]

Who made the decision to omit these stanzas and why? In the *PRB Journal*, William remarks that it was his decision to publish his sister's 'short song of 8 lines' (*PRB Journal* 47). Rossetti writes to William in January 1850 that she 'must not—object' to the publication of the poem in *The Germ* (*Letters* 1: 30). This equivocal remark suggests that Rossetti was passive in deferring to her brother's editorial choices, but at the same time implies that she had the power to veto his decisions. Was she also agreeing to the omission of the first three stanzas to her poem? What was the rationale behind these omissions?

We may never know the answer to these questions, but we can gauge their effect on the gendering of the poetic voice of 'Ellen Alleyn'. While the original poem identifies a clearly male speaker, the shorter version of the poem, when connected to a feminine pseudonym, seems to identify a melancholy female voice. The poem is no longer about a man's lament for his dead lover but about a woman's suppressed desire for the 'roses' of youth and 'laurels' of fame. Regardless of who made the decision to excise the opening stanzas of the poem, the effect was to create an aura of feminine melancholy and mystery around the name 'Ellen Alleyn'. This construction of Rossetti's literary persona complemented the many other images of repining and dejected women published in the journal. As Barbara Garlick points out, these images 'reinforced the patriarchally defined separate spheres of the day by figuring the centrality of the female other and by confining this other within certain literary and metaphorical framing devices' (108). These devices included 'focus[ing] on the dangers of active female sexuality and conversely the erotic promise of virginity' (109). [14]

The pseudonym 'Ellen Alleyn' thus performed many functions in *The Germ*. It functioned as a marketing technique—a strategy for adding mystery and romanticism to the journal. It also served to conceal Rossetti's identity, thus providing her with the privacy to write without fear of public exposure. However, the pseudonym also served as an obstacle to the poetic fame Rossetti desired by denying her the authorial name that would ensure her visibility as an emerging poet. Rossetti's pseudonym thus functioned to suppress and facilitate her authorial anxieties and desires, while at the same time constructing the kind of femininity that would further the PRB's artistic objectives.

The inclusion of Christina Rossetti's feminine pseudonym on the list of contributors—along with Frederick Stephens' pseudonym 'Laura Savage' on number four—also performed the function of complicating the gendering of the periodical as a whole. During this period, few literary periodicals published the names of contributors, let alone a mix of masculine and feminine names on the table of contents. Consequently, for some mid-Victorian critics, *The Germ*'s mixed-gender list of contributors seemed out of place in a literary periodical. One reviewer, for example, remarked that the 'natural prejudice' against poetry journals by young people is not 'diminished by the knowledge that it [*The Germ*] is the production of young gentlemen *and* ladies' (Cox 94; italics mine). Perceived as a heterosocial textual space, *The Germ* did not seem to fit within the gender configurations many readers associated with contemporary periodicals. The inclusion of the names of male and female contributors on the journal's title page struck some reviewers as a violation of conventional gender codes. For example, a review published in *The Guardian* soon after the demise of *The Germ* refers to the journal as a production of the Pre-Raphaelite 'fraternity' but then proceeds to quote from Christina Rossetti's poem 'Repining', which had been published under her feminine pseudonym ('Art and Poetry' 623). It is perhaps the mix of gender significations that causes the writer to lament the lack of manliness in the production as a whole. He writes, 'Want of purpose may be easily charged against

164   FIRST-PERSON ANONYMOUS

them as a fault, and with some justice; but it is a very common defect of youthful poetry, which is sure to disappear with time, if there be anything real and manly in the poet' (623). Critics thus defined the effeminacy of the periodical based on the writing style of its contributors.[15] However, their response might also have been prompted by the periodical's mixed-gender list of contributors and the many representations of women in the periodical. Within this context, the name 'Ellen Alleyn' may have served as a marker of the periodical's 'effeminacy' but it also served as a useful marketing device that capitalized on the literary public's interest in the 'abused woman author' as a literary trope and as an object of social concern.

Finding a Name

Whatever function the pseudonym 'Ellen Alleyn' might have had as a marketing device for *The Germ* as a literary periodical, it still had the effect of suppressing the name 'Christina Rossetti' within the journal as a whole. As I have pointed out, Rossetti's contributions to *The Germ* and the construction of her authorial identity were to some extent mediated by the editorial activities of her brothers. It was perhaps these limitations that led Rossetti to seek another venue for more freely exploring her struggle with authorial ambition: her semi-autobiographical novella, *Maude*.[16] Written in 1849-50, during the same period as *The Germ*, *Maude* tells the story of a melancholy woman author who has an intense desire for literary fame. These literary ambitions are written on her body as frailty and illness. When a cousin comes upon Maude at work, she is greeted with the following tableau:

> Maude was seated at a table surrounded by the old chaos of stationary; before her lay the locking manuscript-book, into which she had just copied something. That day she had appeared more than usually animated: and now supporting her forehead upon her hand, her eyes cast down till the long lashes nearly rested upon her cheeks, she looked pale, languid, almost in pain (23).

While in some sense this description seems to hystericize Maude, characterizing her ambition as an self-destructive impulse, it also functions so as to draw attention to the plight of women authors in mid-Victorian society, who cannot develop their talent due to constraining definitions of female behavior. After all, the only way Maude can escape domestic responsibilities and claim time to write is by retiring to her room after 'complaining of a headache, and promising either to wrap herself in a warm shawl or to go to bed' (22). This fib allows her a little undisturbed writing time before being discovered by her cousin Agnes.

Maude's retreat to her bedroom is just one example of her generalized fear of public display. She refuses to recite her poetry at a dinner party and carefully guards her poems in the 'locking manuscript-book' (21, 23). Ashamed of her own vanity, she contemplates taking the veil. Yet even though she claims to be humiliated by public adulation, Maude devotes most of her free time to writing, engages in *bouts rimés* competitions, and eagerly circulates her poems among friends. These poems are displayed in the text of the story as evidence of Maude's tortured literary genius. When the young author becomes fatally ill as a result of a carriage accident, she asks her cousin to destroy the poems 'never intended to be seen' (41). This ending is tragic in the sense that it emphasizes the loss of Maude and her brilliant poetry, which like the work of Sappho, can only be recalled through the brief fragments that escaped the flames.

While seemingly an act of destruction, the burning of Maude's poems also acts as an incitement to further knowledge. The reader, having viewed only the small selection of poems included in the narrative, wonders about the poems that have been excluded. These missing fragments are described from Agnes' point of view:

> The locked book she never opened: but had it placed in Maude's coffin, with all its words of folly, sin, vanity; and, she humbly trusted, of true penitence also. She next collected the scraps of paper found in her cousin's desk and portfolio, or lying loose upon the table; and proceeded to examine them. Many of these were mere fragments, many half-effaced pencil scrawls, some written on torn backs of letters, and some full of incomprehensible abbreviations. Agnes was astonished at the variety of Maude's compositions (42).

Both 'half-effaced' and 'incomprehensible', Maude's writings cannot be understood by the common reader. Similarly, Rossetti's own unpublished writings, the mass of compositions not included in *Maude*, are inaccessible to the public and are thus constructed as objects of interest and desire. Teased by incomplete knowledge, readers long to read the 'sinful' and 'vain' poems that have been denied to them.

What the final passages of *Maude* accomplish, then, is to draw attention to the selection process behind the construction of Maude's—and Rossetti's—miscellaneous texts. As an 'edited' text, *Maude* can be seen as a sister document to *The Germ*. Like *The Germ*, *Maude* includes selections of poetry (in this case, all written by Rossetti) and highlights issues of self-naming, female death, and literary fame. But unlike *The Germ* and many of the documents associated with the PRB, *Maude* depicts a Rossetti as the active editor of her own miscellaneous text, which is both a novella and a collection of poetry that she has selected. As in *The Germ*, Rossetti arguably tells the story of her own struggle with authorship in the voice of a persona (in this case, the protagonist Maude), but the difference is that she has more control over how this image is presented to readers. She is the undisputed editor of the text. The voice of this editor intrudes in the narrative in order to assert control over the presentation of the story's details:

> it was the amazement of everyone what could make her [Maude's] poetry so broken-hearted as was mostly the case. Some pronounced that she wrote very foolishly about things she could not possibly understand; some wondered if she really had any secret

166   FIRST-PERSON ANONYMOUS

source of uneasiness; while some simply set her down as affected. Perhaps there was a degree of truth in all these opinions. But I have said enough: the following pages will enable my readers to form their own estimate of Maude's character (5).

Like an editor, Rossetti offers an anthology of work for her readers. And though she claims that they should form their own opinion of Maude's poetry, the remainder of the novella is heavily slanted toward emphasizing Maude's genius and the tragedy of her early demise. Unlike in *The Germ*, Rossetti is both hidden as a fictional character and exposed as an editorial 'I' who arranges the story and poems that follow.

Sadly, Rossetti's *Maude* did not immediately find an audience. It remained unpublished until 1897, three years after Rossetti's death. It therefore offered only a private response to the publicly received *Germ*. However, it did offer Rossetti an alternative literary space where she could assert more artistic control in working inside and outside of a literary persona and where she could explore the contradictions between her desire for obscurity and literary fame. Thus, although in *Maude* Rossetti expressed pessimism about women's opportunities for poetic achievement, she also constructed a self-authorizing narrative that enabled her to assess her own limitations and desires as a poet at the beginning of her career.

Though in *Maude* Rossetti expressed doubts about her own potential as a writer, she continued to pursue publication throughout the 1850s. Interestingly, her first publishing venue after *The Germ* was a journal written and edited by women: *The Bouquet from Marylebone Gardens* (1851-55).[17] Intended for aristocratic female readers, *The Bouquet* included primarily fiction and poetry. As a way of further emphasizing the journal's ladylike tone, contributors published their work under flower pseudonyms. As 'Calta' (Marigold), Christina Rossetti published four pieces: three poems, 'Versi', 'L'Incognita', and 'Purpurea Rosa' as well as a fragment of an epistolary novel, *Corrispondenza Famigliare*. Like *Maude, Corrispondenza* foregrounds Rossetti's conflict between the desire for literary fame and the fear of public exposure. The novel is comprised of the correspondence between Angela-Maria de'Ruggieri, an exiled Italian girl attending a boarding school in England, and Emma Ward, her rich and superficial British cousin. In the course of the narrative, Angela-Maria's anxieties over her missing father are described as are Emma's shallow reflections on dress and display. In the crisis of the novel, Emma volunteers to write an Italian poem for the Countess of Crawley's album. Soon she realizes she is not up to the challenge and begs her cousin to 'pen me a few stanzas' (282). Angela-Maria obliges her but insists that she be allowed to 'remain anonymous' (282). One inscribed and circulated, the poem is admired by all of Emma's aristocratic friends. When Emma insists that she 'did not deserve such praise', her words are misinterpreted as feminine modesty (284). Guiltily, she writes to Angela-Maria:

Don't scold me for my unwilling deceit, my dear. It is now too late to correct the mistake. Nobody would believe me unless I were to reveal the name of the true author, and I know you don't want me to do that. I hope that very soon the verses will be forgotten, and then the wrong of a moment will matter no longer. I shall continue to declare myself unworthy of such praise, and it won't be my fault if I'm not believed (285).

Just two paragraphs later, the narrative concludes without providing an adequate explanation for who should be held responsible for the conflict. On one hand, Emma's vanity seems to have been the cause of the conundrum. She claims to be able to write verse in Italian and when caught in the lie, borrows another's work, presenting it as her own. But it is Angela-Maria's insistence on anonymity that enables Emma to lie in the first place and to perpetuate this falsehood in the future. Thus the story seems to suggest that both disingenuous display and selfless anonymity are inadequate models of female authorship. If interpreted as two sides of Rossetti's authorial identity—the English self who desires recognition and the Italian self who desires anonymity—we see that in combination these selves produce only social confusion and dissimulation.

Since the narrative curtails just after the conflict is introduced, it is difficult to know what kind of resolution Rossetti might have had in mind. Indeed, as Jan Marsh points out, it is difficult to surmise why Rossetti abandoned the novel and stopped contributing to the *Bouquet*. It is possible, as Marsh suggests, that she may not have felt an 'affinity with a journal that printed the scorecard of the Eton and Harrow match' (*Christina Rossetti* 135). After all, as a contributor to *The Germ*, Rossetti had taken part in a literary project with much higher literary aspirations. The genre of aristocratic silver fork fiction may not have suited her style. Indeed, with its satirical treatment of Emma's upper-class lifestyle, *Corrispondenza* seems to poke fun at aristocratic fiction *and* lady-journalism. After all, Rossetti's poems published in *The Bouquet* are mediated by 'Calta' just as Angela-Maria's poem published in the Countess' album is mediated by Emma. Clearly, an aristocratic ladies' periodical was not the right venue for the development of Rossetti's poetic craft.

However, it is also possible that Rossetti did not complete the novel because she had decided to abandon the model of pseudonymous authorship that had shaped her early career. During the 1850s, she published a number of poems under her own name in periodicals such as the *National Magazine* and *Once a Week*[18] as well as in anthologies such as *Nightingale Valley*, the *Pictorial Calendar of the Seasons*, and the *Dusseldorf Artist's Album*.[19] At the same time, she attempted without success to publish in prestigious mainstream periodicals: *Blackwood's Magazine* and *Fraser's Magazine* (*Letters* 1: 98-9, Marsh, *Christina Rossetti* 157).[20] These publishing efforts demonstrate Rossetti's growing commitment to establishing a name for herself as a poet. In her letters of the period, she expresses a desire for recognition of her work. After reading a book by a fellow poet in 1853, she writes to her friend Amelia Barnard Heimann, 'How very grand, to be published in Germany and New York, as well as in England. I wonder if I shall ever attain such eminence' (1: 71). Yet at the same time Rossetti seemed to feel some anxiety about putting her name

168   FIRST-PERSON ANONYMOUS

before the public. In a letter to her brother William, she complains about her poems being published with her signature in *Beautiful Poetry*: 'It is a ghastly circumstance to find ourselves ranked amongst the beautiful poets of England: an additional and by me totally unexpected mishap is that our names are printed' (1: 80).

By the early 1860s, however, Rossetti's reservations about signed publication were clearly outweighed by her desire for critical recognition. In 1861, she made the decision to pursue signed publication in *Macmillan's Magazine* (1859-1900). *Macmillan's* was a literary magazine styled after *Blackwood's* that published poetry, fiction, and reviews as well as articles on contemporary culture and politics. But what made *Macmillan's* distinctive was that it was one of the first mainstream Victorian literary periodicals to publish most contributions with authorial signature. Indeed, as Laurel Brake points out, 'it was with the founding of *Macmillan's Magazine* that a general march toward signature in the Victorian periodicals began' (21). Thomas Hughes outlines the reasoning behind sighed publication in an article titled 'Anonymous Journalism', published in *Macmillan's* in 1861:

> The notion that he [the writer] is to put aside his own individuality, that he is to 'reflect' the opinions of a journal, or, indeed, that he is to 'reflect' anything, is about as mischievous a one as a man can have in his head when he sits down to write; and it is this which lowers the character of so much of our public writing (160).

Hughes' use of masculine pronouns suggests a distinctly male identity for the contemporary writer. However, the journal as a whole emphasized women's participation by publishing the names of prominent women writers. This included Dinah Mulock Craik, Elizabeth Gaskell, Harriet Martineau, Charlotte Younge, Caroline Norton, and Frances Power Cobbe. Thus, by extension, the female author was also an 'individual' who did not have to represent or 'reflect' the editorial views of the magazine. Rather, her name functioned as a marker of individuality and as a marketing device for the magazine. Since Alexander Macmillan often published books by his periodical writers, he used his magazine to build their reputations and visibility, thereby promoting future book sales.[21]

Rossetti was no doubt partly attracted to *Macmillan's* due to the fact that editor David Masson was a family friend; however, she may also have been looking forward to publishing under her own name in a high-profile literary periodical. In January of 1861 Rossetti submitted a selection of poems to Masson, who quickly agreed to publish 'Up-hill'. The critical acclaim brought on by the publication of this and other poems in the magazine led Alexander Macmillan to offer to publish her first signed collection of poetry, *Goblin Market and Other Poems* (1862). Gabriel, who served as Christina's agent throughout the negotiations with Macmillan, wrote to her, 'I saw [Alexander] Macmillan last night, who has been congratulated by some of his contributors on having got a poet at last in your person, and read aloud your lively little Song of the Tomb with great satisfaction' (*Family Letters* 2: 162-63). Interestingly, Gabriel reports Macmillan as having said

CHRISTINA ROSSETTI   169

he had 'gotten a poet' rather than a poem. Clearly, she was to be the next 'name', whose notoriety would help to build the publisher's reputation and sales.

Signed publication in *Macmillan's* thus represented a turning point in Rossetti's career where she finally came into her own as a professional writer. Indeed, in 1863, she writes to Macmillan, 'No one is more aware than myself that what slight footing I have gained in the world of letters has its foundation in your Magazine' (*Letters* 1: 174). At this stage of Rossetti's career, there is much less apology and self-effacement in her commentary on her own work. In a letter to William, she mentions that she has agreed to serve at the Highgate Penitentiary but only on the condition that she 'have leisure to attend to proofs' of her forthcoming book (1: 151). Increasingly confident in her ability to direct her own career, she even dickers with Macmillan over the payment for her poems (1: 173, 174). Indeed, Rossetti's connection with *Macmillan's Magazine* initiated the most productive phase of her career.[22] Twenty-one of her poems appeared in *Macmillan's* during the 1860s, and she published poems under her signature in variety of other periodicals, including *Argosy* and the *English Woman's Journal.* During the following decades, Alexander Macmillan was the publisher for many of Rossetti's books, including *The Prince's Progress and Other Poems* (1866) and *A Pagent and Other Poems* (1881). The critical acclaim that followed the publication of these works established Rossetti as one of the most important poets of her generation.

She became a 'name' on the British literary scene, yet in much of her later poetry, she seems to problematize the correspondence between her name and the personae of her poetry. As Antony Harrison observes, much of Rossetti's work 'abjures both didacticism and sincerity, actively resisting autobiographical readings' (*CR in Context* 17).[23] This is especially evident in Rossetti's sonnet sequence *Monna Innominata* (Unnamed Lady), published in *A Pagent and Other Poems* in 1881. In her preface to the sequence, she suggests that her title refers to the women of the past who, instead of merely serving as muses to great male poets, might have written love poetry themselves. She writes, 'one can imagine many a lady as sharing her lover's poetic aptitude, while the barrier between them might be one held sacred by both, yet not such as to render mutual love incompatible with mutual honor' (229). The sonnet sequence is thus defined as the utterance of Christina Rossetti, whose name appears on the volume's title page, but also as an expression of a multitude of women from the past, whose voices have hitherto been silent. The object of the sonnet sequence, though defined as a man, is equally vague. Is he Christina Rossetti's inaccessible lover or 'everyman' from the past who might have been the object of women's love poetry? The poems themselves offer no particularizing detail that would help the reader to answer this question with any certainty. Indeed, as William Whitla points out, at the end of the sequence, 'the lady [speaker] sinks once more into the anonymity of the *monna innominata*, leaving her inner identity, her roles, and her relationship to her beloved enduring and beguiling puzzles to the reader' (131). The effect of the preface and sequence, then, is to call into question the identity of both speaker and object, lover and beloved.[24] When read without the biographical information imposed on the sequence—in other words, without knowledge of the supposed romance between Rossetti and Charles Cayley—the poems are difficult to interpret as autobiographical.[25]

Such indeterminacy was of course also characteristic of much periodical discourse of the Victorian period, where specificities of gender and identity were complicated and obscured. In *Monna Innominata*, Rossetti was perhaps looking back nostalgically to the 1850s, when she was primarily an anonymous and pseudonymous poet, a 'donna innominata'. In other words, this sequence can be viewed as Rossetti's attempt to recreate a sense of indeterminacy in her work, to identify herself once more as a poet whose work is read without the assumption of a direct correspondence between the authorial name and the autobiographical lyric 'I'. As Susan Conley points out, 'anonymity has a subversive power, in being able to resist the kinds of appropriations to which a name is subject' (375). In *Monna Innominata*, Rossetti recaptures this sense of 'subversive power' by employing poetic devices that would remove the sequence from the category of autobiographical poetry. Rossetti enforced a separation between her work and private life not only through her use of poetic techniques but also by avoiding public appearances.[26] As Antony Harrison demonstrates, by the end of her life she had developed a 'reputation in both England and America as a saintly, reclusive writer of highly wrought and effective poems (both secular and devotional) as well as six widely read books of religious commentary' ('CR and Sage Discourse' 88).

After her death, Rossetti's work continued to receive critical acclaim. Early twentieth-century textbooks and encyclopedias refer to her in laudatory terms, calling her the 'greatest of English poetesses' (Patrick 646) and referring to her work as the 'greatest body of religious verse in English since Herbert and Crashaw and Vaughan' (H. Walker 507). Of course, in addition to this laudatory rhetoric, most posthumous assessments also depict Rossetti as a melancholy 'feminine' poet who works in minor genres. However, on the whole her work is defined as being important to the study of Victorian literature. Indeed, as Virginia Blain points out, Rossetti is the only Victorian woman poet 'never entirely to have slipped out of view' ('Introduction' 8). Part of the reason for the continuing visibility of Rossetti's life and work in the late nineteenth and early twentieth centuries was that William Michael Rossetti made efforts to keep the memory of his sister alive after her death by editing, publishing, and reprinting her work. The posthumous publication of *New Poems* (1896) and *Poetical Works* (1904) re-energized the critical reception of Rossetti's poetry. In these works, William published introductions that reinterpreted his sister's work from a biographical perspective. Rossetti's biographical introduction to *Poetical Works* established many of the stereotypes about Rossetti that remain with us today: that she was pure, unsophisticated, overscrupulous in her religious beliefs, and tortured by amatory self-denial. In a sense, William Michael Rossetti resurrected 'Ellen Alleyn', the female genius whose 'hushed life drama' was tortured by unconsummated passion but whose heart remained 'pure, duteous, concentrated, loving, and devoted' ('Memoir' liii, lxxi).

Though many contemporary critics claimed to disapprove of posthumous biography, they still relished the details provided by William Michael Rossetti's biographical introductions. For example, though *National Review* critic Arthur Benson claims to have some reservations about the intrusiveness of literary biography, he proceeds to explore 'the secrets of a buoyant and tender soul', an investigation which is justified by the fact that 'the same autobiographical savour haunts all her work as haunted the eager dramas of Charlotte Brontë' (756). This comparison is interesting considering that Brontë, like Rossetti, was the special target of biographical criticism after her death. As an exemplar of the 'abused woman author' Brontë serves as a trope for a particular kind of woman author whose life is inseparable from her work. Indeed, for many critics, Rossetti is first and foremost a 'poetess', whose work demonstrates a particularly feminine biography and sensibility. As Theodore Watts-Dunton, a critic for the *Athenaeum,* puts it, readers 'feel that at every page of her writing the beautiful poetry is only the outcome of a life whose almost unexampled beauty fascinates them', and consequently, she comes to represent the 'ideal Christian woman of our own day' (208).

However, to claim that Rossetti's authorial identity was wholly circumscribed and essentialized by her brother and the critics who reviewed his publications is to miss the complexities that surrounded the construction of her authorial identity in the periodical press during the late nineteenth and early twentieth centuries. For many of these critics, as for Virginia Woolf, Rossetti's was a 'complex song' that could not easily be explained or contained by a biographical reading (243). Indeed, most critics of the period emphasize their inability to fully 'see' or understand Rossetti. Thus, at the same time that critics attempted to 'make visible' the connections between Rossetti's poetry and biography, they simultaneously pointed to her 'invisibility' as a woman and poet. That is, at the same time that critical reviews attempted to ground Rossetti's poetry in her biography, they also argued that her poetry could not be located in any particular historical context. For example, critic Paul More, after giving a biographical reading of Rossetti's poems, writes, 'into that region of rapt stillness it seems almost a sacrilege to penetrate with inquisitive, critical mind; it is like tearing away the veil of modesty' (820). Indeed, he remarks, her spiritual removal from the world was reinforced by her physical isolation within the domestic sphere, as if she were a 'cloistered nun' (820). For More, as for many other critics, literary criticism was a self-consciously voyeuristic process, an act of metaphorically gazing upon female poet and then looking away as a gesture of atonement.

For the critic, then, to look upon the woman poet's biographical details is akin to looking upon her body. And paradoxically it is her resistance to this gaze, her disappearance, as it were, that ensures her critical reputation. As one critic for the *Saturday Review* puts it, 'how genuinely and by how many she, not having been seen, was loved' ('Miss Rossetti's Poems' 196). This sense of physical invisibility is shown as the outcome of her connection with the spiritual realm, her ability to see the 'Invisible' (196). For some readers, this sense of invisibility becomes a kind

172 FIRST-PERSON ANONYMOUS

of fictionality. The writer, when separated from the world, becomes a textual construction who can be compared only to characters in the literary realm. To one critic Rossetti is like Dante Gabriel Rossetti's Blessed Damozel, 'circled with a company of singers, yet holding herself aloof in chosen loneliness of passion' (P. More 816). To another she is like Dorothea Brooke, whose 'finer feelings' were destined 'to end in petty collisions with the petty people around [her]' ('Christina Rossetti's *Poems*' 127-28). The name 'Christina Rossetti' for these critics thus becomes a fictional construct, an identity only knowable or understandable through literary reference.

It is tempting to agree with Tricia Lootens, that late Victorian critics, by focusing on the 'invisibility' of Rossetti's work and historical persona, 'attempted to exonerate an artist of the onus of having created art' and 'deprived Rossetti's verse of the worldliness necessary to make it live' (182). However, read from another perspective, the 'disappearance' of Christina Rossetti in critical discourse of the late nineteenth and early twentieth centuries may help to explain why she achieved canonicity whereas many other women poets of the period did not. Because Rossetti's poetry was defined as being ahistorical and non-topical, it was afforded a higher status in the masculine canon. Critics often emphasized her lack of philanthropic or political motivation, using this as justification for her canonical status. Inevitably in these accounts Elizabeth Barrett Browning is presented as Rossetti's anti-type.[27] For example, Alice Law, writing for the *Westminster Review*, argues that while Barrett Browning's poetry demonstrates a 'noble-minded desire to remedy crying abuses of the day', it is Rossetti who achieves the 'supreme expression of poetic art' (452). Likewise, Paul More argues that it is Rossetti's transcendent femininity which makes her work rise above 'Mrs. Browning—her political ideas, her passion for reform, her scholarship' (420). On one hand, these critical accounts marginalize Barrett Browning due to the 'masculine' quality of her verse, but they express a broader trend in literary criticism of the period toward downgrading philanthropic, socially engaged models of female authorship. As noted in chapter five, the social problem novel, reformist periodical, and other genres associated with women's rise to prominence in the field of letters were marked as old fashioned by the 1860s, and the model of cultured authorship, epitomized by George Eliot, came to be defined as the ultimate achievement for women writers.

Located outside the realm of overtly political or philanthropic writing, Rossetti, too, was able to achieve stature in the literary canon as it was comprised at the end of the Victorian era. The play between Rossetti's biographically situated 'feminine' identity and her otherworldly, ahistorical identity seemed to place her simultaneously both inside and outside the realm of the 'poetess'. Paradoxically, as Susan Conley points out, Victorian critics argue that it is Rossetti's willingness to be 'merely a woman' that enables her to achieve the 'masculine-gendered status of "poet"' (381). As much as 'femininity' was viewed as a retreat from the public world—a kind of decontextualization—so was the poetry of the 'feminine' writer made valuable due to its lack of grounding in the material world. In this way,

Rossetti, like Eliot, enters the realm of 'culture' by at once claiming a name and problematizing its historical referentiality. By the end of the century, then, Eliot and Rossetti represent two complementary but distinct models of sage writing—the pseudonymous, cultured woman writer and the named, invisible woman writer. In both cases, the authorial name comes to represent a second self that is connected to but not interchangeable with the historical author.

Such representations of the woman writer would not have been possible without the complex narrative conventions and definitions of authorship associated with Victorian print media. The convention of anonymous and pseudonymous publication in the periodical press during the Victorian period provided women with a model of authorship that countered the tendency toward high-profile signed book publication. The diffusion of authorial identity enabled them to break out of narrow definitions of female authorship, writing on an expanded array of topics from a variety of narrative positions. As they moved between forms of signed and unsigned publication, they discovered ways to capitalize on the conventions of various print media as a way of alternately managing, controlling, publicizing, and suppressing their authorial identities. Women writers did not imagine celebrity and obscurity as an either/or proposition. They strove to keep the divisions between public and private, name and absence, visibility and invisibility, continually in play. The movement toward signed periodical publication and the corresponding movement toward high-culture canon formation brought the issue of women's authorship to a crisis point, where women were challenged to develop ever more innovative ways of evading narrowly defined categories of female authorship. As we have seen, Eliot and Rossetti represent two responses to the dilemma of how to assume a name in a literary culture that requires signature as a marker of literary value while at the same time retaining the indeterminacy associated with anonymous and pseudonymous models of authorship, thereby resisting constrictive definitions of the female author. Their authorial identities remain with us today, not as puzzles to be solved or as selves to be recovered but as complex texts in the history of authorship during the Victorian period.

Notes

1 See also A. Chapman's theoretical discussion of the tendency of critics—past and present—to impose autobiographical readings on Victorian women's poetry (37-45).

2 For further discussion of the genealogy of the term 'poetess', see Conley and Blain ('Letitia Elizabeth Landon').

3 Rossetti's views on the Woman Question are complex and contradictory. She was associated with the Langham Place Group and contributed to a variety of women's causes, including anti-vivisectionist and social purity campaigns (Marsh, *Christina Rossetti* 433-36, 516-19). Yet in 1889 she signed a petition against women's suffrage (554-55). Rossetti's poetry does not assume a consistent polemical stance on the Woman

Question; in fact, she published many poems that would seem to fit into the category of anti-feminist verse (e.g., 'The Lowest Room'). However, as Antony Harrison has pointed out, Rossetti employs the sage discourse of high Anglicanism as a way of subtly challenging patriarchal institutions and ideologies ('Christina Rossetti and the Sage Discourse').

4   Rossetti's most important philanthropic work was with fallen women in the St. Mary Magdalene Penitentiary (see Marsh, *Christina Rossetti* 218-28). As D'Amico has pointed out, some of these experiences undoubtedly influenced the subject matter of her poetry. However, I would argue that her work is not overtly engaged in the discourse on urban investigation, nor is it associated with middle-class radicalism or the popular literature movement.

5   See 'Christina Rossetti's *Poems*', published in *Catholic World* in 1876.

6   William Michael Rossetti excluded some references to Christina Rossetti's poems from his printed version of the *PRB Journal*, published in *Pre-Raphaelite Diaries and Letters* in 1900 (see Fredeman's critical apparatus to the *PRB Journal,* 168-73). For example, the following passage was excluded from the 1900 volume: 'I copied out for next number another poem of our Sister's, 'Sweet Death', as it seems doubtful whether there will be an odd corner adapted to either of the little things I had before selected' (*PRB Journal* 44). Apparently, Gabriel expurgated some references to Elizabeth Siddal from the original manuscript of the *PRB Journal*. William explains his brother's expurgations in *Dante Gabriel Rossetti: His Family Letters* (1: 136).

7   Significantly, the letters I cite in this paragraph did not appear in William Rossetti's *The Family Letters of Christina G. Rossetti.*

8   *The Germ*'s anonymity was apparently successful in masking the individual identities of contributors. A Mr. Bellamy wrote to William after the publication of the first number of *The Germ* asking to be introduced to the author of the poems, supposing them to have been written by a single poet. This error apparently delighted Christina Rossetti. She wrote to William, 'Mr. Bellamy is rather grand; perhaps he would be somewhat startled at an introduction to seven bards where he only imagined one!' (*Letters* 1: 34).

9   This and all other quotes from *The Germ* are taken from the Ashmolean Museum's reprint of the periodical.

10 See Marsh for a discussion of Rossetti's early interest in Gothic fiction (*Christina Rossetti* 30).

11 When in January of 1850 William proposed that Christina's 'A Pause of Thought' be published in *The Germ*, she claimed that the poem's subject matter 'baffled all my efforts at recollection' (*Letters* 1: 34). William later wrote that the poem demonstrated how 'at that early age, [Christina] aspired ardently after poetic fame, with a keen sense of "hope deferred"' ('Introduction' 21).

12 For a discussion of the symbolic meanings of ivy, see Steven Olderr.

13 These omitted stanzas are included in Crump's textual notes to *The Complete Poems* (1: 242-3).

14 For additional analysis of the images of women in *The Germ* and early Pre-Raphaelitism, see Jan Marsh (*Pre-Raphaelite*), and Linda Peterson ('Restoring').

15 The charge of 'effeminacy' would be transformed into a charge of sexual impropriety when Robert Buchanan called *The Germ* 'an unwholesome periodical' in his notorious 1871 article, 'The Fleshly School of Poetry' (446).

16 See Linley for a discussion of the ways in which Rossetti uses *Maude* as a means of exploring the vexed category of the poetess as a 'site not only for the ongoing interrogation of what it means to write as a woman, but also for the development of strategies that might in fact undo the gender of women's writing' (287).

17 Marsh provides a useful overview of Rossetti's connection with the *Bouquet* (*Christina Rossetti* 131-35).

18 Though Christina's 1857 Contribution to *Once a Week*, 'In the Round Tower at Jhansi, June 8, 1857', was intended to be published under her name, it was mistakenly attributed to Caroline G. Rossetti (*Letters* 1: 162).

19 Crump's notes to *The Complete Poems of Christina Rossetti* provide publication information for Rossetti's work. During the 1850s, she published in the following periodicals: *The Crayon, The National Magazine, Once A Week,* and *Our Paper*. She also contributed to the following gift books and anthologies: *Dusseldorf Artist's Album, Nightingale Valley, Beautiful Poetry, Marshall Ladies' Daily Remembrancer, Pictorial Calendar of the Seasons,* and *Midsummer Flowers for the Young*.

20 During roughly the same period as these unsuccessful attempts at publication, Rossetti hints in a letter to her brother William that she would like to pursue publishing opportunities in the *The Artist* (1855). She writes, 'I am glad the *Artist* has hatched at last, and hope it in its turn will lay golden eggs ... I wish I could get into *Delphic* connection [referring to Thomas Delf, editor of the *Artist*] ... Do you think there would be any possibility of such a thing? I have plenty of time down here [in Frome], and can work hard on occasion' (*Letters* 1: 88). Apparently, this effort at publication was unsuccessful as well.

21 See the introduction to *Macmillan's Magazine* in Houghton, *The Wellesley Index to Victorian Periodicals*.

22 See Harrison, *Christina Rossetti in Context* (3,14).

23 Alison Chapman also provides insightful theoretical discussion of the problem of autobiographical 'recovery' of Rossetti from her literary remains. She writes that Rossetti's 'poetics typically inscribe a subjectivity that vacillates between presence and absence and a subjectivity that, furthermore, seems to have erased its own historical context (although there are exceptions to this)' (8).

24 See Whitla and Conley for detailed readings of the ambiguity and indeterminacy in Rossetti's preface.

25 Most autobiographical readings are based on William Michael Rossetti's notes to the poem, published in *Poetical Works*, in which he identifies Charles Cayley as the 'man' in the sequence. See Whitla for a discussion of how biographical readings of the poem are problematized by the sequence's 'ambiguity and concealment of meaning' (85).

26 Paradoxically, she must retreat to the domestic sphere in order to claim a broader context for her poetry. See Susan Conley's fascinating discussion of Rossetti's obscurity, both as 'poetic practice' and 'lifestyle' (378).

27 See Lootens for an analysis of the 'competitive canonization' of Barrett Browning and Rossetti (158-82).

Afterword

In 1877, the *British Medical Journal* published a postmortem analysis of Harriet Martineau's remains. In this report, medical analyst Thomas Greenhow recounts the discovery of a 'vast tumor', thirty inches in circumference, attached to one of Martineau's ovaries (449). He then describes the dissection that followed:

> The disease was in the left ovary. The uterus was small and unaffected. The right ovary was normal. The liver was elevated into the chest by pressure from below, but otherwise appeared normal. The kidneys showed nothing remarkable. The intestines nearly entirely occupied the upper cavity of the abdomen, the stomach being much pushed up, and to the right overlapping the liver a good deal. The diaphragm was much arched, by which the cavity of the chest was much diminished. There must of necessity been considerable interference with the action both of the lungs and heart from pressure (449-50).

In addition to describing the dissection of Martineau's body, Greenhow tells the story of her long and highly publicized struggle with terminal disease, her temporary 'cure' by mesmerism in 1844, and her eventual death in 1876. Greenhow finds the case 'interesting' not only because of the tumor's unusual size but also because he believes an analysis of Martineau's remains might 'serve in some degree to explain some of the peculiarities of character which were apparent during her remarkable career' (450). In this way, the 'peculiarities' of Martineau's professional persona, presumably her outspokenness and radicalism, came to be inextricably connected to her diseased body. By extension, her career, like her body, could be taken apart, examined, and exposed to the public eye.

The postmortem analysis of Martineau's remains can be seen as an analogy for the widespread and invasive critical interest in the lives of women authors during the late nineteenth century. As women novelists and journalists became increasingly involved in mass-market publishing, the female author once again became a social identity that must be theorized, represented, and understood.[1] By century's end, the woman writer and the barriers that impeded her progress were never more visible. Yet ironically, the desire to expose and analyze the woman author was accompanied by a desire to enforce her obscurity. In the last decades of the nineteenth century, countless Victorian women authors disappeared from literary history.

More than any other event in late nineteenth-century culture, the death and critical reconstruction of Harriet Martineau highlighted the contradictory status of women in the literary establishment. An analysis of the critical response to her death reveals the ways in which the investigatory discourse on the woman author was translated into the critical desire to embody the woman author—to analyze the private facts of her body, biography, and domestic life. In one sense, this discourse served to create newly visible role models for aspiring women writers; however, as we will see, it also served to exclude women's writing from the emerging high-culture literary canon.

178   FIRST-PERSON ANONYMOUS

As the longest living terminal patient and social radical, Martineau had in many ways outlived her time, but in the years just following her death, Martineau's memory for a short time haunted writers as they struggled to come to terms with their own changing roles within the literary establishment. The number of biographies, testimonials, critical appraisals, and speeches written on Martineau's behalf just after her death testified to public's desire to 'embody' Martineau—to connect the literary icon to the private woman.[2] The attempt to investigate the 'real' life of Martineau was also an attempt to singularize her identity—to finally know her and to mobilize her image in the service of two causes: the formation of the British feminist movement and the project of establishing the high-culture literary canon. By the end of the century, her image was marginalized and subsumed by both.

Some women activists used the occasion of Martineau's death to mark the beginning of a new era of women's rights and opportunity. In a speech to the Sunday School Lecture Society in 1877, for example, Florence Fenwick Miller draws attention to the connection between Martineau's work and the progress of society as a whole:

> In an earlier age, a Harriet Martineau would have been impossible. Her existence, and the work she did, are at once tokens and results of civilization and progress. The development of mind has brought the moment for the exercise of the power which resides in the physically weak (*Lessons* 29).

For Fenwick Miller, as for many late Victorian women activists, Martineau's career served as an example of women's potential for positive contributions in the political realm.[3] Fenwick Miller writes,

> Yes, Harriet Martineau's life teaches a most valuable lesson to men—both to those who oppose and to those who support the giving of a political existence to women. To those who oppose it, she has shown the fallacy of their confidently-expressed belief about women; she has shown them that it is impossible to predict the action of others in a position in which they never yet have been seen; she has shown them that their audacious certainties about the necessary influence of sex upon thought are so many ignorant and contemptible assumptions (*Lessons* 28).

The politicization of Martineau's image by women activists would seem to have ensured a lasting place for her work in the history of the women's movement; ironically, it led to her disappearance in literary history. Though activists such as Fenwick Miller acknowledged Martineau's many contributions to the Woman Question and other political issues, they stressed that it was the 'story of her life's work', not her work itself, which would have a lasting impact on society (*Lessons* 27).[4]

Part of what made Martineau's story serve as a replacement for her work was the fact that much of her *oeuvre* was published anonymously. Though some critics acknowledged that Martineau had contributed vast numbers of articles to the *Daily News*, the *Westminster Review, Household Words,* and other periodicals, they for the most part viewed these works as ephemeral. Likewise, her signed works were viewed as period pieces, the useful and sometimes controversial literature of an earlier age. G. A. Simcox, for example, remarks, 'the fine writing and thinking which are fatiguing to a reader now, were very likely elevating then, not only to the writer, but to her restricted public' (522). Similarly, Margaret Oliphant writes of Martineau's *Society in America* and *Retrospect of Western Travel*, 'So far as our recollection of them goes, they are not very remarkable books; but the world has changed so completely since then, that the interest has, of course, very nearly gone out of them' ('Harriet' 490).

In formulating definitions of 'great' literature, critics found the didacticism of Martineau's work out of step with new definitions of literary value. Abraham Hayward, for example, observes, 'What a pity it is that Miss Martineau should have tried to persuade herself and others that political economy, considered as a science, is a fit subject for fiction!' (498). Oliphant, for her part, believed that Martineau had been 'very much overrated as a writer; and indeed, except in the single fact that her Political Economy stories really met a public need, we find it very difficult to understand on what her great reputation was founded' (496). Through their analysis of Martineau's fiction, both critics imply that her work lacks those qualities that constitute canonical nineteenth-century literature: it is didactic instead of artistic, topical instead of timeless.

But perhaps what contributed the most to the effacement of Martineau's achievements at the end of the nineteenth century were autobiographical works that emanated from her own pen. Throughout her lifetime, Martineau had attempted to carefully construct her public image—by writing essays in retaliation against what she saw as unjust appraisals of her work and character and by controlling who had knowledge of her authorship of specific works. She, like Johnstone, Gaskell, Eliot, and Rossetti, had always been careful to avoid direct forms of self-representation lest she be accused of vanity and egotism. At the end of her life, she attempted to continue this project of indirect self-representation by writing her own obituary, which was published in the *Daily News* just after her death. Written in the third person, it reviews the high and low points of Martineau's life and character, remarking, 'But none of her novels or tales have, or ever had, in the eyes of good judges or in her own, any character of permanence' (*On Women* 39). Amusingly enough, she punctuates such self-effacing commentary with plugs for her *Autobiography,* which was scheduled to be released to the public shortly after her death. She writes, 'Harriet Martineau's forthcoming Autobiography will of course tell the story of the struggle she passed though to get her work published in any manner and on any terms' (38).

Ironically, Martineau attempts to perform the ultimate act of self-effacement by writing her own obituary in an anonymous journalistic voice while at the same time performing the ultimate act of self-advertisement by puffing her own book. In the end, the anonymity Martineau was attempting to maintain in writing this obituary was lost. After her death, the editors of the *Daily News* retitled it 'An Autobiographic Memoir' and printed it with Martineau's by-line. In this way, her attempt at self-reconstruction had the effect of turning her into a public spectacle— the woman author who would vainly write her own obituary and puff her own book while posing as a anonymous journalist.

180   FIRST-PERSON ANONYMOUS

The 'unmasking' of Harriet Martineau was of course carried out not only by the editors of the *Daily News* but by Martineau herself. Although Martineau adhered to this de-personalized model of women's authorship at various points in her career, her *Autobiography* in many ways undermined these efforts. By presenting herself as a great woman of letters, she suggested that the details of her private life could provide moral instruction and insight into the development of Victorian politics and culture. Autobiographies of Leigh Hunt (1850), John Stuart Mill (1873), and John Henry Newman (1864) had certainly served as capstones to prestigious literary careers. Though such narratives might facilitate the canonization of the male author by making connections between his public and private identities, for a woman they had the opposite effect.

By drawing attention to her life as a 'real' woman, Martineau succeeded in singularizing a complex public image that for many years had been constructed and reconstructed in periodical reviews and in her own signed and unsigned texts. Consequently, what survived into the twentieth century were Martineau's self-representations in her *Autobiography*. As Margaret Oliphant remarked in 1877,

> Had some kind fairy set fire benevolently to the piles of printed paper so easily disposed of in one stage, so indestructible in another, which have now at last made their way into the world, and are unhappily no longer within the reach of burning, the reputation of Miss Martineau would have settled down into that mellow glow of universal acceptance which lasts longer than more special crowns ('Harriet' 473).

It is impossible to know whether Martineau would have found the 'mellow glow of universal acceptance' had she not written the *Autobiography*, but it does seem likely that, as Oliphant suggests, Martineau's reputation suffered as a result of its publication.

As many contemporary critics noticed, Martineau's *Autobiography* succeeded in creating and solidifying negative stereotypes about her life and character. Martineau came to be seen as the crotchety and self-righteous spinster who popularized the ideas of her male contemporaries. Margaret Oliphant called the *Autobiography* a 'terrible instrument of self-murder' ('Harriet' 472). Similarly, Florence Fenwick Miller commented on its self-destructiveness:

> No one who knew her considers that she did herself justice in the *Autobiography*. It is hard and censorious; it displays vanity, both in its depreciation of her own work, and in its recital of the petty slights and insults which had been offered to her from time to time; it is aggressive, as though replying to enemies rather than appealing to friends; and no one of either the finer or the softer qualities of her nature is at all adequately indicated. It is in short, the least worthy of her true self of all the writings of her life (*Harriet* 233-34).

Martineau's harsh self-representations in the *Autobiography* also disturbed George Eliot, who had in some sense modeled her early career after Martineau's example of influential obscurity and indirect activism. Eliot writes to Cara Bray in 1877, 'You must read Harriet Martineau's Autobiography ... . The account of her childhood and early youth is most pathetic and interesting, but as in all books of

AFTERWORD

181

the kind, the charm departs as the life advances, and the writer has to tell of her own triumphs' (*Letters* 6: 353). Is it not wrong, Eliot seems to ask, for Martineau to display her 'triumphs' before the world? Certainly Eliot was not adverse to constructing her own public image as a Victorian sage in the later years of her career, yet she had always resisted forms of direct self-representation in her writing (I. Taylor 177-93). She no doubt felt that such representations would expose the details of her private life to public scrutiny and would demystify the relationship between the complex narrative voice of her work and her private, embodied self.

In her *Autobiography,* Martineau constructs this 'embodied' authorial self by dwelling on her physical state at various points of her literary career.[5] As Dorothy Mermin has noticed, the *Autobiography* suggests that 'Martineau's triumphantly self-sufficient career is founded in incompleteness and deprivation' that is 'located in the first instance in her body' (101). The connection between Martineau's literary achievements and physical incapacitation is reinforced in the 'Memorials' compiled by Maria Chapman, which include many of Martineau's final letters describing her struggle with physical pain (527-60). This image of the ailing, 'embodied' author is also constructed in memorial letters written by Henry Atkinson, who tells Chapman that under hypnosis Martineau had once uttered, 'I shall become an apostle of pain!' (qtd. in Chapman 589). As the 'apostle of pain', Martineau thus comes to stand for the suffering and abused woman author, whose work can be understood only within the context of painful biographical details. Just as Gaskell's *Life* came to be viewed as the real story of Charlotte Brontë, Martineau's *Autobiography* came to be seen as the authoritative source of knowledge about her gender, life, and persona. As such, her work became interesting only inasmuch as it illuminated that essential identity. It was just the kind of author- and gender-based critical appraisal that Martineau had fought against throughout her career—yet it was a legacy that she had helped to create.

Another reason Martineau's *Autobiography* served to efface her work within literary history was that it constructed an image of the woman of letters that by the 1870s had become largely obsolete. While the *Autobiography* presented anonymous journalism as an integral, productive facet of a woman writer's career, most contemporaneous images of the woman writer and journalist were less optimistic. As Penny Boumelha points out, at the end of the nineteenth century, most novels that featured women journalists as characters depicted their careers as lives of drudgery and obscurity.[6] Marian Yule in George Gissing's *New Grub Street* (1891), for example, reflects on the meaninglessness of her journalistic work in this way:

> She kept asking herself what was the use and purpose of such a life as she was condemned to lead. When already there was more good literature in the world than any mortal could cope with in his lifetime, here was she exhausting herself in the manufacture of printed stuff which no one even pretended to be more than a commodity for the day's market. What unspeakable folly! To write—was not that the joy and privilege of one who had an urgent message for the world? (89).

182 FIRST-PERSON ANONYMOUS

Anonymity does not provide a means for Marian to maneuver for higher stature within the literary establishment; it is a state of being that classes her with all of the other journalistic hacks who fuel the market for literary goods. Unlike Martineau, she produces no 'urgent message for the world', only the endless pages needed to satisfy the public's desire for literary commodities.

The pessimism about women's literary careers expressed in novels of the late nineteenth century was partly caused by the gradual disappearance of genres that had enabled the rise of the woman of letters at mid-century: the social problem novel and the anonymous periodical. But the lack of optimism about women's careers as writers was also part of a larger anxiety among authors about the loss of a receptive audience for their work.[7] As Leslie Stephen remarked in 1881, the new man of letters

> becomes famous, not to be the cherished companion of the day, but to be mobbed by a crowd. He may become a recluse, nowhere more easily than in London; but then he can hardly write effective essays upon life; or he may throw himself into some of the countless 'movements' of the day, and will have to be in too deadly earnest for the pleasant interchange of social persiflage with a skilful blending of lively and severe. The little friendly circle of sympathetic hearers is broken up for good or bad, dissolved into fragments and whirled into mad confusion (64-65).

The sense of dislocation and confusion within literary culture was in part caused by the expansion of the commercial print trade and mass reading audiences during the last decades of the nineteenth century.[8] Viewing themselves as a cultured minority within the commercial marketplace, writers began to formalize their efforts toward self-advocacy and professionalization.[9] Walter Besant's professional advocacy group, the Society of Authors, was established in 1883 and in 1890 began publishing *The Author,* a periodical designed specifically for an audience of professional writers (Colby, 'Harnessing').[10] Nicknamed the Society for the Prevention of Cruelty to Authors, Besant's organization was based on the conception of the author as a marginalized member of society, whose interests could only be represented through self-help and collective action (Colby 113). Though women were included in the Society of Authors, they also founded their own advocacy groups in the 1890s, most notably the Institute of Women Journalists (1895) and the Society of Women Journalists (1899).[11] As Sally Mitchell, Margaret Beetham, and Elaine Showalter have demonstrated, the increasing professionalization of women writers at the end of the century corresponded with expanded employment opportunities for women in newspaper writing, women's periodicals, new woman novels, and sensation fiction.[12]

However, at the same time that women were gaining increased access to professional writing careers, they were simultaneously marginalized within the high-culture literary establishment. As Tuchman and Fortin have shown, the high-culture novel came to be defined as a 'male preserve' at the end of the nineteenth century (5). Correspondingly, they contend, 'women were identified with mass audiences, passive entertainment, and flutter—popular culture' (78).[13] In judging the literary achievements of their age, high-culture critics such as Leslie Stephen,

Matthew Arnold, and John Morley most often selected men as prototypical great British authors. For example, John Morley included no women in his series of critical biographies, *English Men of Letters* (1878-92); instead, he selected Byron, Burns, Carlyle, Coleridge, De Quincey, Dickens, Hawthorne, Keats, Lamb, Landor, Macaulay, Scott, Shelley, Southey, Thackeray, and Wordsworth as the nineteenth century's representative men. The exclusive masculinity of Morley's collection is interesting considering that it was inspired by two 'feminine' sources: Harriet Martineau's *Biographical Sketches* (1869) and Morley's own article on George Eliot published in *Macmillan's Magazine* (1866).[14] In 1877, Morley did try to persuade George Eliot to write a biography of Shakespeare for his collection; apparently, he felt that it was acceptable for women to contribute to project but not to be otherwise represented within the canon of English authors.[15] Eliot declined the honor. When the *English Men of Letters* project was revived in a second series (1902-19), however, George Eliot finally did make an appearance—as one of only four women authors whose biographies were included in the 67 volumes of Morley's series as a whole.[16] By this time, most of the other great nineteenth-century women of letters—including Harriet Martineau, Christian Johnstone, and Elizabeth Gaskell, as well as Margaret Oliphant, Dinah Mulock Craik, and Anne Mozley—had disappeared from literary history.

Yet their absence in literary history is less cause to lament than it is cause to wonder. For paradoxically the disappearance of the Victorian woman author was contemporaneous with her appearance as a major force within the field of letters— a legacy that remains with us into the present day. As anonymous and pseudonymous writers, women capitalized on the conventions of periodical journalism in order to expand the audience and subject matter of women's writing as well as to exert influence on public policy, including the Woman Question and the Condition-of-England Question. Located within the context of anonymous journalism, women developed complex authorial identities that were not subject to the biographical discourse surrounding the female author. These experiences led women to adopt strategies in their signed works of poetry, fiction, and non-fiction that would enable them to resist confining stereotypes associated with female authorship. At the same time, they sometimes made use of the discourse on the woman author as a means of marketing their work. The movement toward signed publication in the periodicals and the corresponding proliferation of literary biographies challenged women writers to find ever more innovative ways of claiming a 'name' in the high-culture literary canon without narrowly defining their work as the outgrowth of a conventionally 'feminine' biographical identity.

The simultaneous appearance and disappearance of the woman author at the end of the nineteenth century had important implications for the history of women's writing. The image of the woman as grub street hack eventually gave way to the image of Virginia Woolf, who, as Alison Booth has shown, continued in the tradition of women's writing established by George Eliot (*Greatness*). However, this was a tradition established not only by George Eliot but by Martineau, Johnstone, Gaskell, Rossetti, and countless other women writers who constructed complex narrative identities through the convention of anonymous and pseudonymous journalism and who revised and complicated these journalistic

184 FIRST-PERSON ANONYMOUS

forms in their signed works of fiction, non-fiction, and poetry. While some definitions of the woman author proved to be less 'visible' in literary history than others, they were nonetheless transformative within the overall history of women's writing, activism, and enfranchisement. By working in the interstices between high-culture literary production and popular print culture—that is, by simultaneously writing for the anonymous periodical press and engaging in high-profile literary careers—women writers were able to complicate notions of 'feminine' writing and identity, redefining themselves within and against the narrative and social conventions of their age.

Paradoxically, it was their absence as conventionally defined women—their experiments in anonymity, pseudonymity, and other narrative forms designed to complicate notions of single authorship—that enabled their vast but still largely unrecognized contributions to literary history. Our desire to understand and to record these contributions has led to a renaissance in Victorian studies that has now lasted over twenty-five years. The expansion of our efforts of literary recovery to incorporate women's achievements in journalistic publishing promises to provide a more nuanced and complex view of women's literary careers during the nineteenth century. Such efforts will enable us to investigate the careers of the hundreds of women whose work in journalism has been lost to literary history. These efforts will also help us to understand the ways women worked within and across diverse genres and print media as they made their way in a male-dominated profession.

However, I do not believe that our only goal should be to 'recover' the lost lives, works, and names of women within the journalistic press and within literary history in general. Indeed, we must be careful that we do not reimpose narrow definitions of 'female writing' on Victorian women's work. As Alison Chapman puts it, we must continually ask ourselves whether our effort to recover a lost tradition of women's writing is 'really an unproblematic uncovering of lost, forgotten and silenced works, or is it somehow always a re-covering?' (2). Do we reimpose biographical interpretations on women's writing as a way of organizing and understanding their achievements? In order to avoid this process of 're-covering' women's writing, we must be aware of our own roles as critics embedded in an institutional matrix that reinforces and relies upon notions of the author as an intentional, single-gendered agent in literary history. One of the goals of this book has been to provide the tools for reading the Victorian women writer simultaneously as named and unnamable, creator and creation, writer and text. This approach is premised on the idea that women were both agents and constructed identities within Victorian print media who at once privileged and undermined notions of individual, celebrity authorship in their work.

As we continue our study of Victorian authorship, our object must not be merely to 'make visible' a separate canon or tradition of women's journalism or literature but to interrogate notions of obscurity and fame themselves in the history of women's writing. This will enable us to understand the contradictory impulses that made women desire simultaneous careers as famous novelists and anonymous journalists and that made them embrace and resist the label of 'female author'. We must learn to appreciate women's self-effacement in the nineteenth-century tradition—not only as a patriarchally imposed requirement but also as a gesture of

AFTERWORD

185

self-empowerment. In rethinking women's use of anonymous and pseudonymous identities in their work, we must acknowledge that women's manipulation of authorial gender was not only an expression of their 'anxiety of authorship' but also was part of wider cultural controversies over individualized authorship within Victorian society. Further investigation of the identity politics associated with Victorian print media will enable us to develop a greater understanding of the obstacles women faced within the nineteenth-century literary establishment—but also the opportunities they created for themselves within the changing field of professional publication.

Notes

1   Much of this discursive activity was centered on women's sensation fiction and the new woman novel. See Boumelha ('Woman of Genius'), Beetham (115-30), Showalter (153-4, 182-3), and Helsinger et al. (3: 111-70).

2   See, for example, M. W. Chapman and Fenwick Miller (*1885*).

3   Martineau''s *Autobiography* was especially influential in this regard. As Mitzi Myers has argued, it can be read as an 'emancipation proclamation of a female philosopher' that provided a model of how women could overcome adversity and engage in influential writing careers ('Harriet' 53). See also Peterson, who argues that the *Autobiography* 'raised questions for women writers about gender and genre, about their relationship to dominant (male) literary traditions and the desirability of creating an autobiographical literature of their own' (*VictorianAutobiography* 124).

4   This sentiment was echoed by Margaret Oliphant, who remarked in 1877 that Martineau's 'own stout heart, and unfailing resolution, and confidence in her project [*Illustrations of Political Economy*], form a chapter in literature much more interesting than a dozen mediocre stories like Ella of Graveloch' ('Harriet' 484).

5   See, for example, Martineau's discussion of her childhood illnesses (1: 10-11), deafness (1: 74-75), the first onset of her disease in 1839 (2: 147-52); and its return in 1854 (2: 430-35).

6   Boumelha ('Woman of Genius') and Cross (194-98) both discuss of images of the woman writer in novels of the *fin de siècle*. Examples include Rhoda Broughton, *A Beginner* (1894), Mary Chomondeley, *Red Pottage* (1899), Marie Corelli, *The Sorrows of Satan* (1895), E. M. Forester, *A Room with a View* (1908), George Gissing, *New Grub Street* (1891), Sarah Grand, *The Beth Book* (1897), George Meredith, *Diana of the Crossways* (1885), Charlotte Riddell, *A Struggle for Fame* (1883), Anthony Trollope, *The Way We Live Now* (1875), and Charlotte Yonge, *The Two Sides of the Shield* (1885).

7   Heyck (190-220), Huyssen (52-53), and Eagleton (45-67).

8   Williams (*Long Revolution* 194-99).

9   See Besant's 'Literature as a Career' (1892) for further elucidation of this position. Besant identifies the barriers that prevent men and women of letters from achieving status as professionals within the literary marketplace.

10 The first Society of Authors in England was established by Charles Dickens in 1843. See Besant, 'Society of British Authors' (1889).

11 See Mitchell (109) and Beetham (128).

12 Beetham (128-29) and Showalter (154-57).

13 Andreas Huyssen also examines the feminization of mass culture at the end of the nineteenth century and explores the relationship of this trend to the development of the modernist sensibility (44-62).

14 See Nadel (32, 40-41). In his discussion of Morley's positivist approach to biography, Nadel suggests even more ways that Martineau's biographical writing might have served as a model for Morley's series (38-41). As Linda Peterson has pointed out, Martineau's *Autobiography* was one of the first examples of positivist autobiography published in England (*Victorian* 136-55). Thus, since Martineau's *Autobiography* was published just one year before the start of Morley's series, it may also have served as an important model. Ironically, even though Martineau's biographical criticism influenced the shape of Morley's project, her biography was never included in it.

15 Nadel provides useful information about the *English Men of Letters* series and about Morley's interchange with Eliot over her possible contribution (34-5). Apparently, a volume on Gaskell was proposed for the series but never published (Shorter 3). Morley apparently was able to convince one woman to write a volume for the first series: Margaret Oliphant published her biography of Sheridan in 1883. Women authors were not otherwise 'represented' in the first series of Morley's *English Men of Letters* published by Macmillan. Interestingly enough, Macmillan republished a series of 'classic' women's novels in the 1890s edited by Anne Ritchie Thackeray (Peterson, 'No Finger Posts' 44). During roughly the same time period, W. H. Allen published a series titled *Eminent Women*, which included book-length biographies of Martineau and Eliot.

16 Other biographies of women authors included in the second series were Emily Lawless' *Maria Edgeworth* (1904), Austin Dobson's *Fanny Burney* (1903), and Francis Ware Cornish's *Jane Austen* (1913).

Works Cited

Altick, Richard. *The English Common Reader: A Social History of the Mass Reading Public, 1800-1900*. Chicago: U of Chicago P, 1957.

—. *Lives and Letters: A History of Literary Biography in England and America*. New York: Knopf, 1965.

Anderson, Carol, and Aileen Riddell. 'The Other Great Unknowns: Women Fiction Writers of the Early Nineteenth Century'. *A History of Scottish Women's Writing*. Eds. Douglas Gifford and Dorothy McMillan. Edinburgh: Edinburgh UP, 1997. 179-95.

Anderson, William. *The Scottish Nation; Or the Surnames, Families, Literature, Honours, and Biographical History of the People of Scotland*. 3 vols. Edinburgh: Fullarton, 1863.

'Anonymous Journalism'. *Saturday Review* 20 Nov. 1858: 499-500.

'Appreciation of Literary Merit'. *Eliza Cook's Journal* 7 August 1852: 231-33.

Arnold, Matthew. *Culture and Anarchy*. New Haven: Yale UP, 1994.

'*Art and Poetry* Review'. *Guardian* 8 (1850): 623.

'Authoresses'. *Saturday Review* 11 November 1865: 601-3.

Babbage, Benjamin Herschel. *Report to the General Board of Health on a Preliminary Inquiry into the Sewerage, Drainage, and Supply of Water, and the Sanitary Condition of the Inhabitants of the Hamlet of Haworth*. London: Clowes, 1850.

Bamber, Linda. 'Self-defeating Politics in George Eliot's *Felix Holt*'. *Victorian Studies* 18 (1975): 419-35.

Barthes, Roland. 'The Death of the Author'. *Authorship from Plato to the Postmodern: A Reader*. Ed. Seán Burke. Edinburgh: Edinburgh UP, 1995. 125-30.

Beard, J. R. '*Mary Barton*'. *British Quarterly Review* 9 (1849): 117-36.

Becker, Lydia. 'Female Suffrage'. *Contemporary Review* 4 (1867): 307-16.

Beer, Gillian. *George Eliot*. Bloomington: Indiana UP, 1986.

Beetham, Margaret. *A Magazine of Her Own?: Domesticity and Desire in the Woman's Magazine, 1800-1914*. New York: Routledge, 1996.

Benson, Arthur. 'Christina Rossetti'. *National Review* 24 (1895): 753-63.

Bertram, James. *Some Memories of Books, Authors, and Events*. London: Constable, 1893.

Besant, Walter. 'The First Society of British Authors'. *Essays and Historiettes*. Port Washington, NY: Kennikat, 1970. 271-307.

—. 'Literature as a Career'. *Essays and Historiettes*. Port Washington, NY: Kennikat, 1970. 308-36.

Bick, Suzann. 'Clouding the "Severe Truth": Elizabeth Gaskell's Strategy in *The Life of Charlotte Brontë*'. *Essays in Arts and Sciences* 11 (1982): 33-47.

'Biographic Sketches: Hannah More'. *Chambers' Edinburgh Journal* 3 (22 February 1834): 29.

Blain, Virginia. Introduction. *Victorian Women Poets: A New Annotated Anthology*. Ed. Virginia Blain. London: Longman, 2001. 1-16.

—. 'Letitia Elizabeth Landon, Eliza Mary Hamilton, and the Genealogy of the Victorian Poetess'. *Victorian Poetry* 33 (1995): 31-51.

Bode, Rita. 'Power and Submission in *Felix Holt*'. *Studies in English Literature* 35.4 (1995): 769-88.

Bodenheimer, Rosemarie. *The Politics of Story in Victorian Social Fiction*. Ithaca: Cornell UP, 1988.

—. *The Real Life of Mary Ann Evans: George Eliot, Her Letters and Fiction*. Ithaca: Cornell UP, 1994.

Booth, Alison. *Greatness Engendered: George Eliot and Virginia Woolf.* Ithaca: Cornell UP, 1992.

—. 'Not All Men Are Selfish and Cruel: *Felix Holt* as a Feminist Novel'. *Gender and Discourse in Victorian Literature and Art.* Eds. Antony Harrison and Beverly Taylor. DeKalb: Northern Illinois UP, 1992. 143-60.

Boumelha, Penny. 'George Eliot and the End of Realism'. *Women Reading Women's Writing.* Ed. Sue Roe. New York: St. Martin's, 1987. 15-35.

—. 'The Woman of Genius and the Woman of Grub Street: Figures of the Female Writer in British *Fin-de-Siècle* Fiction'. *English Literature in Transition* 40.2 (1997): 164-80.

Brady, Kristin. *Women Writers: George Eliot.* New York: St. Martin's, 1992.

Brake, Laurel. *Subjugated Knowledges: Journalism, Gender and Literature.* New York: New York UP, 1994.

Brantlinger, Patrick. *The Spirit of Reform: British Literature and Politics, 1832-67.* Cambridge: Harvard UP, 1977.

'The British Press: Its Growth, Liberty, and Power'. *North British Review* 30 (1859): 367-402.

Brougham, Henry. 'Memoirs of Lady Hester Stanhope'. *Quarterly Review* 76 (1845): 430-59.

Brown, Ford. *Fathers of the Victorians: The Age of Wilberforce.* Cambridge: Cambridge UP, 1961.

Brown, Homer Obed. *Institutions of the English Novel.* Philadelphia: U of Pennsylvania P, 1997.

Browning, Elizabeth Barrett. *Aurora Leigh: A Poem.* Chicago: Academy Chicago Publishers, 1992.

Buchanan, Robert. 'The Fleshly School of Poetry: Mr. D. G. Rossetti'. *The Pre-Raphaelites.* Ed. Jerome Buckley. New York: Modern Library, 1968. 437-60.

—. 'Immorality in Authorship'. *Fortnightly Review* 6 o.s. (15 Sept. 1866): 289-300.

Burke, Seán, ed. *Authorship from Plato to the Postmodern: A Reader.* Edinburgh: Edinburgh UP, 1995.

Burness, Catriona. '"Kept some steps behind him": Women in Scotland, 1780-1920'. *A History of Scottish Women's Writing.* Eds. Douglas Gifford and Dorothy McMillan. Edinburgh: Edinburgh UP, 1997. 103-118.

Caine, Barbara. 'Feminism, Journalism and Public Debate'. *Women and Literature in Britain, 1800-1900.* Ed. Joanne Shattock. Cambridge: Cambridge UP, 2001. 99-118.

—. *Victorian Feminists.* Oxford: Oxford UP, 1992.

'The Cant of Criticism'. *Fraser's Magazine* 19 (1839): 95-103.

Carlyle, Thomas. 'Biography'. *Critical and Miscellaneous Essays.* Vol. 4. London: Chapman and Hall, 1891. 51-66.

—. 'Characteristics'. *Critical and Miscellaneous Essays.* Vol. 4. London: Chapman and Hall, 1891. 1-38.

—. *Chartism.* New York: Millar, 1885.

—. *Collected Letters of Thomas and Jane Welsh Carlyle.* Ed. Charles Sanders. 28 vols. Durham: Duke UP, 1970.

—. 'Jean Paul Friedrich Richter Again'. *Critical and Miscellaneous Essays.* New York: Appleton, 1870. 196-219.

—. 'On Heroes, Hero-Worship, and the Heroic in History: The Hero as Poet'. *English Prose of the Victorian Era.* Eds. Charles Harrold and William Templeman. New York: Oxford UP, 1938. 182-196.

—. *Sartor Resartus.* Oxford: Oxford UP, 1987.

—. 'Schiller, Goethe, and Madam de Staël'. *Fraser's Magazine* 5 (1832): 171-76.

—. 'Signs of the Times'. *Scottish and Other Miscellanies.* London: Dent, 1915. 223-45.

WORKS CITED   189

—. 'Sir Walter Scott'. *Scottish and Other Miscellanies*. London: Dent, 1915. 54-111.

Carroll, David. *George Eliot and the Conflict of Interpretations: A Reading of the Novels*. Cambridge: Cambridge UP, 1992.

—. *George Eliot: The Critical Heritage*. New York: Barnes & Noble, 1971.

Casey, Ellen Miller. 'Edging Women Out?: Reviews of Women Novelists in the *Athenaeum*, 1860-1900'. *Victorian Studies* 39.2 (1996): 151-71.

Chadwick, Edwin. *Report on the Sanitary Condition of the Labouring Population of Great Britain*. Edinburgh: Edinburgh UP, 1965.

Chapman, Alison. *The Afterlife of Christina Rossetti*. London: Macmillan, 2000.

Chapman, Maria Weston. 'Memorials to Harriet Martineau'. *Autobiography of Harriet Martineau*. Boston: Osgood, 1877. Vol. 2. 137-596.

Chorley, Henry. *The Authors of England: A Series of Medallion Portraits of Modern Literary Characters*. London: Charles Tilt, 1838.

—. '*Mary Barton*'. *Athenaeum* 21 Oct. 1848: 1050-51.

Christ, Carol. 'The Hero as Man of Letters: Masculinity and Victorian Non-Fiction Prose'. *Victorian Sages and Cultural Discourse: Renegotiating Gender and Power*. Ed. Thaïs Morgan. New Brunswick: Rutgers UP, 1990. 19-31.

'Christina Rossetti's *Poems*'. *Catholic World* 24 (1876): 122-29.

Cobbe, Frances Power. 'What Shall We Do with Our Old Maids?' *Fraser's Magazine* 66 (1862): 594-610.

Colby, Robert. 'Harnessing Pegasus: Walter Besant, *The Author*, and the Profession of Authorship'. *Victorian Periodicals Review* 23.3 (1990): 111-20.

Colby, Robin. '*Some Appointed Work to Do*': Women and Vocation in the Fiction of Elizabeth Gaskell*. Westport: Greenwood, 1995.

Cole, Lucinda. '(Anti)Feminist Sympathies: The Politics of Relationship in Smith, Wollstonecraft, and More'. *ELH* 58 (1991): 107-40.

Collet, Collet D. *History of the Taxes on Knowledge: Their Origin and Repeal*. 2 vols. London: Fisher Unwin, 1899.

Colley, Linda. *Britons: Forging the Nation, 1707-1837*. New Haven: Yale UP, 1992.

Conley, Susan. '"Poet's Right": Christina Rossetti as Anti-Muse and the Legacy of the "Poetess"'. *Victorian Poetry* 32 (1994): 365-86.

Conolly, Matthew. *Biographical Dictionary of Eminent Men of Fife*. Cupar: Orr, 1866.

Cook, Eliza. 'A Word to My Readers'. *Eliza Cook's Journal* 1 (1849): 1.

Corbett, Mary Jean. *Representing Femininity: Middle-Class Subjectivity in Victorian and Edwardian Women's Autobiographies*. New York: Oxford UP, 1992.

Courtney, Janet. *The Adventurous Thirties: A Chapter in the Women's Movement*. London: Oxford UP, 1933.

Cox, Edward. 'Poetry and the Drama'. *The Critic* 15 February 1850: 94-95.

Craig, David. 'Fiction and the Rising Industrial Classes'. *Essays in Criticism* 17 (1967): 64-74.

Craik, Dinah Mulock. 'To Novelists—and a Novelist'. *Macmillan's Magazine* 3 (1861): 441-48.

—. 'A Woman's Thoughts About Women'. *Maude, On Sisterhoods, and A Woman's Thoughts About Women*. Ed. Elaine Showalter. New York: New York UP, 1993. 59-216.

Croker, John Wilson. 'Conduct of Ministers'. *Quarterly Review* 65 (1839): 283-314.

—. 'Miss Martineau's *Morals and Manners*'. *Quarterly Review* 63 (1839): 61-72.

Croker, John Wilson, John Gibson Lockhart, and George Poulett Scrope. 'Miss Martineau's Monthly Novels'. *Quarterly Review* 49 (1833): 136-152.

Cross, Nigel. *The Common Writer: Life in Nineteenth-Century Grub Street*. Cambridge: Cambridge UP, 1985.

190   FIRST-PERSON ANONYMOUS

'Culture'. *Saturday Review* 16 June 1866: 711-12.

D'Albertis, Deirdre. '"Bookmaking Out of the Remains of the Dead": Elizabeth Gaskell's *The Life of Charlotte Brontë'. Victorian Studies* 39.1 (1995): 1-31.

—. *Dissembling Fictions: Elizabeth Gaskell and the Victorian Social Text.* New York: St. Martin's, 1997.

D'Amico, Diane. '"Equal Before God": Christina Rossetti and the Fallen Women of Highgate Penitentiary'. *Gender and Discourse in Victorian Literature and Art.* Eds. Antony Harrison and Beverly Taylor. DeKalb: Northern Illinois UP, 1992. 67-83.

Dallas, E. S. 'Currer Bell'. *Blackwood's Edinburgh Magazine* 82 (1857): 77-94.

—. 'Popular Literature—The Periodical Press'. *Blackwood's Edinburgh Magazine* 85 (1859): 96-112, 180-95.

David, Deirdre. *Intellectual Women and Victorian Patriarchy: Harriet Martineau, Elizabeth Barrett Browning, George Eliot.* Ithaca: Cornell UP, 1987.

Davis, Lennard. *Factual Fictions: The Origins of the English Novel.* New York: Columbia UP, 1983.

Delaura, David. 'Heroic Egotism: Goethe and the Fortunes of *Bildung* in Victorian England'. *Johann Wolfgang Von Goethe: One Hundred and Fifty Years of Continuing Vitality.* Eds. Ulrich Goebel and Wolodymyr Zyla. Lubbock: Texas Tech P, 1984. 41-60.

De Quincey, Thomas. *Works.* 16 vols. Edinburgh: Black, 1862-74.

Donoghue, Frank. *The Fame Machine: Book Reviewing and Eighteenth-Century Literary Careers.* Stanford: Stanford UP, 1996.

Doody, Margaret. 'George Eliot and the Eighteenth-Century Novel'. *Nineteenth-Century Fiction* 35.3 (1980): 260-91.

Dowden, Edward. 'George Eliot'. *Contemporary Review* 20 (1872): 403-22.

Downing, Harriet. 'Remembrances of a Monthly Nurse'. *Fraser's Magazine* 14 (1836): 398-407, 531-44, 722-32.

Duncan, Ian. *Modern Romance and Transformations of the Novel: The Gothic, Scott, Dickens.* Cambridge: Cambridge UP, 1992.

DuPlessis, Rachel Blau. *Writing Beyond the Ending: Narrative Strategies of Twentieth-Century Women Writers.* Bloomington: Indiana UP, 1985.

Eagleton, Terry. *The Function of Criticism from the* Spectator *to Post-Structuralism.* London: Verso, 1984.

Easson, Angus. 'Domestic Romanticism: Elizabeth Gaskell and *The Life of Charlotte Brontë'. Durham University Journal* 73 (1981): 169-76.

—. 'Elizabeth Gaskell and the *Athenaeum*: Two Contributions Identified'. *Modern Language Review* 85.4 (1990): 829-32.

—, ed. *Elizabeth Gaskell: The Critical Heritage.* London: Routledge, 1991.

'The *Edinburgh Tales'. Athenaeum* 9 August 1845: 788.

'Edinburgh Tales' (advertisement). *Tait's Edinburgh Magazine* 12 n.s. (1845).

Eisenstein, Zillah. *The Radical Future of Liberal Feminism.* Boston: Northeastern UP, 1981.

Eliot, George. 'Address to Working Men, by Felix Holt'. *George Eliot: Selected Critical Writings.* Ed. Rosemary Ashton. Oxford: Oxford UP, 1992. 338-354.

—. *Felix Holt, the Radical.* London: Dent, 1983.

—. *The George Eliot Letters.* Ed. Gordon Haight. 9 vols. New Haven: Yale UP, 1954-78.

—. *Scenes of Clerical Life.* London: Penguin, 1985.

—. 'Silly Novels by Lady Novelists'. *Selected Essays, Poems and Other Writings.* Eds. A. S. Byatt and Nicholas Warren. London: Penguin, 1990. 140-63.

—. 'Thomas Carlyle'. *Essays of George Eliot.* Ed. Thomas Pinney. New York: Columbia UP, 1963. 212-15.

WORKS CITED

Eliot, George, and John Chapman. 'Prospectus of the *Westminster and Foreign Quarterly Review'*. *Selected Essays, Poems and Other Writings*. Eds. A. S. Byatt and Nicholas Warren. London: Penguin, 1990. 3-7.

Empson, William. 'Mrs. Marcet-Miss Martineau'. *Edinburgh Review* 57 (1833): 1-39.

'English Journalism'. *Fraser's Magazine* 34 (1846): 631-40.

Erickson, Lee. *The Economy of Literary Form: English Literature and the Industrialization of Publishing, 1800-1850*. Baltimore: Johns Hopkins UP, 1996.

Feltes, N. N. 'One Round of a Long Ladder: Gender, Profession, and the Production of *Middlemarch'*. *English Studies in Canada* 12.2 (1986): 210-228.

'Female Authorship'. *Fraser's Magazine* 33 (1846): 460-66.

'The Female Character'. *Fraser's Magazine* 7 (1833): 591-601.

'Female Education and Modern Match-Making'. *Fraser's Magazine* 13 (1836): 308-16.

Fenwick Miller, Florence. *Harriet Martineau*. Boston: Roberts, 1885.

—. *The Lessons of a Life: Harriet Martineau*. London: Sunday Lecture Society, 1877.

Ferris, Ina. 'Translation from the Borders: Encounter and Recalcitrance in *Waverley* and *Clan-Albin'*. *Eighteenth-Century Fiction* 9.2 (1997): 203-22.

Figes, Eva. *Sex and Subterfuge: Women Writers to 1850*. New York: Persea, 1988.

Forster, John. *'Mary Barton: A Tale of Manchester Life'*. *Examiner* 4 November 1848: 708-9.

Foster, Shirley. *Victorian Women's Fiction: Marriage, Freedom and the Individual*. Totowa, N.J.: Barnes & Noble, 1985.

Foucault, Michel. 'What is an Author?' *The Foucault Reader*. Ed. Paul Rabinow. New York: Pantheon, 1984. 101-20.

Frawley, Maria. 'Harriet Martineau in America: Gender and the Discourse of Sociology'. *Victorian Newsletter* 81 (1992): 13-20.

Fryckstedt, Monica. 'The Early Industrial Novel: *Mary Barton* and Its Precursors'. *Bulletin of John Rylands University Library of Manchester* 63.1 (1980): 11-30.

Fulford, Roger. *Votes for Women: The Story of a Struggle*. London: Faber and Faber, 1957.

Gallagher, Catherine. *The Industrial Reformation of English Fiction, 1832-67*. Chicago: U of Chicago P, 1985.

—. *Nobody's Story: The Vanishing Acts of Women Writers in the Marketplace, 1670-1820*. Berkeley: U of California P, 1994.

Garlick, Barbara. 'The Frozen Fountain: Christina Rossetti, the Virgin Model and Youthful Pre-Raphaelitism'. *Virginal Sexuality and Textuality*. Ed. Lloyd Davis. Albany: State U of New York P, 1993. 105-127.

Gaskell, Elizabeth. 'A Fear for the Future'. *Fraser's Magazine* 59 (1859): 243-48.

—. 'The Golden Legend'. *The Athenaeum* 13 Dec. 1851: 1303-4.

—. *The Letters of Mrs. Gaskell*. Eds. J. A. V. Chapple and Arthur Pollard. Manchester: Mandolin, 1997.

—. 'Life in Manchester: Libbie Marsh's Three Eras'. *Howitt's Journal* 1 (1847): 310-13, 334-36, 345-47.

—. *The Life of Charlotte Brontë*. London: Dent, 1974.

—. *Mary Barton*. London: Penguin, 1985.

—. 'Robert Gould Shaw'. *Macmillan's Magazine* 9 (1863): 113-17.

—. 'Sermons and Sermonizers'. *Fraser's Magazine* 55 (1857): 84-94.

—. 'Shams'. *Fraser's Magazine* 67 (1863): 265-72.

—. 'Spiritual Alchemy; or Trials Turned to Gold'. *The Athenaeum* 13 Dec. 1851: 1306.

Gaskell, Elizabeth, and William Gaskell. 'Sketches Among the Poor'. *Blackwood's Edinburgh Magazine* 41 (1837): 48-50.

'Genius and the Public'. *Fraser's Magazine* 18 (1838): 379-96.

Gérin, Winifred. *Elizabeth Gaskell, a Biography*. Oxford: Clarendon, 1976.

The Germ: The Literary Magazine of the Pre-Raphaelites. 1850. Oxford: Ashmolean Museum, 1992.

Gilbert, Sandra, and Susan Gubar. The Madwoman in the Attic: The Woman Writer and the Nineteenth-Century Literary Imagination. New Haven: Yale UP, 1979.

Gillies, Mary. 'A Labourer's Home'. Howitt's Journal 1 (1847): 61-4.

Ginsberg, Michael Peled. 'Pseudonym, Epigraphs and Narrative Voice: Middlemarch and the Problem of Authorship'. ELH 47 (1980): 542-58.

Gissing, George. New Grub Street. Boston: Houghton Mifflin, 1962.

Greenhow, Thomas. 'Termination of the Case of Miss Harriet Martineau'. British Medical Journal 14 April 1877: 449-50.

Grogan, Claire. 'Mary Wollstonecraft and Hannah More'. Lumen 8 (1994): 99-108.

Haight, Gordon. George Eliot: A Biography. Oxford: Oxford UP, 1968.

Hardy, Barbara. Particularities: Readings in George Eliot. Athens: Ohio UP, 1982.

Harrison, Antony. 'Christina Rossetti and the Sage Discourse of Feminist High Anglicanism'. Victorian Sages and Cultural Discourse: Renegotiating Gender and Power. Ed. Thaïs Morgan. New Brunswick: Rutgers UP, 1990. 87-104.

—. Christina Rossetti in Context. Chapel Hill: U of North Carolina P, 1988.

Harrison, Brian. 'Press and Pressure Group in Modern Britain'. The Victorian Periodical Press: Samplings and Soundings. Eds. Joanne Shattock and Michael Wolff. Leicester: Leicester UP, 1982. 261-95.

Hayward, Abraham. 'Harriet Martineau's Autobiography'. Quarterly Review 143 (1877): 484-526.

'Health of Towns Association'. Howitt's Journal 1 (24 Apr. 1847): 237-38.

Helsinger, Elizabeth, Robin Lauterbach Sheets, and William Veeder. 3 vols. The Woman Question: Society and Literature in Britain and America, 1837-83. New York: Garland, 1983.

Hennell, Sara. Letter to Harriet Martineau, 29 October 1859. Harriet Martineau Papers, HM 431. Birmingham University Library.

Herstein, Sheila. 'The English Woman's Journal and the Langham Place Circle: A Feminist Forum and Its Women Editors'. Innovators and Preachers: The Role of the Editor in Victorian England. Ed. Joel Wiener. Westport, Conn.: Greenwood, 1985. 61-76.

Heyck, Thomas. The Transformation of Intellectual Life in Victorian England. New York: St. Martin's, 1982.

Hiller, Mary Ruth. 'The Identification of Authors: The Great Victorian Enigma'. Victorian Periodicals: A Guide to Research. 2 vols. Eds. Rosemary Van Arsdel and J. Don Vann. New York: MLA, 1978. 123-47.

Hobart, Ann. 'Harriet Martineau's Political Economy of Everyday Life'. Victorian Studies 37.2 (1994): 223-51.

Hoecker-Drysdale, Susan. Harriet Martineau: First Woman Sociologist. Oxford: Berg, 1992.

Horne, R. H. Exposition of the False Medium and Barriers Excluding Men of Genius from the Public. London: Effingham Wilson, 1833.

Houghton, Walter, ed. The Wellesley Index to Victorian Periodicals: 1824-1900. 5 vols. Toronto: U of Toronto P, 1966-89.

Howitt, William. 'Visit to a Working Man'. Howitt's Journal 2 (16 Oct. 1847): 242-44.

Howitt, William, and Mary Howitt. 'The Weekly Record'. Howitt's Journal 1 (9 Jan. 1847): 1-2.

—. 'William and Mary Howitt's Address to Their Readers'. Howitt's Journal 1 (2 Jan. 1847): 1-2.

Hughes, Thomas. 'Anonymous Journalism'. Macmillan's Magazine 5 (1861): 157-68.

Hunter, Shelagh. Harriet Martineau: The Poetics of Moralism. Aldershot, UK: Scolar, 1995.

WORKS CITED

Huyssen, Andreas. *After the Great Divide: Modernism, Mass Culture, Postmodernism.* Bloomington: Indiana UP, 1986.

Hyde, Michael. 'The Role of "Our Scottish Readers" in the History of *Tait's Edinburgh Magazine'. Victorian Periodicals Review* 14.4 (1981): 135-40.

'The Identity of Journalism'. *Saturday Review* 26 Jan. 1856: 224-25.

Janowitz, Anne. 'The Chartist Picturesque'. *Politics of the Picturesque: Literature, Landscape, and Aesthetics Since 1770.* Eds. Stephen Copley and Peter Garside. Cambridge: Cambridge UP, 1994. 261-81.

Jaszi, Peter, and Martha Woodmansee. Introduction. *The Construction of Authorship: Textual Appropriation in Law and Literature.* Eds. Peter Jaszi and Martha Woodmansee. Durham: Duke UP, 1994. 1-13.

Jenkins, Ruth. *Reclaiming Myths of Power: Women Writers and the Victorian Spiritual Crisis.* Lewisburg: Bucknell UP, 1995.

Jerdan, William. *National Portrait Gallery of Illustrious and Eminent Personages of the Nineteenth Century.* 5 vols. London: Fisher, 1830-34.

Jessop, Ralph. 'Viragos of the Periodical Press: Constance Gordon-Cumming, Charlotte Dempster, Margaret Oliphant, and Christian Isobel Johnstone'. *A History of Scottish Women's Writing.* Eds. Douglas Gifford and Dorothy McMillan. Edinburgh: Edinburgh UP, 1997. 216-31.

Johnstone, Christian Isobel. 'A Chapter of Popular Poetry'. *Tait's Edinburgh Magazine* 6 n.s. (1839): 581-97.

—, ed. *Edinburgh Tales.* 3 vols. Edinburgh: William Tait, 1845-6.

—. 'The Experiences of Richard Taylor, Esq'. *Edinburgh Tales.* 3 vols. Edinburgh: William Tait, 1845-6. 1-152.

—. 'High Living and Mean Thinking'. *Tait's Edinburgh Magazine* 2 o.s. (1833): 442-44.

—. 'Miss Fanny Kemble's American Journal'. *Tait's Edinburgh Magazine* 2 n.s. (1835): 465-80.

—. 'Miss Martineau's *Illustrations of Political Economy'. Tait's Edinburgh Magazine* 1 o.s. (1832): 612-18.

—. 'Mrs. Hugo Reid's *Plea for Woman'. Tait's Edinburgh Magazine* 11 n.s. (1844): 423-28.

—. 'On Periodical Literature'. *Tait's Edinburgh Magazine* 3 o.s. (1833): 491-96.

—. 'Tam Glen's Letters to Political Characters'. *Tait's Edinburgh Magazine* 2 n.s. (1835): 539-41.

—. 'Twelve Months in the British Legion; by an Officer of the Ninth Regiment'. *Tait's Edinburgh Magazine* 3 n.s. (1836): 693-700.

—. 'Union of Johnstone's and Tait's Magazines'. *Johnstone's Edinburgh Magazine* 1 (1834): 529-30.

—. 'What Shall We Do With Our Young Fellows?' *Tait's Edinburgh Magazine* 1 n.s. (1834): 527-30.

—. 'What Is Going On'. *Tait's Edinburgh Magazine* 1 n.s. (1834): 419-30.

Johnstone, Christian, and William Tait. 'To Our Subscribers'. *Tait's Edinburgh Magazine* 1 n.s. (1834): 289.

Judd, Catherine. 'Male Pseudonyms and Female Authority in Victorian England'. *Literature in the Marketplace: Nineteenth-Century Publishing and Reading Practices.* Eds. John Jordan and Robert Patten. Cambridge: Cambridge UP, 1995. 250-68.

Kent, Christopher. 'The Higher Journalism and Mid-Victorian Clerisy'. *Victorian Studies* 13 (1969): 181-98.

Kestner, Joseph. *Protest and Reform: The British Social Narrative by Women, 1827-67.* Madison: U of Wisconsin P, 1985.

Kingsley, Charles. 'Recent Novels'. *Fraser's Magazine* 39 (1849): 417-32.

Kinnear, J. Boyd. 'Anonymous Journalism'. *Contemporary Review* 5 (1867): 324-39.

Kirkpatrick, Kathryn. 'Sermons and Strictures: Conduct-Book Propriety and Property Relations in Late Eighteenth-Century England'. *History, Gender and Eighteenth-Century Literature*. Ed. Beth Tobin. Athens: U of Georgia P, 1994. 198-226.

Kröller, Eva-Marie. 'First Impressions: Rhetorical Strategies in Travel Writing by Victorian Women'. *Ariel: A Review of International English Literature* 21.4 (1990): 87-99.

Krueger, Christine. 'The "Female Paternalist" as Historian: Elizabeth Gaskell's *My Lady Ludlow*'. *Rewriting the Victorians: Theory, History, and the Politics of Gender*. Ed. Linda Shires. New York: Routledge, 1992. 166-83.

—. *The Reader's Repentance: Women Preachers, Women Writers, and Nineteenth-Century Social Discourse*. Chicago: U of Chicago P, 1992.

Lansbury, Coral. *Elizabeth Gaskell*. Boston: Twayne, 1984.

Latané, David. 'The Birth of the Author in the Victorian Archive'. *Victorian Periodicals Review* 22.3 (1989): 109-117.

Law, Alice. 'The Poetry of Christina G. Rossetti'. *Westminster Review* 143 o.s. (1895): 444-53.

Leary, Patrick. '*Fraser's Magazine* and the Literary Life, 1830-1847'. *Victorian Periodicals Review* 27.2 (1994): 105-121.

Leighton, Angela, and Margaret Reynolds. Introduction. *Victorian Woman Poets: An Anthology*. Eds. Angela Leighton and Margaret Reynolds. Oxford: Blackwell, 1995. xxv- xl.

Lewes, George Henry. 'The Condition of Authors in England, Germany, and France'. *Fraser's Magazine* 35 (1847): 285-95.

—. '*Ruth* and *Villette*'. *Westminster Review* 3 n.s. (1853): 474-91.

'The Life and Correspondence of Mrs. Hannah More'. *Athenaeum* 16 August 1834: 601-603; 23 August 1834: 620-22; 6 September 1834: 654-56.

Linley, Margaret. 'Dying to Be a Poetess: The Conundrum of Christina Rossetti'. *The Culture of Christina Rossetti: Female Poetics and Victorian Contexts*. Athens: Ohio UP, 1999. 285-314.

Lister, T. H. 'Mrs. Gore's *Women as They Are; or, Manners of the Day*'. *Edinburgh Review* 51 (1830): 444-62.

Lockhart, John Gibson. 'Life of Hannah More'. *Quarterly Review* 52 (1834): 416-41.

Lootens, Tricia. *Lost Saints: Silence, Gender, and Victorian Literary Canonization*. Charlottesville: U Press of Virginia, 1996.

Lovell, Terry. *Consuming Fiction*. London: Verso, 1987.

Ludlow, John. '*Ruth*'. *North British Review* 19 (1853): 151-74.

Maclise, Daniel. 'The Fraserians'. *Fraser's Magazine* 11 (1835): 1.

—. 'Miss Harriet Martineau'. *Fraser's Magazine* 8 (1833): 577.

—. '*Regina's* Maids of Honor'. *Fraser's Magazine* 13 (1836): 80.

Maginn, William. 'Miss Harriet Martineau'. *Fraser's Magazine* 8 (1833): 576.

—. 'Mrs. Norton'. *Fraser's Magazine* 3 (1831): 222.

—. 'Novels of the Season'. *Fraser's Magazine* 4 (1831): 8-25.

Mahoney, Francis. 'Miss Landon'. *Fraser's Magazine* 8 (1833): 433.

Maidment, Brian. 'Magazines of Popular Progress and the Artisans'. *Victorian Periodicals Review* 17.3 (1984): 83-94.

Malkin, Arthur Thomas. *The Gallery of Portraits: with Memoirs*. 7 vols. London: Knight, 1833-37.

Marks, Patricia. 'Harriet Martineau: *Fraser's* Maid of (Dis)Honor'. *Victorian Periodicals Review* 19.1 (1986): 28-34.

Marsh, Jan. *Christina Rossetti: A Writer's Life*. New York: Viking, 1995.

—. *Pre-Raphaelite Women: Images of Femininity in Pre-Raphaelite Art*. London: Artus, 1987.

WORKS CITED

Martineau, Harriet. 'The Achievements of the Genius of Scott'. *Tait's Edinburgh Magazine* 2 o.s. (1833): 445-60.

—. *Autobiography*. 2 vols. London: Virago, 1983.

—. *Deerbrook*. Garden City: Dial, 1984.

—. 'Criticism on Women'. *London and Westminster Review* 32 o.s. (1839): 454-75.

—. 'Female Industry'. *Edinburgh Review* 109 (1859): 293-336.

—. 'Female Writers on Practical Divinity'. *Monthly Repository* 17 o.s. (1822): 593-96, 746-50.

—. *Harriet Martineau on Women*. Ed. Gayle G. Yates. New Brunswick: Rutgers UP, 1985.

—. *How to Observe Morals and Manners*. New Brunswick: Transaction, 1989.

—. *Illustrations of Political Economy*. 9 vols. London: Fox, 1832-34.

—. Letter to Charles Bracebridge, 21 November 1859 (hand-copied extract). Harriet Martineau Papers, HM 83. Birmingham University Library.

—. Letter to Helen Tagart, 3 January 1824. Harriet Martineau Papers, 1800-1994 (bulk 1821-1875), BANC MSS 92/754z, 4/76. The Bancroft Library, University of California Berkeley.

—. 'Literary Lionism'. *London and Westminster Review* 32 o.s. (1839): 261-81.

—. 'Middle-Class Education in England'. *Cornhill Magazine* 10 (1864): 549-68.

—. 'Miss Sedgwick's Works'. *London and Westminster Review* 6 n.s. (1837): 42-65.

—. 'Notes Toward an Iconography of Harriet Martineau'. Harriet Martineau Papers, 1800-1994 (bulk 1821-1875), BANC MSS 92/754z, 11/45. The Bancroft Library, University of California Berkeley.

—. *The Rioters*. London: Houlston, 1827.

—. *Selected Letters*. Ed. Valerie Sanders. Oxford: Clarendon, 1990.

—. *Society in America*. New Brunswick: Transaction, 1981.

—. '*Villette*'. *Daily News* 3 February 1853: 2.

Masson, David. 'Pre-Raphaelitism in Art and Literature'. *British Quarterly Review* 16 (1852): 197-220.

McCarthy, Justin. 'Novels with a Purpose'. *Westminster Review* 26 n.s. (1864): 24-49.

Mermin, Dorothy. *Godiva's Ride: Women of Letters in England, 1830-1880*. Bloomington: Indiana UP, 1993.

Meteyard, Elizabeth. 'A Woman's Pen'. *English Woman's Journal* 1 (1858): 246-59.

Meynell, Alice. 'Christina Rossetti'. *New Review* 12 (1895): 201-6.

'*The Mill on the Floss*'. *Saturday Review* 9 (14 April 1860): 470-71.

Miller, Nancy. 'Changing the Subject: Authorship, Writing, and the Reader'. *Feminist Studies: Critical Studies*. Ed. Teresa de Lauretis. Bloomington: Indiana UP, 1986. 102-20.

Mineka, Francis. *The Dissidence of Dissent:* The Monthly Repository, *1806-38*. Chapel Hill: U of North Carolina P, 1944.

'Miss Edgeworth's Tales and Novels'. *Fraser's Magazine* 6 (1832): 541-58.

'Miss Fanny Kemble and Her Critics'. *Fraser's Magazine* 12 (1835): 327-37.

'Miss Rossetti's Poems'. *Saturday Review* 81 (1896): 194-7.

Mitchell, Sally. 'Careers for Girls: Writing Trash'. *Victorian Periodicals Review* 15.3 (1992): 109-13.

Moers, Ellen. *Literary Women: The Great Writers*. New York: Oxford UP, 1985.

Moi, Toril. *Sexual/Textual Politics: Feminist Literary Theory*. London: Routledge, 1985.

Moncrieff, James. 'Secret Voting and Parliamentary Reform'. *Edinburgh Review* 112 (1860): 266-93.

Monnickendam, Andrew. 'The Good, Brave-hearted Lady: Christian Johnstone and National Tales.' *Atlantis* 20.2 (1998): 133-47.

196 FIRST-PERSON ANONYMOUS

—. 'The Odd Couple: Christian Johnstone's Reviews of Maria Edgworth and Walter Scott.' *Scottish Literary Journal* 27.1 (2000): 22-38.

More, Hannah. *Strictures on the Modern System of Female Education.* 2 vols. London: Cadell and Davies, 1811.

—. *The Works of Hannah More.* 9 vols. London: Fisher, Fisher, and Jackson, 1838-43.

More, Paul. 'Christina Rossetti'. *Atlantic Monthly* 94 (1904): 815-21.

Morley, John. 'Anonymous Journalism'. *Fortnightly Review* 8 o.s. (1867): 287-92.

—. 'George Eliot's Novels'. *Macmillan's Magazine* 14 (1866): 272-79.

'Mrs. Johnstone'. *Tait's Edinburgh Magazine* 24 n.s. (1857): 573-75.

Myers, Mitzi. 'Hannah More's Tracts for the Times: Social Fiction and Female Ideology'. *Fetter'd or Free?: British Women Novelists, 1670-1815.* Eds. Mary Anne Schofield and Cecilia Macheski. Athens: Ohio UP, 1985. 264-84.

—. 'Harriet Martineau's *Autobiography*: The Making of a Female Philosopher'. *Women's Autobiography: Essays in Criticism.* Ed. Estelle Jelinek. Bloomington: Indiana UP, 1980. 53-70.

—. '"A Peculiar Protection": Hannah More and the Cultural Politics of the Blagdon Controversy'. *History, Gender and Eighteenth-Century Literature.* Ed. Beth Tobin. Athens: U of Georgia P, 1994. 227-57.

Myers, Sylvia. *The Bluestocking Circle: Women, Friendship, and the Life of the Mind in Eighteenth-Century England.* Oxford: Clarendon, 1990.

Nadel, Ira. *Biography: Fiction, Fact and Form.* New York: St. Martin's, 1984.

Nesbitt, George. *Benthamite Literary Reviewing: The First Twelve Years of the* Westminster Review. New York: AMS, 1966.

Newman, F. W. 'Capacities of Women'. *Westminster Review* 28 n.s. (1865): 352-80.

Nord, Deborah Epstein. *Walking the Victorian Streets: Women, Representation, and the City.* Ithaca: Cornell UP, 1995.

'Notes Towards an Iconography of Harriet Martineau'. Harriet Martineau Papers, 1800-1994 (bulk 1821-1875), BANC MSS 92/754z, 11/45. The Bancroft Library, University of California Berkeley.

Olderr, Steven. *Symbolism: A Comprehensive Dictionary.* Jefferson, NC: McFarland, 1986.

Oliphant, Margaret. 'The Condition of Women'. *Blackwood's Edinburgh Magazine* 83 (1858): 139-54.

—. 'Harriet Martineau'. *Blackwood's Edinburgh Magazine* 121 (1877): 472-96.

—. 'Mill on the Subjection of Women'. *Edinburgh Review* 130 (1869): 572-602.

—. 'Modern Novelists—Great and Small'. *Blackwood's Edinburgh Magazine* 77 (1855): 554-568.

Onslow, Barbara. *Women of the Press in Nineteenth-Century Britain.* London: Macmillan, 2000.

'Opinions of the Press on the *Edinburgh Tales*' (advertisement). *Tait's Edinburgh Magazine* 12 n.s. (1845).

Palmegiano, E. M. *Women and British Periodicals, 1832-67: A Bibliography.* New York: Garland, 1976.

Parker, Pamela Corpron. 'Fictional Philanthropy in Elizabeth Gaskell's *Mary Barton* and *North and South*'. *Victorian Literature and Culture* 25.2 (1997): 321-331.

Parkes, Bessie Rayner. *Essays on Women's Work.* London: Strahan, 1865.

—. 'The Profession of the Teacher'. *English Woman's Journal* 1 (1858): 1-13.

—. 'A Review of the Last Six Years'. *Barbara Leigh Smith Bodichon and the Langham Place Group.* Ed. Candida Lacey. New York: Routledge, 1987. 215-22.

Patrick, David. *Chambers's Cyclopaedia of English Literature.* 3 vols. London: Chambers, 1903.

'Periodicals'. *Eliza Cook's Journal* 1 (1849): 182.

WORKS CITED

Peterson, Linda. 'Harriet Martineau: Masculine Discourse, Female Sage'. *Victorian Sages and Cultural Discourse: Renegotiating Gender and Power.* Ed. Thaïs Morgan. New Brunswick: Rutgers UP, 1990. 171-86.

—. 'Harriet Martineau's *Household Education:* Revising the Feminine Tradition'. *Bucknell Review* 34.2 (1990): 183-94.

—. '"No finger posts—no guides": Victorian Women Writers and the Paths to Fame'. *A Struggle for Fame: Victorian Women Artists and Authors.* Eds. Linda Peterson and Susan Casteras. New Haven: Yale Center for British Art, 1994. 35-47.

—. 'Restoring the Book: The Typological Hermeneutics of Christina Rossetti and the PRB'. *Victorian Poetry* 32.3-4 (1994): 209-32.

—. *Victorian Autobiography: The Tradition of Self-Interpretation.* New Haven: Yale UP, 1986.

'The Philanthropy of the Age in Its Relation to Social Evils'. *Westminster Review* 35 n.s. (1869): 437-57.

Pichanick, Valerie. 'An Abominable Submission: Harriet Martineau's Views on the Role and Place of Woman'. *Women's Studies* 5 (1977): 13-32.

Pinney, Thomas. *The Essays of George Eliot.* 4 vols. London: Routledge, 1963.

Poovey, Mary. *Making a Social Body: British Cultural Formation, 1830-64.* Chicago: U of Chicago P, 1995.

—. *Uneven Developments: The Ideological Work of Gender in Mid-Victorian England.* Chicago: U of Chicago P, 1988.

'Practical Reasoning Versus Impracticable Theories'. *Fraser's Magazine* 19 (1839): 557-92.

'Present Aspects and Tendencies of Literature'. *British Quarterly Review* 21 (1855): 157-81.

'Public Patronage of Men of Letters'. *Fraser's Magazine* 33 (1846): 58-71.

Pykett, Lyn. 'George Eliot and Arnold: The Narrator's Voice and Ideology in *Felix Holt, the Radical'*. *Literature and History* 11.2 (1985): 229-40.

Redinger, Ruby. *George Eliot: The Emergent Self.* New York: Knopf, 1975.

Riede, David. 'Transgression, Authority and the Church of Literature in Carlyle'. *Victorian Connections.* Ed. Jerome McGann. Charlottesville: UP of Virginia, 1989. 88-120.

Riley, Denise. *'Am I That Name?'*: *Feminism and the Category of 'Women' in History.* Minneapolis: U of Minnesota P, 1988.

Roebuck, John. 'Madame Roland'. *Westminster Review* 15 o.s. (1831): 69-89.

—. 'Useful Knowledge'. *Westminster Review* 14 o.s. (1831): 365-94.

Rogers, Katharine. *Feminism in Eighteenth-Century England.* Urbana: U of Illinois P, 1982.

Rosenberg, Philip. *The Seventh Hero: Thomas Carlyle and the Theory of Radical Activism.* Cambridge: Harvard UP, 1974.

Rossetti, Christina. *The Complete Poems of Christina Rossetti.* Ed. Rebecca Crump. London: Penguin, 2001.

—. *Corrispondenza Famigliare. Christina Rossetti: Poems and Prose.* Ed. Jan Marsh. London: Dent, 1994. 275-85.

—. *The Letters of Christina Rossetti.* 3 vols. Ed. Antony Harrison. Charlottesville: University Press of Virginia, 1997.

—. *Maude, On Sisterhoods, and A Woman's Thoughts About Women.* Ed. Elaine Showalter. New York: New York UP, 1993.

—. *Monna Innominata: A Sonnet of Sonnets. Christina Rossetti: Poems and Prose.* Ed. Jan Marsh. London: Dent, 1994. 229-37.

Rossetti, Dante Gabriel. *Dante Gabriel Rossetti: His Family Letters with a Memoir by William Michael Rossetti.* 2 vols. New York: AMS, 1970.

—. *The Letters of Dante Gabriel Rossetti.* 4 vols. Eds. Oswald Doughty and John Wahl. Oxford: Clarendon, 1965-67.

Rossetti, William Michael. Introduction. *The Germ: The Literary Magazine of the Pre-Raphaelites.* Oxford: Ashmolean Museum, 1992. 5-30.

—. 'Memoir'. *The Poetical Works of Christina Georgina Rossetti.* Ed. William Michael Rossetti. London: Macmillan, 1928. xlv-lxxi.

—. *The P.R.B. Journal: William Michael Rossetti's Diary of the Pre-Raphaelite Brotherhood, 1849-1853.* Ed. William Fredeman. Oxford: Clarendon, 1975.

Rubenius, Aina. *The Woman Question in Mrs. Gaskell's Life and Works.* Uppsala: Lundequistska, 1950.

Sanders, Valerie. *Eve's Renegades: Victorian Anti-Feminist Women Novelists.* New York: St. Martin's, 1996.

—. *Reason Over Passion: Harriet Martineau and the Victorian Novel.* Sussex: Harvester P, 1986.

Schor, Hilary. *Scheherezade in the Marketplace: Elizabeth Gaskell and the Victorian Novel.* New York: Oxford UP, 1992.

Shattock, Joanne. *Politics and Reviewers: The* Edinburgh *and the* Quarterly *in the Early Victorian Age.* London: Leicester UP, 1989.

Shorter, Clement. Introduction. *'My Diary': The Early Years of My Daughter Marianne.* By Elizabeth Cleghorn Gaskell. London: Shorter, 1923.

Showalter, Elaine. *A Literature of their Own: British Women Novelists from Brontë to Lessing.* Princeton: Princeton UP, 1977.

Simcox, G. A. 'Miss Martineau'. *Fortnightly Review* 21 n.s. (1877): 516-37.

Smith, Adam. *The Theory of Moral Sentiments.* Indianapolis: Liberty Fund, 1982.

Smith, Olivia. *The Politics of Language, 1791-1819.* Oxford: Clarendon, 1984.

Smith, Sidonie. *Subjectivity, Identity and the Body: Women's Autobiographical Practices in the Twentieth Century.* Bloomington: Indiana UP, 1993.

Smith, William, and P. M. Moir. 'Mrs. Hemans'. *Blackwood's Edinburgh Magazine* 64 (1848): 641-58.

Stein, Richard. *Victoria's Year: English Literature and Culture, 1837-38.* Oxford: Oxford UP, 1987.

Stephen, Leslie. 'The Essayists'. *Men, Books, and Mountains: Essays by Leslie Stephen.* Minneapolis: U of Minnesota P, 1956. 45-73.

Stoneman, Patsy. *Elizabeth Gaskell.* Bloomington: Indiana UP, 1987.

Sutherland, J. A. *Victorian Novelists and Publishers.* Chicago: U of Chicago P, 1976.

Swindells, Julia. *Victorian Writing and Working Women: The Other Side of Silence.* Minneapolis: U of Minnesota P, 1985.

Tait, William. 'Advertising in Scotland'. *Tait=s Edinburgh Magazine* 3 n.s. (1836): 190-200.

—. *'Johnstone's Edinburgh Magazine'. Tait's Edinburgh Magazine* 3 o.s. (1833): 783-94.

Taylor, Barbara. *Eve and the New Jerusalem: Socialism and Feminism in the Nineteenth Century.* New York: Pantheon, 1983.

Taylor, Harriet. 'The Enfranchisement of Women'. *Westminster Review* 55 o.s. (1851): 289-311.

Taylor, Ina. *A Woman of Contradictions: The Life of George Eliot.* New York: Morrow, 1989.

Thackeray, William Makepeace. 'Half-a-Crown's Worth of Cheap Knowledge'. *Fraser's Magazine* 17 (1838): 279-90.

Tholfsen, Trygve. *Working Class Radicalism in Mid-Victorian England.* New York: Columbia UP, 1977.

Thompson, Nicola. 'Responding to the Woman Questions: Rereading Noncanonical Victorian Women Novelists'. *Victorian Women Writers and the Woman Question.* Ed. Nicola Thompson. Cambridge: Cambridge UP, 1999. 1-23.

—. *Reviewing Sex: Gender and the Reception of Victorian Novels*. New York: New York UP, 1996.

Tillotson, Kathleen. *Novels of the Eighteen-Forties*. Oxford: Oxford UP, 1961.

'A Triad of Novels'. *Fraser's Magazine* 42 (1850): 574-90.

Trodd, Anthea. *Domestic Crime in the Victorian Novel*. New York: Macmillan, 1989.

Trollope, Anthony. 'On Anonymous Literature'. *Fortnightly Review* 1 o.s. (1865): 491-98.

Tuchman, Gaye, and Nina Fortin. *Edging Women Out: Victorian Novelists, Publishers and Social Change*. New Haven: Yale UP, 1989.

Turner, Mark. '*Saint Paul's Magazine* and the Project of Masculinity'. *Nineteenth-Century Media and the Construction of Identities*. Eds. Laurel Brake, Bill Bell, and David Finkelstein. Houndmills: Palgrave, 2000.

Tush, Susan R. *George Eliot and the Conventions of Popular Women's Fiction: A Serious Literary Response to the 'Silly Novels by Lady Novelists'*. New York: Lang, 1993.

Uglow, Jenny. *Elizabeth Gaskell: A Habit of Stories*. London: Farrar Straus, 1993.

—. *George Eliot*. London: Virago, 1987.

Unsworth, Anna, and A. Q. Morton. 'Mrs Gaskell Anonymous: Some Unidentified Items in *Fraser's Magazine*'. *Victorian Periodicals Review* 14.1 (1981): 24-29.

Vanden Bossche, Chris. *Carlyle and the Search for Authority*. Columbus: Ohio State UP, 1991.

Walker, Cheryl. 'Feminist Literary Criticism and the Author'. *Critical Inquiry* 16 (1990): 551-71.

Walker, Hugh. *The Literature of the Victorian Era*. Cambridge: Cambridge UP, 1910.

Walkowitz, Judith. *City of Dreadful Delight: Narratives of Sexual Danger in Late-Victorian London*. Chicago: U of Chicago P, 1992.

Warhol, Robyn. *Gendered Interventions*. New Brunswick: Rutgers UP, 1989.

Watt, Ian. *The Rise of the Novel: Studies in Defoe, Richardson and Fielding*. Berkeley: U of California P, 1957.

Watts-Dunton, Theodore. '*New Poems* by Christina Rossetti'. *Athenaeum* 15 Feb. 1896: 207-9.

Webb, R. K. *Harriet Martineau: A Radical Victorian*. New York: Columbia UP, 1960.

Welsh, Alexander. *George Eliot and Blackmail*. Cambridge: Harvard UP, 1985.

'What is Education?' *Penny Magazine* 16 June 1832: 109-110.

Whitla, William. 'Questioning the Convention: Christina Rossetti's Sonnet Sequence "Monna Innominata"'. *The Achievement of Christina Rossetti*. Ed. David Kent. Ithaca: Cornell UP, 1987. 82-131.

Wiener, Joel. Introduction. *Innovators and Preachers: The Role of the Editor in Victorian England*. Ed. Joel Wiener. Westport: Greenwood, 1986. xi-xix.

Williams, Raymond. *Culture and Society, 1780-1950*. New York: Harper and Row, 1958.

—. *The Long Revolution*. Westport: Greenwood, 1975.

Willmott, R. A. '*Homes and Haunts of the British Poets*'. *Fraser's Magazine* 35 (1847): 210-27.

Wollstonecraft, Mary. *A Vindication of the Rights of Woman*. Ed. Carol Poston. New York: Norton, 1975.

Woolf, Virginia. 'I Am Christina Rossetti' *The Common Reader, Second Series*. London: Hogarth P, 1965. 237-44.

Woolford, John. 'Periodicals and the Practice of Literary Criticism, 1855-64'. *The Victorian Periodical Press: Samplings and Soundings*. Eds. Joanne Shattock and Michael Wolff. Leicester: Leicester UP, 1982. 109-42.

Yates, Gayle Graham. Introduction. *Harriet Martineau on Women*. New Brunswick: Rutgers UP, 1985. 1-27.

Yeazell, Ruth. 'Why Political Novels Have Heroines: *Sybil, Mary Barton,* and *Felix Holt'*. *Novel, A Forum on Fiction* 18.2 (1985): 126-44.

Zimmerman, Bonnie. '*Felix Holt* and the True Power of Womanhood'. *ELH* 46 (1979): 432-51.

Index

(References to illustrations are in **bold**)

abolitionist movement 18, 32 n.13
'abused woman author' 103-9, 111, 130,
    153, 154
Adams, Sara F. 34 n.42
Aiken, Lucy 27
Anderson, William 63, 68
Anglicanism, high 173 n.3
anonymous publication
    Christian Johnstone 62, 73, 78 n.6
    commercial reasons 126-7
    criticism of 5
    debate, contemporary 149 n.12
    E.S. Dallas on 131
    and gender 126
    George Eliot 117, 121
    and *The Germ* 155, 163, 174 n.8
    Harriet Martineau 38, 57-8, 178-9
    and identity 6
    and literary recovery 184
    in periodicals 57
    Thomas Hughes on 133, 168
    Walter Scott 126
    and women 1-2, 113 n.19, 131-2
    see also pseudonymous publication
anti-Catholicism 18, 32 n.13
Argosy 169
Arnold, Matthew 117, 130, 136, 183
    on culture 149 n.20
The Artist 175 n.20
Athenaeum 76, 108, 171
Atkinson, Henry 181
Austen, Jane 37, 49
Austin, Sarah 27
The Author 182
author
    Barthes on 7
    Carlyle on 15, 18-20
    defining 16-17
    as educator 16
    female 18
        marginality 182-3
        model 23-4
        in novels 185 n.6
        oppression 103-9, 111, 130, 153,
            154, 164

        subject matter 23-4, 118
        and the Woman Question 100-
            12, 137, 153
    hardships 106-7
    identification, and *Howitt's Journal*
        86-7
    male 6
    Michel Foucault on 6
    model, Hannah More as 23-4
    organizations 182
    portraiture 18, 24, **28-9**, 32 n.12, 34 n.41,
        42
    role 6, 9
    signatures, and *Macmillan's*
        Magazine 168
    see also authorship
authorship
    and Christian Johnstone 77
    and class 17
    and Elizabeth Gaskell 83
    and gender 6, 17-18, 129
    and Harriet Martineau 35-7, 44
    identity 7
        Christina Rossetti 171-3
    and masculinity 16, 132-3
    professionalization 182
    see also author

Babbage, Benjamin, *Report to the
    General Board of Health* 105-6
Barbauld, Anna L. 38
Barley Wood 22-3
Barthes, Roland, on the author 7
Becker, Lydia 149 n.18
Beetham, Margaret 2, 27, 66, 182
Benson, Arthur 171
Bentley's Miscellany 61
Bertram, James 63, 69, 72
Besant, Walter 182
biography
    literary 171-2, 178
    positivist 186 n.14
Blackwood, John 126-7
Blackwood's Magazine 4, 11, 17, 27, 63,
    65, 104, 110, 117, 167

202   FIRST-PERSON ANONYMOUS

gender balance 121
masculinity 81
readership 121
Blain, Virginia 170
bluestockingism 21, 58
   meaning 33 n.23, 37
Boaden, James, *Memoirs of Mrs.*
   Inchbald 17
Bode, Rita 144, 151 n.31
Bodenheimer, Rosemarie 125
Bodichon, Barbara 145, 146
Booth, Alison 137, 183
Boumelha, Penny 181
The Bouquet from Marylebone Gardens
   12, 166, 167
Brake, Laurel 6, 168
Bray, Cara 180
Bremer, Fredrika 87, 102
Bright, John, MP 149 n.20
British Medical Journal 177
British Mother's Magazine (1845-55) 61
British Quarterly Review 4, 99
Brontë, Branwell 106, 110
Brontë, Charlotte 98, 102, 104-5
   books
      Jane Eyre 107, 126
      Shirley 109
      Villette 100
   Christina Rossetti, compared 171
   as oppressed author 107-9
Brooke, Dorothea 172
Brougham, Henry 114 n.26
Broughton, Rhoda, *A Beginner* 185 n.6
Browning, Elizabeth Barrett 102, 154,
   172
   Aurora Leigh 100, 106, 115 n.33
Buchanan, Robert 175 n.15
Burns, Robert 183
Busk, Mary M. 27
Butler, Josephine 57, 60 n.26-7
Buxton, Priscilla 27
Byron, George G., Lord 14, 183

canon, literary
   formation 18, 173
   and Harriet Martineau 178-9
Carlyle, Thomas 9, 38, 72, 183
   articles
      'Biography' 20
      'Characteristics' 15, 19
      'On Hero Worship: The Hero as
         Poet' 32 n.18
      'Schiller, Goethe, and Madame

         de Staël' 32 n.15
      'Signs of the Times' 32 n.17, 62
   on the author 15, 18-20
   feminism 20
   on *Life of Sir Walter Scott* 19
   on *Mary Barton* 97
   Sartor Resartus 31 n.2, 32 n.20, 148 n.3
   on Walter Scott 19
Carter, Elizabeth 21
Casey, Ellen 3
Cayley, Charles 170, 175 n.25
Chadwick, Edwin, *Report on the*
   Sanitary Condition 61, 81
Chamber's Edinburgh Journal 129
Chapman, Alison 184
Chapman, Maria 181
Chartism, and women 18
Chomondeley, Mary, *Red Pottage* 185 n.6
Chorley, Henry
   Memorials of Mrs Hemans 17
   The Authors of England 18
Christ, Carol 18
Christian Lady's Magazine 27, 61
class, and authorship 17
Cobbe, Frances P. 146, 168
Cobbett, William 16, 38
Cole, Lucinda 22, 51
Coleridge, Samuel T. 15, 183
colonialism
   and Florence Nightingale 33 n.29
   and Harriet Martineau 47-8
commodification, literature 14, 19, 30
   n.2, 182
Condition-of-England Question 10, 61,
   137, 183
   contemporary publications on 61
   and the periodical press 61
   and the Woman Question 77, 81-2
Conley, Susan 170, 172
Contagious Diseases Acts 57, 60 n.26,
   146
Contemporary Review 131
Cook, Eliza 4, 77, 154
   biographical information 78 n.12
copyright law 17, 30 n.9
Corbett, Mary Jean 17, 39
Corelli, Marie, *The Sorrows of Satan* 185
   n.6
Corn Laws 61, 86
Cornish, Francis W., *Jane Austen* 186 n.16
Coventry Herald and Observer 118
Craik, Dinah Mulock 101, 148 n.9, 168,
   183

INDEX 203

'A Woman's Thoughts About
    Women' 129
The Crayon 175 n.19
Critical Review 31 n.8
Croker, John W. 24, 42, 59 n.17
    Life of Samuel Johnson 16
culture
    and George Eliot 119, 130-1, 143,
        146, 147
    meaning 149 n.20

Daily News 57, 101, 178, 179, 180
Dallas, E.S. 128
    on anonymous publication 131
David, Deirdre 39
Davies, Emily 150 n.25
De Quincey, Thomas 183
    on Christian Johnstone 68
De Staël, Germaine 21, 22, 32 n.15
Dickens, Charles 183
    David Copperfield 106
    Oliver Twist 61
    Sketches by Boz 61
Dobson, Austin, *Fanny Burney* 186 n.16
    domesticity
    in *Mary Barton* 90-8
    and women 27
Dowden, Edward 128
Downing, Harriet, 'Remembrances of a
    Monthly Nurse' 29
Dublin Review 26

Eclectic Review 97
Edinburgh Review 4, 27, 41, 57
Edinburgh Tales 10, 63, 72-3, 75-7
    advertisement for **74**
Edinburgh Weekly Chronicle 10, 62
'editorial we' 30, 69
educator, author as 16
Eisenstein, Zillah 57
Eliot, George 1, 112
    anonymous publication 117, 121
    articles
        'Felix Holt's Address to
            Working Men' 11
        'Silly Novels by Lady Novelists'
            11, 117, 118-21, 148 n.1
        'The Influence of Rationalism' 136
        'Thomas Carlyle' 32 n.19
    books
        Adam Bede 125, 126
        Felix Holt, the Radical 11, 118,
            131, 136-47, 151 n.28

The Mill on the Floss 126-7,
    128-9
Romola 130
Scenes of Clerical Life 117, 125
and culture 119, 130-1, 143, 146, 147
on Harriet Martineau 180-1
narrative voice 129-30, 148 n.10
periodical journalism 118-31
pseudonymous publication 125, 126-
    8, 136, 147
stories
    'Amos Barton' 11,122-4
    'Lifted Veil' 126
sub-editor, *Westminster Review* 101,
    117, 118
on women novelists 118-21
Eliza Cook's Journal (1848-54) 61, 77
Elliott, Ebenezer 65, 86
Ellis, Sarah S., *The Women of England*
    35
Emerson, Ralph W. 'Literary Ethics' 44
enfranchisement, women 133-4, 138,
    146, 173 n.3
English Woman's Journal 4, 110, 133, 169
Evans, Marian (George Eliot) 111, 127-8
    see also Eliot, George

Factory Acts 61
Feltes, N.N. 130
feminism 33 n.23-4, 102
    Harriet Martineau 56-7, 79 n.16
    liberal 57
    proto-feminism 2-3, 57
    Thomas Carlyle 19
Fenwick Miller, Florence, on Harriet
    Martineau 178, 180
Foreign Quarterly Review 26
Forster, E.M., *A Room with a View* 185 n.6
Fortin, Nina 3
Fortnightly Review 5, 131, 132, 136
Foster, Shirley 148
Foucault, Michel, on the author 6
Fox, Eliza 102
Fox, William J. 37, 45
'The Fraserians' 26, **27**
Fraser's Magazine 4, 17, 24, 25, 26, 27,
    30, 41, 48, 102, 103, 107, 108,
    118, 167
    masculinity 81
Frawley, Maria 45

Gallagher, Catherine 7, 96, 136, 137
Garlick, Barbara 163

Gaskell, Elizabeth 1, 77, 101, 168, 183
  and authorship 83
  books
    The Life of Charlotte Bronte 11,
      83, 103-12, 115 n.38,
      122, 128, 130
    Mary Barton 10, 82, 84, 90-8,
      99, 105, 108, 126
    Ruth 98, 99, 100
  'A Fear for the Future' 102-3
  Langham Place Group 114 n.21
  poem, 'Sketches Among the Poor'
    83
  pseudonymous publication 87, 91,
    125
  reformist journalist 82-90
  stories
    'Christmas Storms and Sunshine'
      84
    'Hand and Heart' 84
    'Life in Manchester: Libbie
      Marsh's Three Eras' 84,
      87-9
    'Martha Preston' 84
    'The Last Generation in
      England' 84
    'The Sexton's Hero' 84
  urban investigator 97-8
  and the Woman Question 82-3, 102-3
Gaskell, Peter, *Artisans and Machinery* 61
gender
  and anonymous publication 126
  and authorship 6, 17-18, 129
  balance
    Blackwood's Magazine 121
    Howitt's Journal 81
    People's Journal 81
The Germ 11, 154
  and anonymous publication 155,
    163, 174 n.8
  and Christina Rossetti 154-64
  frontispiece **159**
  origins 155
  and the Woman Question 155
Gilbert, Sandra, *The Madwoman in the
  Attic* 6
Gillies, Mary, 'A Labourer's Home' 84
Girton College 150 n.25
Gissing, George, *New Grub Street* 181,
  185 n.6
Goethe, Johann Wolfgang von 15
Gore, Catherine 4, 73
  Temptation and Atonement 72

The Banker's Wife 69
  Women as They Are 33 n.34
Gothicism 158, 174 n.10
governesses 51-2
Grand, Sarah, *The Beth Book* 185 n.6
Greenhow, Thomas 177
Grimstone, Mary L. 27
The Guardian 163
Gubar, Susan, *The Madwoman in the
  Attic* 6

Hall, Agnes 27
Harrison, Antony 169, 170
Haworth Parsonage 105, 114 n.25
Hawthorne, Nathaniel 183
Hayward, Abraham 179
Heimann, Amelia B. 160, 167
Hemans, Felicia
  feminine style 101
  'The Burial in the Desert' 24
Hennell, Sara 125-6
Hering, Catherine 34 n.42
Highgate Penitentiary 169
Hobart, Ann 57, 60 n.22 & 25
Household Words (1850-9) 77, 101, 178
Howitt, Mary 72, 77, 84, 86, 87
  Sketches of Natural History 69
Howitt, William 72, 84, 86, 87
Howitt's Journal (1847-8) 4, 10, 61, 77, 84
  and author identification 86-7
  gender balance 81
  and social reform 84-5
  title page **85**
Hughes, Thomas, on anonymous
    publication 133, 168
Hunt, Leigh 63, 67, 180
  'Blue-Stocking Revels' 59 n.7
Hunt, William Holman 155
  The Germ, frontispiece **159**
Huyssen, Andreas 186 n.13

iconography, Hannah Moore 22-3, 33
  n.29
identity
  and anonymous publication 6
  and authorship 7
Infant Custody Act (1839) 35
Institute of Women Journalists 182
Inverness Courier 10, 62
ivy, symbolism 162, 174 n.12

James, Henry 139
Jameson, Anna 27, 102

INDEX

Jerdan, William, *National Portrait Gallery* 18, 22
Jerrold's Shilling Magazine 61
Johnstone, Christian I. 1, 8, 183
  anonymous publication 62, 73, 78 n.6
  articles
    'High Living and Mean Thinking' 65-6
    'On Periodical Literature' 65
    'Tam Glen' 68
    'What is Going On' 68
    'What Shall We Do With Our Young Fellows' 67
  as author 77
  biographical information 78 n.7
  books
    Blanche Delamere 73
    Clan-Albin 62
    Cook and Housewife's Manual 62
    Elizabeth de Bruce 62
    The Experiences of Richard Taylor, Esq. 75-6
    Nighean Ceard 72, 73
    Violet Hamilton 73
  De Quincey on 68
  editor
    Edinburgh Tales 63, 72-7
    Edinburgh Weekly Chronicle 62
    Inverness Courier 62
    Johnstone's Edinburgh Magazine 62, 63, 66, 75
    Schoolmaster and Edinburgh Weekly Magazine 62, 66
    Tait's Edinburgh Magazine 62, 63, 65-6, 67-9, 71-2
  influence 77
  on periodical journalism 65-6
  pseudonymous publication 78 n.6 & 18
  on the Woman Question 69-71, 77
Johnstone's Edinburgh Magazine (1833-4) 10, 62, 63
  readership 66-7
journalism
  as apprenticeship 8-9
    periodicals 2
  and women 1, 26-9, 183
  reformist, Elizabeth Gaskell 82-90

Kay-Shuttleworth, James, *Moral and Physical Condition of the Working Classes* 61
Keats, John 15, 183

Kemble, Fanny 26
  Journal of a Residence in America 25, 78 n.15
Kinder, Letitia 27
Kingsley, Charles 115 n.37

Lamb, Charles 183
Landon, Letitia E. 24, 27
Landor, Walter S. 183
Langham Place Group
  Christina Rossetti 154, 173 n.3
  Elizabeth Gaskell 114 n.21
Latané, David 6
Law, Alice 172
Lawless, Emily, *Maria Edgworth* 186 n.16
Leader 118
Leary, Patrick 27
Leighton, Angela 153
Lewes, George H. 98, 107, 109, 126, 136
Lewis, Sarah, *Woman's Mission* 35
Linley, Margaret 153
literature
  commodification 15, 19, 31 n.2, 182
  social purpose 16, 19
Lockhart, John G. 24
  Memoirs of the Life of Sir Walter Scott 17, 19
London and Westminster Review 35, 38, 43
Lootens, Tricia 172
Lovett, William 86
Ludlow, John 98

Macaulay, Thomas B. 183
Maclise, Daniel 24
  illustrations
    'Miss Harriet Martineau' **42**
    '*Regina's* Maids of Honour' **29**
    'The Fraserians' **28**
Macmillan, Alexander 168, 169
Macmillan's Magazine 5, 12, 129, 131, 147, 154, 169, 183
  and authors' signatures 168
Madge, Travers 84
Maginn, William 15, 24
Mahoney, Francis 24
Maidment, Brian 61-2, 66
Malkin, Arthur, *Gallery of Portraits* 18
Manchester 88-9, 91, 92, 94, 98, 99
Marcet, Jane 18
marginality 56
  female author 182-3
Marks, Patricia 25
marriage, Harriet Martineau on 47

206   FIRST-PERSON ANONYMOUS

marriage plot 49-50, 60 n.21
Married Women's Property Acts 102, 133
Marsh, Jan 167
Martineau, Harriet 1, 18, 24, 27, 30, 63,
      69, 101, 102, 121, 146, 168, 183
   anonymous publication 38, 57-8,
      178-9
   articles
     'Criticism on Women' 42-3
     'Female Industry' 57
     'Female Writers on Practical
     Divinity' 38
     'Literary Lionism' 43-4
     'On Female Education' 39
   author models 38-9
   and authorship 35-7, 44
   books
     Autobiography 35-6, 38, 37, 41,
      46, 48, 49, 179, 180, 181,
      185 n.3, 186 n.14
     Biographical Sketches 183
     Deerbrook 9, 35, 48-58, 60 n.22
     How to Observe Morals and
      Manners 9, 35, 45-8, 49,
      50, 53, 56
     Illustrations of Political
      Economy 9, 24, 40, 41,
      43, 49, 59 n.12, 71
     Retrospect of Western Travel
      179
     Society in America 9, 35, 45-6,
      48, 179
   caricature 41, **42**
     and colonialism 47-8
   criticism of 41-2
   feminism 56-7
   Florence F. Miller on 178, 180
   George Eliot on 180-1
   and the literary canon 178-9
   literary models 38
   Margaret Oliphant on 179, 180
   on marriage 47
   on Mary Wollstonecraft 37
   and masculine discourse 38-9
   postmortem analysis 177
   reputation 177-82
   self-development 36-7
   on social progress 46-7
   on unmanliness 43
   on the Woman Question 35-6, 40,
     56, 57-8
   on women's status 46-7
masculine discourse, and Harriet

Martineau 38-9
masculinity
   and authorship 17, 132-3
   Blackwood's Magazine 81
   Fraser's Magazine 81
Masson, David 168
Matrimonial Causes Act 133
Matthews, Anne 27
meliorism 56
   vs revolution 86
Meredith, George, *Diana of the*
     Crossways 185 n.6
Mermin, Dorothy 181
mesmerism 177
Meteyard, Eliza 69
   Scenes in the Life of an Authoress 72
   'A Woman's Pen' 110-11
Mill, John S. 63, 134, 136, 146, 180
Millais, John E. 155
Mitchell, Sally 182
Mitford, Mary R. 24, 37, 72, 87
Mohl, Madame 102
Moncreiff, James 150 n.27
Montague, Elizabeth 21
Monthly Repository 4, 27, 38, 39
Monthly Review 31 n.8
Moore, Thomas, *Life of Byron* 17
More, Hannah 21, 38, 66
   books
     An Estimate of the Religion of
      the Fashionable World
      33 n.25
     Cheap Repository Tracts 22, 33
      n.28, 38
     Coelebs in Search of a Wife 22
     Memoirs 22
     Strictures on Female Education
      21-2
     Works 22
   iconography 22-3, 33 n.29
   as model author 23-4, 33 n.31
   Sunday School Movement 22
More, Paul 171, 172
Morgan, Sydney 30
Morley, John 135, 136
   English Men of Letters 183, 186 n.15
   Mother's Friend (1848-59) 61
Mozley, Anne 5, 101, 183

National Magazine 167, 175 n.19
National Review 171
New Woman 177, 185 n.1
Newman, F.W. 149 n.16

INDEX

Newman, John H. 180
Nicoll, Robert 65, 73
Nightingale, Florence, and colonialism
33 n.29
Nord, Deborah E. 82
North British Review 98, 100
Norton, Caroline 35, 58 n.2, 168
A Voice from the Factories 23
novel, social problem 135, 140
decline 150 n.21
examples 113 n.10
Felix Holt 137-9
Mary Barton 90
Ruth 98
Nussey, Ellen 104

Oliphant, Margaret 4, 5, 101, 110, 121, 183
on Harriet Martineau 179, 180
Once a Week 167, 175 n.18-19
Onslow, Barbara 2
Opie, Amelia 69
Our Paper 175 n.19

Palmegiano, E.M. 2
paper, machine-made 31 n.3
Parkes, Bessie R. 2, 4, 101, 110
Essays on Women's Work 132
Patmore, Coventry 155
Penny Magazine 16, 31 n.7
People's Journal 4, 61, 77
gender balance 81
periodical press
access to 27
anonymity 57
availability 15, 31 n.4
Christian Johnstone on 65-6
and the Condition-of-England
Question 61
literary 4, 5
reformist 61, 77, 81, 112 n.4-5
religious 4
and social reform 61-2
women journalists 2, 26-30, 183
Peterson, Linda 38, 39
'poetess' 147, 153, 171, 172, 175 n.16
poets, women, stereotypes 153-4
Poor Law 61
Poovey, Mary 17, 81
portraiture, authors 18, 24, **28-9**, 32 n.12,
34 n.41, **42**
Pre-Raphaelite Brotherhood 11, 154, 155
Pre-Raphaelite Brotherhood Journal 156
printing technology 15, 31 n.3

professionalization, authorship 182
pseudonymous publication
Anthony Trollope on 132-3
Christian Johnstone 78 n.6 & 18
Christina Rossetti 158, 160, 163-4, 166
Elizabeth Gaskell 87, 91, 125
function 148 n.7
George Eliot 125, 126-8, 136, 147
and literary recovery 184
see also anonymous publication
publishing industry 6

Quarterly Review 4, 41, 107

radical press 16
reading practices 34 n.38, 86, 108-9
Reeve, Henry 57
Reform Act
(1832) 18
(1867) 134, 145
reformism, middle-class, and the
working classes 86, 87, 89, 90,
91-2, 111
'*Regina's* Maids of Honour' **29**
Reid, Marion, *A Plea for Woman* 69-71
*Report of the Children's Employment
Commission* 61
Research Society for Victorian
Periodicals 2
revolution, vs meliorism 86
Reynolds, Margaret 153
Riddell, Charlotte, *A Struggle for Fame*
185 n.6
Rigby, Elizabeth 101, 108
Riley, Denise 3
Roberts, William, *Memoirs of Mrs.
Hannah Moore* 17
Robinson, Henry C. 98
Robson, Anne 99
Roebuck, John 63
Romanticism 15
Rossetti, Caroline G. 175 n.18
Rossetti, Christina 1, 147, 183
authorial identity 171-3
books
Corrispondenza Famigliare 154,
166-7
Goblin Market and Other Poems
168
Maude 154, 164-6, 175 n.16
New Poems 170
A Pageant and Other Poems 169
Poetical Works 170, 175 n.25

*The Prince's Progress and Other
Poems* 169
Verses 156
Charlotte Brontë, compared 171
as fictional construct 171-2
Langham Place Group 154, 173 n.3
poems
'A Pause of Thought' 158, 160,
161, 174 n.11
'A Testimony' 158, 161
'Dream Land' 157, 158
'In the Round Tower at Jhansi'
175 n.18
'L'Incognita' 166
'The Lowest Room' 174 n.3
Monna Innominata 169-70
'Purpurea Rosa' 166
'Song' 158, 161-2
'Sweet Death' 174 n.6
'Up-hill' 168
'Versi' 166
pseudonymous publication 158, 160,
163-4, 166
reputation 170-1
The Germ 154-64
the Woman Question 173 n.3
Rossetti, Dante Gabriel 154, 155, 160,
168-9
Rossetti, William M. 155, 156, 160, 162,
169, 170, 171

St. Mary Magdalene Penitentiary 174 n.4
St. Paul's Magazine 149 n.17
Sanders, Valerie 2
Sartain's Union Magazine 84
Saturday Review 128, 171
*Schoolmaster and Edinburgh Weekly
Magazine* 10, 62
readership 66
Scott, Walter, Sir 15, 18, 183
anonymous publication 126
Scott, William B. 155
sexuality, fallen women 174 n.4
Shelley, Percy B. 114, 183
Showalter, Elaine 100, 182
A Literature of Their Own 6
Siddal, Elizabeth 174 n.6
Simcox, G.A. 179
Sinnett, Jane 4, 121
Smith, Adam, *Theory of Moral
Sentiments* 50-1, 60 n.23
Smith, Caroline S. 34 n.42
social problem novel *see* novel, social

problem
social purpose, literature 16, 19
social reform
and *Howitt's Journal* 84-5
and the periodical press 61-2
Society of Authors 182, 186 n.10
Society for the Diffusion of Useful
Knowledge 16, 31 n.7
Society of Women Journalists 182
sociological investigation 9, 45, 46-8
see also urban investigation
Somerville, Mary 18
Southey, Robert 183
stamp duty 15, 26, 31 n.5
Stein, Richard 46
Stephen, Leslie 182
Stephens, Frederick 163
Stowe, Harriet B., *Uncle Tom's Cabin* 100
style, feminine 101
Sunday School Lecture Society 178
Sunday School Movement, Hannah
More 22
The Sunday School Penny Magazine 84
sympathy 139

Tagart, Helen 38
Tait, William 40, 63, 67, 69
Tait's Edinburgh Magazine 10, 35, 38,
62, 63, 66, 71-2
masculinity 67-9
poetry 65
popularity 65
title page **64**
women's novels, serialisation 72
Taylor, Emily 34 n.42
Taylor, Harriet 34 n.42
'The Enfranchisement of Women' 69,
133-4
Taylor, Helen 146
Thackeray, Anne R. 186 n.15
Thackeray, William M. 9, 183
'Half-a-Crown' 16
Pendennis 106
Thornton, Elizabeth, *Truth and
Falsehood* 72
The Times 30 n.3, 125
Tonna, Charlotte, *Helen Fleetwood* 113
n.10
Trimmer, Sarah 66
Trollope, Anthony
on pseudonymous publication 132-3
The Way We Live Now 185 n.6
Trollope, Frances, *Domestic Manners of*

INDEX

the Americans 24
Tuchman, Gaye 3
Tush, Susan 148

Uglow, Jenny 98, 104
Unitarianism 36, 96, 113 n.14
unmanliness, Harriet Martineau on 43
urban investigation 81-2, 84, 87, 88, 93,
    97-8, 111, 114 n.26, 138-9, 174 n.4
voyeurism 54

Walker, Cheryl 7
Walkowitz, Judith 57
Watts-Dunton, Theodore 171
Wellesley Index to Victorian Periodicals
    26, 63
Westminster Review 4, 27, 101, 117, 133,
    178
Whitla, William 169
Williams, Raymond 96
Willmott, R.A. 114 n.26
Wollstonecraft, Mary
    Harriet Martineau on 37
    Vindication of the Rights of Woman 21
'woman', connotations 3
Woman Question 3, 9, 10, 30, 183
    Christian Johnstone on 69, 77
    and Christina Rossetti 173 n.3
    and the Condition-of-England
        Question 77, 81-2
    and Elizabeth Gaskell 82-3, 102-3
    and the female author 100-12, 137, 153
    and *The Germ* 155
    Harriet Martineau on 35-6, 40, 56,
        57-8

and legislative campaigns 133
    publications 35
Woman as She Is and Should Be 35
women
    and anonymous publication 1-2, 113
        n.19, 131-2
    and Chartism 18
    and domesticity 27
    education, Harriet Martineau on 39
    enfranchisement 133-4, 138, 146,
        173 n.3
    novelists, George Eliot on 118-21
    and periodical journalism 1, 26-30, 183
    poets, stereotypes 153-4
    private vs public careers 132-3
    status
        Harriet Martineau on 46-7
        in literary establishment 177-8
women's movement 3
women's rights *see* Woman Question
Woolf, Virginia 171, 183
Woolner, Thomas
    poems
        'My Beautiful Lady' 157-8
        'Of My Beautiful Lady in Death'
        158
Wordsworth, William 32 n.31, 183
working classes, and middle-class
    reformism 86, 87, 89, 90, 91-2,
    111

Yates, Gale G., *Harriet Martineau on
    Women* 56
Yonge, Charlotte 168
    The Two Sides of the Shield 185 n.6